*The Last Word on the Gentle Art
of Verbal Self-Defense*

D1015980

# The Last Word on the Gentle Art of Verbal Self-Defense

## Suzette Haden Elgin

PRENTICE HALL PRESS • New York

*Also by Suzette Haden Elgin*

THE GENTLE ART OF VERBAL SELF-DEFENSE

MORE ON THE GENTLE ART OF VERBAL SELF-DEFENSE

Published by Prentice Hall Press
A Division of Simon & Schuster, Inc.
Gulf + Western Building
One Gulf + Western Plaza
New York, NY 10023

PRENTICE HALL PRESS is a trademark of Simon & Schuster, Inc.

**Library of Congress Cataloging-in-Publication Data**

Elgin, Suzette Haden.
    The last word on the gentle art of verbal self-defense.

    Bibliography: p.
    Includes index.
    1. Verbal self-defense.   I. Title.
BF637.V47E432   1986        153.6        86-12195
ISBN 0-13-524067-0

Designed by C. Linda Dingler

Manufactured in the United States of America

# Contents

# Preface

This book is the third in a series on verbal self-defense. The first was an emergency first-aid manual telling you what to do when under verbal attack. The second, still focused on confrontations, extended the system beyond the one-on-one interaction to other language situations. This third book will continue the discussion of both those topics but will bring in a new set of verbal skills: ways to improve your entire language environment so much that verbal abuse will no longer be a part of it.

My thanks go to so long a list of people who have helped me and encouraged me through the development of this series that there is not room enough to include it here. In particular, I want to thank all my students, from whom I have learned so much over the years, and my readers, who have so often written me to share their thoughts and their experiences.

—SUZETTE HADEN ELGIN, PH.D.
*Huntsville, Arkansas*

# 1
# The Blueberry Muffin Interaction

It was summertime, on a farm in Mississippi. Presidential candidate Walter Mondale was there, with his vice-presidential running mate, Geraldine Ferraro. Mondale had set up the meeting on the farm to "introduce Ferraro to the South."[1] Among the people present was Jim Buck Ross, who, after exchanging a few words with Ferraro, asked her, "Can you bake a blueberry muffin?" And Geraldine Ferraro answered, "I sure *can*. Can *you?*"

That exchange was widely reported in the media. And all over America, southerners hearing about it and reading about it looked at one another and sighed and said, "Well . . . *that's* torn it!" It was only the first day of August, with months still to go in the campaign. But southerners knew that unless something unexpected happened, Geraldine Ferraro had just thrown away the southern vote.

Jim Buck Ross had been Mississippi's commissioner of agriculture for more than fifteen years, which indicates that he is a man of stature in that state. But that is not the point. The point is that Jim Buck Ross was seventy years old that day in 1984, and he had the white hair to prove it.

In the South, in much of the Midwest, and in all of rural

America, you do not do what Geraldine Ferraro did that day in Mississippi. If an older person is rude to you in public, you can go home and talk about it just as forcefully as you like. You can make remarks about how that older person's children ought to have the sense to keep their parent home; you can suggest that that older person is a disgrace and a scandal; you can say whatever you please. Other people who were there may well agree with you, and they may go home and speak their minds on the subject, too. But in public, in front of people, *you will be polite to your elders or you will rue the day*. Ferraro obviously thought that the incident revolved around prejudice against women, and especially against a woman running for vice-president. Perhaps the oddest thing about it is that none of the other candidates, all male, would have made that particular mistake.

Ronald Reagan, forty-eight years old and running for office, challenged publicly by a man of seventy with "Can you change a tire?", would have beamed, stuck out his jaw, squared his handsome shoulders, and said, "Yes, sir—I sure can!" Period. Walter Mondale and George Bush would have done the same, although Bush would have phrased it "Yes, sir, you're darn *toot*in' I can!" And I am positive that if Ferraro had heard that Blueberry Muffin Question from a *woman* of seventy she would never have answered it as she did. But she was confused, and it's easy to understand why.

From the very beginning of the 1984 presidential campaign, every time Ferraro picked up a paper or turned on a newscast somebody was hammering away at the topic of sexual gender and the candidates. She was being cutesipated every fifteen minutes, coast to coast, and she was well aware that she was expected to serve as a role model for American women. She was in the Deep South, which is widely viewed as a bastion of male supremacy, that August day, and she was expecting someone to put her down *as a woman*. When the Blueberry Muffin Question came at her, it fit one of the holes in the filter of her expectations, and she instantly concluded that it was the male chauvinist crack she had been listening for. She was uneasy, and off her home turf, and thoroughly fed up with all those gender stories in the media, and she made a mistake. Even if sexism *had* been the main point of the question, her response would have been a mistake.

If you're not from the large section of America that saw the incident this way, you may be thinking, "So she made a little mistake with one older politician. So what?" I'll be happy to tell you so what. The Southern reaction was "Mercy, if she doesn't even know any better than *that*, heaven only knows what she might do in the White House!" And if you're thinking, "Well, we've had rude men in the White House," you are right; but men will excuse other men for being rude. They will not excuse women for it, and that is common knowledge. The thought of Geraldine Ferraro in Washington, challenging the aging Soviet males as she had challenged Jim Buck Ross, was horrifying. Neither Lyndon Johnson, who was famous for his rudeness, nor Harry S Truman, famous for his unbending refusal ever to compromise for politeness' sake, would have made the mistake Ferraro made. Not with an older person of *either* gender.

Please don't misunderstand me, now. If you are thinking, "He had no *right* to put her down like that!", you are quite wrong. I don't think that Jim Buck Ross was trying to be rude. On the contrary, I think his intention was to give Ferraro an opportunity to show off her verbal skills for the press, as he would have done if she had been a young male candidate. But it makes no difference whether I am right about that or not. Because in that situation, even if the older person is boorish or insensitive or downright outrageous, the rule is: YOU WILL BE POLITE. If you care to win the election, that is. And that rule applies just as strictly to males as it does to females. It is a shame that Ferraro was unaware of the rule, or forgot it in the confusion and strain of the moment. And it is unfortunate that by sassing Jim Buck Ross as she did—"I sure *can*. Can *you?*"—she handed him the opportunity to do just what she had been braced for someone to do. He just pointed out that in Mississippi, to his way of thinking, cooking is something that women do. He was all charm and courtly deference, too.

If it *was* his intention to put down women that day, Ferraro made it very easy for him. It's called walking into a sucker punch.

I am sure that later that day Ferraro realized what had happened, and that she would have given a great deal to have the moment back to do over again. *That happens to every single one of us.* We may not be running for vice-president at the time, but it happens in situations that are just as important to us as that election was to Ferraro. We find ourselves involved in a language interaction; we say something that is absolutely the wrong thing to say (or we say the right words, but in the wrong way), and suddenly we're in trouble. We've lost the job or the loan or the promotion or the grant that we were applying for. We've put ill feeling between ourselves and our new inlaws, or our new neighbors, or our child's teacher, or our employees, or someone we had hoped we might marry. We've lost an important opportunity, ruined a vital negotiation, or in any of a hundred other ways simply *goofed.*

If we're lucky, we may have the advantage of knowing what it was that we did wrong, so that we are less likely to do it again. All too often, however, we have no idea what was wrong with our language behavior. We only know, from the reactions of others at the time or from later events, that our foot was firmly in our mouth. For some of us, that seems to happen over and over and over again, and we stay baffled.

Life doesn't have to be like that. You are *not* obliged to go bumbling through the world of language making one mistake after another, or watching people you love do so. It's not true that only a few gifted individuals "born with a silver tongue" are capable of using language with real skill. It's not true that you can improve your verbal skills only by spending years in training with expensive experts. It is—with one exception that will be discussed later—impossible to please everybody; that is the nature of this world. But there's an alternative available to you: that of not *dis*pleasing anybody, unless you freely and deliberately choose to do so. This book will tell you how to achieve that goal, and how to do so honorably, with no sacrifice of your integrity.

This book is about Blueberry Muffin interactions and other linguistic land mines, and how to avoid stepping on them.

## Notes

1. Bernard Weinraub, "Mississippi Farm Topic: Does She Bake Muffins?" *New York Times*, August 1, 1984.

# 2
# *Language as System: An Overview*

*Webster's* defines *system* as "a set or arrangement of things so related or connected as to form a unity or organic whole." The word is familiar to us, because we deal with systems all the time. We talk about the solar system, the highway system, the subway system, the circulatory system, and our stereo system. We are accustomed to the idea that every system will be "systematic"; that is, that it will be orderly, and that it will be governed by rules.

But we tend to have difficulty perceiving our *language* as a system.[1] At a very basic level, we are able to view English as "a set or arrangement" of sounds into syllables, syllables into words, and words into sentences, all according to rules; and we can accept this as orderly and organized. But when we consider language as it is put to use in daily conversation and other language interactions, it becomes harder to see the system. It begins to look as though anything at all might be said, and anything at all might be said in return. Even when we realize that that can't be true, we are inclined to think that although there may be rules tying together the "system" that is English, *we don't know them.* We assume that to be true in the same way that we assume only chemists know the rules

6

for combining chemical substances. We use chemicals every day, just as we use language every day, but we feel that the *rules* are known only to specialists.

I am happy to be able to tell you that this is not true. On the contrary, you yourself are an expert in the use of your language. It is important for you to know that not even one moderately complete grammar has ever been written down for any human language, including English; nevertheless, you know, and you actively use every day of your life, the complete system of rules for your native tongue.

Much of the confusion comes from the fact that, as usually presented to us, English *does* appear disorderly and unsystematic. The typical language-learning sequence for Americans does not lead them to serene confidence in their skill as communicators. It goes like this:

1. They are born speaking no English at all.
2. By the end of their first day of life, they are moving their bodies in synchronized rhythm with the language they hear spoken.
3. At about three months they are babbling, producing all the sounds of English (as well as many sounds from other languages); as this babbling continues, they begin to use the intonation of English fluently. Babies do this so well that parents say, "I could *swear* that what she's saying means something! There's not a single word you can recognize—but it sounds just like English!"
4. At about eighteen months they begin to speak English, and they do so according to an obvious system of rules, not randomly.
5. By the age of five, they speak English fluently and can carry on a conversation just like an adult, although they are not as skilled as an adult, have smaller vocabularies than adults, and may still have trouble with one or two of the sounds of English.
6. At the age of six, having mastered English as a spoken language, they begin learning to read and write it. At the same time, they enter a roughly twelve-year sequence of *courses* in "English." This is when the trouble begins.

Much of the time, people emerge from all this with little taste for reading, a positive dislike for writing, a terror of "public" speaking, a complete lack of confidence in their own language skills, and a disastrous lack of any knowledge of verbal self-defense. As for English "grammar" (the rules of the system), they will tell you they don't know any.

Well, there are rules and then there are rules. Let's look at a typical rule of English grammar that all of us have heard in school, in one form or another: "A pronoun is a word that replaces the noun it refers to, which is called its antecedent." Let's apply that rule to a sequence of English and see what happens.

> **Basic Form for the Sentence:**
> "I'm looking for the little yellow cat, but I can't *find* the little yellow cat."
> **The Same Sentence after Applying the Rule:**
> "I'm looking for the little yellow cat, but I can't *find* the little yellow it."

You see how that "rule" works? Speakers of English do their best to memorize it so that they will pass their English courses, but they certainly do not use it to speak or write English. When they talk or write, they use the *real* rule, not the one they've been taught.

Imagine a system of "arithmetic arts" classes in which you had to learn the rule "Two and two are five." As you got older and went into more advanced classes you would be required to learn the "exceptions" to this rule, such as: "When the moon is full, the sum of two and two will vary inversely with the temperature of the outside air." Imagine that not only did you have to learn such rules, and all their exceptions, you were expected to learn them so well that you could help the next generation of youngsters learn them too. In the real world, where your attempts to make four coats fit five people would never work, the conflict between the facts and the set of "rules" you were required to learn would produce the sort of results we now see for language. The student population would spend twelve years struggling with the alleged system presented, and learn only to dislike almost everything about it.

What we do when we teach English is much like that. It is not much worse than requiring children to learn the "present tense ending" and its definition, and do exercises using that information, and then telling them to be sure to review because "Our new grammar unit starts tomorrow." The results are not good. We end up with fluent speakers of English who say things like this: "I don't know any English grammar because I always hated it in high school and I never took it in college." They are claiming to know nothing about their language as a system, and to be using it essentially in ignorance.

I would like to take a close look at what you *really* know about English, as opposed to what you may think you know and what other people may have convinced you that you know.

1. You would unhesitatingly reject, as not part of English, all of the following sequences:

   a. "Boy the left."
   b. "Brick little a house."
   c. "Walked slowly elephant an by."
   d. "Who fell out of the tree the boy broke his arm."

2. If someone read you a list of allegedly English words that sounded like these—

   a. "chshat"
   b. "mbowl"
   c. "zhory"
   d. "aaeeaaon"

   —you would absolutely refuse to believe that they *were* English words.

3. Suppose that I read you a sequence like the one below, and asked you to complete it for me aloud.

   a. "one glup, two _____"
   b. "one bloog, two _____"
   c. "one grooch, two _____"

You would unhesitatingly add an *s* sound to *glup,* a *z* sound to *bloog,* and a vowel plus a *z* sound to *grooch,* for "two glups, two bloogs, two grooches." And you would not be distracted from adding the *z* sound by the rule that tells you to add *s* or *es.*

Many studies have proved that if you ask English-speaking children as young as three years of age to do such tasks, they can do them very well. Show them a picture of an unidentified buglike critter and say, "Hey, this is a picture of a grooch!" Then show them a picture of two such critters and ask, "What's this a picture of?" The child will say, "That's some more grooches." If you say to this child, "Apply to the hypothetical word *grooch* the regular English rule for plural formation," you will get nowhere at all, of course; but it can easily be demonstrated that the child knows that rule perfectly.

4. Moving on up the ladder of complexity in the system, you would reject both of the following if they were presented to you as examples of English conversation:

a. TOM:  "How long does it take to get from here to Tulsa?"
   MARY:  "There are only seven letters in the word *affable.*"

b. TOM:  "Six dogs will fit in the back of Volkswagen."
   MARY:  "Yes, but there's a lot more rain in the South."

In his book *Gödel, Escher, Bach: An Eternal Golden Braid* (New York: Random House, 1980), Douglas Hofstadter says on page 306: "Despite not being sure how people will react to a joke, we tell it with the expectation that they will do something such as laugh or not laugh—rather than, say, climb the nearest flagpole." And that is true. There may be some language in which the proper response to a joke is to climb a flagpole, but you know that there is no such rule for English.

Part of our difficulty lies in the definition of the word *know.* No one tests you to see if you "know" how to drive a car by asking you to write down the rules for that task or say them aloud. The fact that you can *do* it is accepted as adequate proof that you "know." But the fact that you speak, read, write, and understand English is not accepted as "knowing" in the same way. And if you are told often enough that you don't "know" something, you often come to believe it and to behave as if it were true.

When I taught English grammar classes at a university, I used to give my students two tasks at the beginning of the course. First I'd put a set of ordinary English sentences on the blackboard and ask the students to divide them into "a subject and a predicate." Some of the students would do that pretty well, some would do very badly, and most would fall somewhere in the middle. There would be a lot of disagreement from one student to another, with many statements like "Well, *I* was always taught . . ."

I would then tell the students to drop the original task and say to them, "Assume that you have to divide each of those sentences into two parts and *only* two parts. Tell me where to make the division." They would then, in unanimous agreement and with no apparent difficulty, divide the sentences into their subjects and their predicates. And that is not surprising; after all, as they talked they produced sentence after sentence, each with its own subject and predicate.

You do know the rules, you see. You know them in a way that no scholar of English grammar has ever been able to write down. Not only that, you know the *meta*rules—the rules that tell you which rule to use when, and how to choose between conflicting rules. And you know the rules for the body language of English, too, although you have probably never taken a class in those.

At one time I was doing an informal experiment with American Sign Language. I would tell a group of people that ASL has two different ways to say "I love you," and that I wanted them to watch me show them both ways and tell me what the difference was. I would say, "Now pay *very close attention*," and then sign "I love you" both ways. Over and over again, the women would see the difference immediately; but the men almost never did. This didn't surprise me, because there is much research indicating that women are better at observing body language than men are. But the way the men reacted when I explained the difference between the two signs bewildered me.

Every single one of them, with varying degrees of outrage, claimed that I had "cheated," that I had "tricked" them, and that "it wasn't fair!"

Now that is clearly a *pattern* of some kind, and it caught my attention. I would have expected some of the men to laugh it off, some to be defensive, some to say, "Oh, well, everybody knows women are better at body language," etc. That didn't happen. They *all* claimed they had been tricked, and they were all bitter about it.

I found the explanation for this puzzle by accident one day when I was reading an article in a book about communication between doctors and patients.[2] In the article, Richard M. Frankel states that one of the rules for appropriate behavior when paying attention to a speaker is that you must focus your attention on the speaker's face.

As I read those words, the light suddenly dawned. The difference between the two ASL versions of "I love you" is that one is done with open palms and the other with closed fists; the hands are located over the upper chest. When I said, "Now pay *very close attention*," the men immediately applied Frankel's rule and fixed their attention on my face; of course they missed the difference in the signs! The men were absolutely right. None of them knew how to explain to me what the problem was, just as Frankel was unaware that his rule applied only for men, but they knew that they'd been tricked. And when I stopped giving the instruction to *"pay very close attention,"* the difference between the men and the women disappeared; most men, and most women, saw the difference at once.

The rules we've been discussing will not have been part of your conscious awareness; no one will ever have required you to be tested on them. But it is very easy to bring such rules to conscious awareness if that happens to be something you want. Consider what you would say if I asked you, "What is the rule for forming an English yes/no question?" I've asked that of thousands of English speakers; what they do is look at me and say, "You go . . . ," followed by an English question that can be answered with *yes* or *no*. When I tell them that that's a fine *example* of a yes/no question, and it proves they know how to form one, but it isn't a *rule*, they are helpless—until I write down a problem for them like the one below, with labels added so they can talk about it conveniently.

### Finding the Rule for Forming English Yes/No Questions

Please look at the following sentences:

1. John will go to the beach.
2. John go will to the beach?
3. Will John go to the beach?
4. Will go John to the beach?
5. Go John will to the beach?
6. Will go to John the beach?
7. John will have gone by now.
8. Will John have gone by now?
9. Will have John gone by now?
10. Have John will gone by now?
11. Will have gone John by now?
12. Have gone will John by now?

INSTRUCTIONS: In all of the sequences above, *John* is the subject and the rest of the sentence is the predicate; the words *will* and *have* are auxiliary verbs. Some of the sentences are not acceptable in English; please put an asterisk beside those. Compare them with the sentences that *are* acceptable. How are they different? When you have decided, write the rule.

---

Given that problem, speakers of English provide the following rule: "Put the first auxiliary verb to the left of the subject of the sentence." And that is correct.

Certainly you don't need to be able to say or write that rule. You know how to form the questions without being able to state the rule. But there are areas of language behavior where conscious knowledge of exactly that kind can be extremely valuable to you. In this book we will discuss many of these areas.

The difference between this kind of knowledge and the knowledge that chemists have about combining chemicals will now be clear. All children learn their native language. They don't have to be taught it, and they use it properly even when we oblige them to learn an assortment of "rules" for using it that don't work very well. You never forget your language, even if you don't use it for years; you do not have to practice it and review your knowledge. A knowledge of chemistry is not like that. If someone puts a set of chemicals before you and tells you to combine them into some compound, you won't be able to do it unless you are a chemist. The knowledge you have of your language as a system is a different *kind* of knowledge from that needed for doing chemistry; linguists call it "internalized" knowledge.

Since you know it so well, it seems that it should be possible to write all of it down, from the simplest rule of the sound system to the most intricate rule of the discourse system. Why hasn't that happened?

We've already looked at a rule of the syntax—the rule for forming English questions that can be answered with *yes* or *no*. Here's a rule from the English sound system, applying to the *g* sound of *go* and the *n* sound of *new:* When a word ends with *g* followed by *n*, don't pronounce the *g*. (This rule accounts for word pairs like *resign, resignation* and *sign, signature;* we can tell that the *g* sound is "really there" because it is pronounced when it's not before a final *n*.) So far, so good; rules like these don't appear to be a major challenge. Let's move on.

Many linguists have been working at the task of writing down rules of discourse. One of the most interesting attempts is that of Labov and Fanshel in the book *Therapeutic Discourse: Psychotherapy as Conversation* (New York: Academic Press, 1977). Here is a typical example from page 78, which they call the "Rule of Requests":

If A addresses to B an imperative specifying an action X at a time $T_1$, and B believes that A believes that
1a.  X should be done (for a purpose Y)
 b.  B would not do X in the absence of the request
2.  B has the ability to do X (with an instrument Z)
3.  B has the *obligation* to do X or is willing to do it
4.  A has the *right* to tell B to do X
then A is heard as making a valid request for action.

You may wonder what purpose such a rule could serve; it may look like nothing more than a way for two professors to show off their scholarly style. But it's that rule, however you want to word it, that distinguishes a sentence like "Please pass the mashed potatoes" from "Go soak your head." It's the rule we need to tell us whether someone who says, "Why don't you make some coffee?" is asking us a question or requesting us to make the coffee. Labov and Fanshel use "Drop dead!" as an exquisitely clear example, saying: "In the case of *Drop dead!* the utterance fails all four conditions: there is usually no real need for the person to drop dead, he cannot do so at will, he has no obligation to do so, and the speaker has no right to tell him to do so."

Labov and Fanshel go on to provide this same sort of detailed formulation for another nineteen discourse rules, including the "Rule for Putting Off Requests," the "Rule for Reinstating Requests," etc. They point out that all native speakers of English know these rules, at a level below conscious awareness, and that they are obligatory in a way that is often a surprise to nonlinguists.

To find out what it's like to bring discourse rules to conscious awareness, you might try working out the rules for appropriate conversation when two strangers with no reason to fear each other find themselves sharing an elevator in a five-story building. You may be amazed at how complicated these rules are, and at the skill with which you are able to work them out; if you try this with a group, you'll find that there are different rules for different dialects. And you'll notice that you know how to exclude large amounts of irrelevant information in advance—*you know what to pay attention to.* For example, you know that in writing the Elevator Discourse Rules you don't have to consider whether the stranger is wearing gloves or not, or the color of the elevator walls.

Obviously, you have superb linguistic skills, and an impressive command of the rules of your language, although writing them all down would take years of time and effort. This is an instance in which *you* are the expert.

This book will show you how to use your skills to accomplish at least the following things:

1. To recognize patterns of verbal abuse in your own speech, so that you can stop using them.
2. To recognize "victim" patterns in your own language behavior, so that you can stop using them.
3. To recognize patterns of verbal abuse in the language behavior of others, so that you will be aware of them and can either

   a. defuse them in advance, thus avoiding the confrontation, or
   b. respond to them effectively if the confrontation is not avoidable.

4. To learn to use patterns of language that will improve the way others perceive you when that perception is based on your language behavior.
5. To learn to eliminate patterns of language behavior that *detract* from the perception others have of you.
6. To learn to interact verbally and nonverbally with others in such a way that your communication is more efficient and more satisfactory.
7. To extend all these skills to the areas of written language and public speaking.

You are equipped to do all these things, no matter what your present level of expertise, *just because you are a native speaker of your language.*

## Is the System Different for Women?

Remember my informal experiment on the two ways for signing "I love you"? I discussed it in detail for two reasons. One was to demonstrate how a rule of grammar that people are not even aware they know can have significant consequences for them in the real world. Another reason was that the experiment showed how easy it is to draw false conclusions from experimental results, especially when there is evidence from other researchers that seems to *support* your conclusions. I knew about the evidence that women are more skilled than men at nonverbal communication, and I concluded that the men's failure to see the difference between the two ASL variants, as well as the women's success, was just more evidence of the same kind. I was completely wrong.

A similar thing happened on a much larger scale some years ago, when research seemed to indicate quite different speech patterns for women, as opposed to men, among speakers of mainstream American English. With the publication of Robin Lakoff's *Language and Woman's Place* (New York: Harper and Row) in the 1970s, this appeared to be thoroughly proved. The information was picked up by the media, and became "news"; it led to a mini-industry of workshops and seminars intended to help women either get rid of their feminine language habits (often called a *genderlect*) or lessen the impact of those habits, especially in the workplace.

Certainly there are differences between male and female language behavior. The male walk and the female walk differ, for example, because male and female anatomy differ. But the "women's speech" that appeared to be so real in early studies turned out not to exist after all. It was a case of misunderstanding.

When important research results are made public, it is the obligation of other researchers to try the same experiments and see if they can duplicate the results; this is necessary because of the natural human tendency to find only what you are looking for. When attempts were made to retest the "women's speech" hypothesis, it quickly became obvious that the set of characteristics said to constitute "women's speech" in America were instead the markers of *subordinate* speech, no matter what the speaker's gender. Men who were being questioned by police officers, witnesses being cross-examined by lawyers, and most other speakers in situations of subordination showed the "women's speech" patterns. And when women were in positions of dominance, they often did *not* show them. The reason that the patterns had seemed to be confined to women was that in America today the subordinate person in an interaction so very often *is* a woman. It was a natural error.

However, that wasn't the end of the matter. Unfortunately, this is one of those situations in which—because people think something is real—there are real-world consequences of their belief. The idea that the speech of women is different from that of men is not new; it is a tradition going back to ancient times. It has always been accompanied in America by a belief that this "women's speech" is childish, irrational, emotional, trivial, disorganized, uninformed, and foolish. On page xiii of her book *Women and Men Speaking* (Rowley, Mass.: Newburg House, 1981), Cheris Kramarae describes the consequences as follows:

> Women's speech is devalued. Women's words are, in general, ignored by historians, linguists, anthropologists, compilers of important speeches, news reporters, and businessmen, among others. People who control public-speaking platforms and public airwaves have effectively restricted women's access to these resources.

There have been many experiments in which subjects are given the text of a speech to read and asked to rank it on a numerical scale for such qualities as logic, coherence, and reliability; if they have been told that it is a speech made by a woman, they consistently rank it lower in those qualities than if they think it is by a man. Similar results are found when subjects hear a speech given by a woman and other subjects hear the *same* speech given by a man; the speech by the woman is always more negatively judged.

The conclusion that there is a "women's speech" that can be demonstrated by linguistic research was news, and it got wide publicity. It fit neatly into the ancient tradition that women spoke differently, and appeared to support it. It was not nearly so newsworthy when it was learned that the language patterns were characteristic not of women but of anyone in a subordinate communication situation. The revised results got little attention outside the scholarly journals. And for so long as people listen to the speech of women, and read the written language of women, with negative preconceptions, the real-world effects will be much the same as if those negative preconceptions were correct.[3]

The grammar rules of the language are not different for women as *women;* they are different for subordinates. So many women are subordinate in so many situations that women spend a great deal of their time following the rules for the subordinate, while men spend most of *their* time following the rules for the dominant. (Focusing attention directly on a speaker's face is apparently not a rule for subordinates, which is what led to the confusion in my own experiment.) But the distribution of subordinates and dominants by sexual gender is a part of the social system, not the language system.[4]

It has been suggested that subordinate individuals are more motivated to become highly skilled at language (perhaps especially at nonverbal communication) because—unlike the dominant and the powerful—they *must* be concerned about the reactions their language behavior causes in others. This is undoubtedly true in some cases; it is surely true when the subordination is so extreme that the dominant individual has the power to do serious physical harm. Then the dominated person is ever alert for the tiny signals of body language that mean the abuser is growing angry. But it is true only for the most crude and ignorant sorts of dominance, because forced compliance is never as satisfactory as willing compliance.

The intelligent person who wants to dominate others knows that, even from the most blatantly selfish point of view, it's far better when people do what you want them to do because of your communication skills than because you have the power to do them harm. People who willingly do what you want will do it faster, more efficiently, for a much longer time, and without any of the conscious or unconscious attempts at sabotage that are the result of feeling coerced. It is therefore to your advantage to learn to use your language with skill, no matter how powerful you may be.

There's no question but that part of Geraldine Ferraro's problem as a public speaker during her vice-presidential campaign came from that built-in conviction in many listeners that female speakers are inherently entitled to less respect than male speakers. But that cannot have been the whole answer. Jeane Kirkpatrick is also a woman; like Ferraro, she is described by the press and by colleagues as "tough." Nevertheless, when Kirkpatrick speaks she is ac-

corded instant respect, even by those who dislike her personally and strongly disagree with her opinions. Many men
dislike Kirkpatrick—very few men interrupt her. What is important to know is: *What's the difference?* Why is Kirkpatrick able somehow to override the prejudice against woman-
as-speaker, while many other women are not? What is it that
some women, and some men, when they find themselves in
the subordinate position in a language interaction, know how
to do that allows them to ignore the rules for subordinate
language behavior?

With your skill as an expert in your language, the information that is provided in this book, and the same sort of practice
that you would put into learning any new activity, you will be
able to find out what these successful speakers know about
language and to use their techniques. You may have grown
accustomed to the idea that you will always be the one who
loses out in any language interaction; you do not have to continue to accept that idea. Put it out of your mind, and go on to
the next chapter of this book.

## Notes

1.   In this book we will be using American English as the example
of "our language"; however, what is said here can usually be extended to any human language.

2.   Richard M. Frankel, "The Laying on of Hands: Aspects of the
Organization of Gaze, Touch, and Talk in a Medical Encounter," Sue
Fisher and Alexandra Dundas Todd, eds., *The Social Organization of
Doctor-Patient Communication* (Washington, D.C.: Center for Applied
Linguistics, 1983), pages 19–54. The rule appears on page 29.

3.   If you try to talk to scientists or scholars about their work and
they seem to you to be reluctant, don't assume that it is because they
think you wouldn't understand. It is usually because it's so hard to
correct or update the results of research once they are a matter of
public knowledge. Researchers know that they can make one casual
careless remark and then—to their horror—find that remark appearing on the morning news in no more than a day or two. This tends to
make them cautious about discussing what they are doing and what
they believe they have learned.

4.  It is true that the average man is more likely to use obscenities than the average woman; it is true that the average woman is more likely to talk about knitting than the average man. But many women *do* use obscenities, and many men almost never do; and there are women who never mention knitting, as well as men who do so routinely. These differences are not due to different rules of language for men and women.

# 3
# Syntonics:
# Linguistic Fine-Tuning

When two radio sets are so well adjusted with respect to each other that they can be used to transmit information effectively and efficiently, they are said to be *syntonic*. The word comes from ancient music theory, and it has to do with being in tune. The first syllable, *syn-*, specifies that it means not just "in tune" but "in tune *with*." And that's very important, because it isn't possible for something to be syntonic in isolation. Even if one of a pair of shortwave radios is taken as the base, and all adjustments are made to the other set, you can't find out if either one is syntonic without turning on both and trying to use them together. *Being syntonic is an interactive matter.*

Because there is no better term in the English language to describe the state of two human beings who are properly "in tune" for successful communication, I call the verbal self-defense system presented in this book *syntonics*. It is exactly the right word.

This book will give you ample and detailed information on syntonics; that is its subject. But it's always easier to understand information if you have a chance to do things with it from the beginning, so that as you read you have something concrete in your own life to tie the information to. For that reason, I'm going to give you a very brief nontechnical intro- duction to syntonics in this chapter, just enough to get your feet wet. Then, in chapter 4, I will describe three techniques that will let you put that information immediately to use. (To do this, I will have to condense the material and move along very quickly. But we will come back to every item in more detail as we go along. And what I say later will be far more clear if you have already begun *using* the information. Don't be concerned, then, if you have questions; they'll be answered in other chapters of this book and in your personal experi- ence.)

## What Is Syntonics?

*Syntonics is a system for putting human beings in tune with one another linguistically so that they are able to communicate with maximum efficiency and effectiveness and satisfaction. It is the science of language harmony.*

In an ideal human language interaction, both persons in- volved would make every effort to adjust to each other in such a way that communication would be at its best. But even in the worst situation, when one person in the interaction expects all adjustments to be made by the other, those adjustments must still be made with reference to the stubborn member of the pair. There is no such gadget as a "syntonometer" that you could put in your mouth to tell you how syntonic you are; the only measure available is in your communication with other people.

You'll notice that I keep talking as if language interactions always involved only two people, which is clearly not true. But every communication—no matter how many people are in- volved—takes place between a speaker and some listener, a writer and some reader, or a signer and some observer. Every utterance, every sequence of body language, has a meaning that is assigned to it by some other person. If you are a teacher, you may say something to a group of thirty students; but each of them will have an individual understanding or misunder- standing of what you said, just as if you had said it thirty times, once to each student in turn. In that sense, every communication event *does* involve only two people. There are differences between the way you plan your language if you are speaking only to one person and the way you plan it for a public talk to a large audience. But the understanding of your words, and the success of the communication, will always be an individual matter between each person who hears you and yourself. Later we'll take up the difference between communicating with individuals and communicating with groups; for now, assume that we are always talking about speaker-listener pairs.

## Miller's Law

One of the most basic concepts used in syntonics, and one of the most important, is expressed in a statement made by cognitive scientist George Miller in an interview in *Psychology Today*.[1] He said:

> In order to understand what another person is saying, you must assume it is true and try to imagine what it could be true of.

Nobody has ever said that better, although many have said it at much greater length and in much more elaborate ways. We will therefore call it Miller's Law throughout this book. But although it's very clear what it *means*, it's not so clear how it's *done*. How do you go about it?

There you are in the middle of an important conversation or interview, and you want to be sure you understand what the other person is saying to you—but at the same time, you have to hold up your own end of the communication. You have to say things, too; and you want to say them so that *you* will be understood. You can't just put the situation on hold while you say to yourself, "Okay . . . let's see now . . . assume that's true . . . what could it be true of?", and then sit there pondering the question at your leisure. There is only one way to participate in a language interaction fast enough and skillfully enough to apply Miller's Law at the same time, and that is to base your language behavior on a *feedback system*.

In his book *The Human Use of Human Beings: Cybernetics and Society,* Norbert Wiener says that feedback "consists of modifying the behavior of a system by reinserting the results of actual (and not just expected) past performance."[2] When you reach for something, you make an estimate about how far it is from you, and on that estimate you base the distance and effort of your reach. If you don't get what you were reaching for the first time, you don't start over from scratch—you take the information from your first try and you *feed it back* into your mind, adjusting your second try to what you learned from the first one.

In every language interaction, the adjustments you make in your language behavior should always be like that: based on the information you get from your listener's reaction to what you say. There are few communication strategies more guaranteed to fail than making such adjustments based upon nothing but your personal determination to talk in a particular way *no matter what happens.* That's like deciding in advance when you reach for an object that you will always reach exactly the same distance, with exactly the same amount of effort, *no matter what happens.* If your language habits have become so fixed and rigid that you follow them without paying any attention to the situation, then the part of your language behavior they cover is not a feedback system. When the furnace in your house comes on because a thermostat has registered a drop in air temperature below its setting, that's a feedback system; if you rig your furnace to come on every three hours no matter what the temperature is, that's not feedback, but an *arbitrary* system. It is not likely to make an efficient or satisfactory use of your energy resources. An arbitrary system for communication is just as wasteful, and just as unsatisfactory.

Let's assume that you want to tune the A string on your guitar to the A of your pitch pipe. You do it like this:

1. Pluck your guitar string and listen to the sound.
2. Blow into the A slot on the pitch pipe and listen to the sound.
3. Compare the two sounds and decide if they were the same or different.

4. If the pitch pipe sounded higher to you than your A string, tighten the string a little bit; if it sounded lower, loosen the string.

5. Repeat this procedure until you no longer hear any difference between the two sounds.

This is an ideal feedback situation. You have an exact target to match—the "Concert A" that the pitch pipe provides. It can be measured by scientific instruments, and it will register exactly 440 cycles per second. When you hear it, your eardrums vibrate at exactly 440 cycles per second. Because that's true for everyone, if you have a dozen people with you during the tuning procedure it's probable that you will all agree about whether the two tones are the same. You can get the feedback information that you need immediately, and you can produce that perfect tone as many times as you want to, without any delay or deviation.

Through all of this, your perceptions are focused on detecting just one thing: *a mismatch between the pitch pipe note and the guitar string note.* That task—comparing two things, deciding if they are the same or different, and making adjustments until you perceive them as the same—is one of the things the human mind does best. George Miller tells us that the mind is a mismatch detector; fortunately, it is also a mismatch *corrector.*

Another situation in which you use feedback is in dressing to be comfortable outside on a cold day. You go through the same sort of steps—putting on clothing, stepping outside to see if you're warm enough, going back in to put on or take off clothing based on your decision, and repeating the sequence until you feel ready to go on about your business. This is not as ideal as tuning a guitar string. The state of your "comfort" is not measurable as so many something or others per second, and people do not agree about it. You have to wait for the feedback information you need, and you can't be sure it won't change; if the sun goes behind a cloud or a wind comes up, the situation is different.

Still, there is a rough and ready consensus about this task. You can be sure that if the temperature is fifteen degrees when you go out the door, it won't go up to ninety degrees or plunge to forty below in any brief interval of time. You can be sure that if it's fifteen degrees outside your door it's approximately fifteen degrees a block away. You can be sure that although people don't agree unanimously on what comfort is, nobody will need three sweaters, two coats, and a blanket, unless they are so sick that they shouldn't go outside anyway. And you can rely on concrete signals from your body if you make a mistake: If you've put on too much clothing, you'll soon begin to sweat, and if you've put on too little, it won't be long before you begin to shiver and your teeth start chattering.

When you tune your guitar string to a pitch pipe or a tuning fork, and when you tune your clothing to the weather outdoors, you take it for granted that you will have enough information available to let you make whatever adjustments you need to make, even though one situation is more ideal for that process than the other. You feel secure in your ability to observe and use the information—and you do use it. You don't set up an arbitrary system in which you always wear an overcoat on Tuesdays and a bathing suit on Thursdays, regardless of the weather and the circumstances.

But what happens when your goal is not to be in tune with a perfect "Concert A" or an approximate "Concert Comfort" but with another human being? How do you proceed? What adjustments do you make? What sort of fine-tuning can you do so that you and the person you are talking with will be syntonic?

The worst possible procedure is to assume that there's nothing you *can* do. People who make this assumption feel that they have only two kinds of feedback information available to them in language interactions: "hunches" or "gut feelings" that are rarely reliable; and the eventual result of the interaction, which may not come along for days or months. If they go through an interview for a bank loan, and a week later they get a letter turning them down, they conclude that their communication was not successful. If they go through a job interview, and they are later hired, they conclude that the communication *was* successful. They say, "I just knew from the look on her face that I wasn't going to get the loan, but they gave it to me!" or "From the sound of his voice I was sure I had the job, but I didn't get it."

It doesn't have to be like that! You are not at the mercy of a completely unpredictable Random Language Demon about which you can't know anything useful. There is a lot of on-the-spot feedback information available to you during any language interaction. You can learn to notice it, to select from it what is useful to you, and to respond to it effectively, without losing track of what's being said. You just need to know what kinds of things to pay attention to. And you need to have some confidence in your ability to do that skillfully.

One reason that this seems hard to do is that a language interaction is so different from the other feedback examples. There is no scientific instrument that will conform syntonicity for you. There's no set of orderly steps you can follow; at best, you say something, the other person says something, then you say something else based on what that person said. But even that is not guaranteed. It may seem that you have little or no control over the responses you get, or the number of chances you have to speak, or even the number of opportunities you have to observe the other person's language behavior. You can't force someone to provide you with just exactly the number of utterances you need until you are satisfied that you have enough information. You don't have any predictable response in yourself, such as shivering or sweating, that you can rely on if you wait a few minutes.

Worst of all, language interaction is a two-way matter. The pitch pipe doesn't make any changes in response to the sound of your guitar string; the weather won't alter itself because you step out into it; but the people you talk with will be constantly making adjustments based on *your* language behavior at the same time that you are trying to adjust to theirs.

Faced with all this, you need a reliable way to judge what's happening *while* it's happening. You need more than guesses, more than hunches. You need ways to get enough information from the other person's utterances to let you decide—on the basis of that information, fed back into the system—what you should say next and how you should say it. You need that information right then, not a week later; and you need a way to get it and analyze it even while much of your attention is taken up by your *own* language behavior.

You can do it. Your mind is so powerful, so skilled, so fast, that you can do it all.

In all the feedback examples discussed above, there is one common ingredient that you are always watching for; it is the same in every case. It is the mismatch—the failure of one thing to be in tune with the other. Different writers have proposed a variety of terms for types of mismatch in language interactions and in daily life. The most common terms are shown in the chart below.

| Column A: Mismatch | Column B: No Mismatch |
| --- | --- |
| incongruence, incongruity | congruence, congruity |
| discord, disharmony | harmony |
| dissonance | assonance |
| disagreement | agreement |
| asynchrony | synchrony |
| asymmetry | symmetry |
| conflict | rapport |

When you read about language interactions, and about related subjects, you will come across all of these terms. Just remember that all the words in Column B are like syntonics—they refer to ways of being *in tune*. All the words in Column A are their opposites, and refer to being *out of tune*. Syntonics is a way of getting from Column A to Column B.

## Notes

1. "Giving Away Psychology in the 80's: George Miller Interviewed by Elizabeth Hall," *Psychology Today*, January 1980, p. 46.

2. Norbert Wiener, *The Human Use of Human Beings: Cybernetics and Society* (New York: Avon Books, 1971), p. 276.

# 4

# *Three Syntonics Techniques*

The three techniques described in this chapter will get you started. They are easily understood, easily remembered, and easily used. They are basic techniques, applicable to every language interaction. Each one involves recognizing a language pattern and responding to it systematically. Each one relies on the principles introduced in Chapter 3.

Your success in using these techniques will give you confidence in your ability to be a highly skilled communicator. *Try them.* Don't feel that you have to wait until you've finished reading this book to put them into practice. Don't worry if you don't see exactly how or why they fit into the system at this point. If you were taking a course in the physical martial arts, you wouldn't feel that you had to sit through the entire course as a passive observer before trying any of the stances and moves being demonstrated. You'd know that the best way to learn was to participate, even if you didn't feel absolutely confident about either the system or your own abilities at that point. Verbal self-defense requires the same kind of participation. The techniques described below are reliable, and their use will lead to a striking improvement in your language environment.

# The Sensory Modes:
## Recognizing Them and Responding to Them

The Sensory Modes correspond to the traditional five senses of sight, hearing, touch, taste, and smell. When human beings process information, and when they express their perceptions of that information, they tend to prefer one of these five Sensory Modes to the others. This is especially true if they are under stress, as in confrontations or emergencies.

The concept of Sensory Mode preference is not new, and there is no way to determine who first thought of it. Every teacher can tell you that some students are "good with their hands" while others "don't remember anything unless they see it in black and white"; any group of parents will agree. Anthropologist Edward T. Hall discussed it at length in his book *Beyond Culture* (New York: Anchor Books, 1977), and its relationship to patterns of language was developed extensively by John Grinder and Richard Bandler in their two books titled *The Structure of Magic: I* and *The Structure of Magic: II* (Palo Alto, Calif.: Science and Behavior Books, 1975 and 1976). As is usual when many individuals from different scientific disciplines are working on similar material, a variety of terminology appears in the literature. Hall speaks of "sensory modalities"; Grinder and Bandler talk of "representational systems"; educators often refer to "learning styles."

A week or two spent with another person will enable you to identify the preferred Sensory Mode by careful observation. But in language interactions you don't have that sort of time available; you need a way to spot the preferred mode quickly and accurately. Fortunately, we have a reliable clue to Sensory Mode preference in the language that people use.

Assume that someone has been asked, "Well, what's your opinion of my proposal? What do you think of it?" Here is a very simple set of responses, one from each of the Sensory Modes.

SIGHT:    "It really looks good to me. I like it."
HEARING:  "It really sounds great to me. I like it."
TOUCH:    "It really feels right to me. I like it."

SMELL:    "I really like the smell of it—it's terrific."
TASTE:    "I really like the taste of it—it's terrific."

Preference for the modes of smell and taste seem to be rare. Either there aren't many people who prefer those two, or the language available for expressing ourselves in those modes in English is very limited, or both. Because taste and smell are intimately connected in the human being (which is why food tastes strange to you when you have a bad cold and can't smell it properly), it may be that there should be only four Sensory Modes, with taste-and-smell as a single category. We really don't know. We do know, however, that most of the time the preferences you will observe in language will be for sight, hearing, or touch.[1]

Recognizing and identifying the Sensory Modes coming at you takes no special training. If you are a fluent speaker of the language, you will be able to do it automatically. When someone complains that he "can't seem to put his finger on the problem" you will know that it is an example of Touch Mode; when someone tells you that she "just doesn't see what the problem is" you will recognize that as use of a Sight predicate. This process is a simple matter of paying attention to a feature of language that you may not have noticed before. Your concern, therefore, is not with identifying the Sensory Mode you hear but with choosing one for your response.

Syntonics has two rules for choosing among the Sensory Modes in language interactions. The first is: IF YOU DON'T KNOW WHICH SENSORY MODE TO USE, DON'T USE ANY OF THEM. If you're asked what you think of someone's idea, and you don't know which Sensory Mode that person prefers, stay with words that can't be classified in any of the five categories. Say, "I think it's excellent," or "In my opinion, it's just fine," and keep your own language neutral until you have more information.

The second rule is: WHEN YOU RECOGNIZE THE SENSORY MODE COMING AT YOU, MATCH IT.

When you match someone's Sensory Mode, that person will perceive you as being "on the same wavelength" or "speaking the same language." This increases the other person's confidence in you and improves the chances for successful communication.

Here are two short dialogues that illustrate the way this works.

## DIALOGUE 1

MARY: "Well, how does my project look to you?"
HELEN: "I like the sound of it. I really do."
MARY: "But do you see what I mean?"
HELEN: "Sure! I said it sounded great—didn't you hear me?"

This is Sensory Mode *mismatch*. Mary is using Sight Mode, and Helen is using Hearing Mode, and they are not communicating well. They are not syntonic.

## DIALOGUE 2

MARY: "Well, how does my project look to you?"
HELEN: "It looks great. It really does."
MARY: "I'm glad you see what I mean."
HELEN: "No problem! It's clear, and I like it."

This is Sensory Mode *matching*. Both Mary and Helen are using Sight Mode, and things are going smoothly for them.

Sensory Mode matching is one of the easiest techniques for improving communication. It is so easy, in fact, that people often object to it, insisting that nothing this simple could possibly work. I assure you, it *does* work. Try it, instead of rejecting it, and see what happens. Objecting to it because it's not difficult is looking a gift horse in the mouth—be *glad* it's easy.

It might seem to you that the quickest way to identify the preferred Sensory Modes, at least among people you know well, would be to just explain the concept and *ask* them. By all means, try that as an experiment; if you find that it works for you, you'll save yourself some time. A good way to begin is with yourself—can you confidently say what your preferred Sensory Mode is? I suggest that you write down your choice, and then pay attention for the next two weeks to the things you say. Get your family and friends to help you. Start with the hypothesis "My preferred Sensory Mode is (<u>Sight, Hearing, Touch, Smell, Taste</u>)," and spend two weeks checking that out. You may be surprised.

In my own case, I was astonished. I would have taken an oath that I was an eye person, with a dominant preference for Sight Mode. I am forever saying "I see" and "You will see that . . ." and "Please look at this example." But when I began paying careful attention to my own speech—especially when I was upset or angry—I found that *Touch* is my preferred mode. Once I knew that, it seemed obvious enough; the things I am best at are typing, playing musical instruments, and needlework and crafts that rely on the hands. But I had a few verbal mannerisms I'd learned from teachers who always said "I see" and "Look here," and that misled me. You may have a similar red herring or two in your speech.

There is also the problem of areas of the English vocabulary where, no matter what your sensory preference, the words considered appropriate are heavily weighted toward sight predicates. Teachers are *expected* to say "I see" rather than "I hear you" or "I get it." To determine someone's true preference, you need to observe language use in a variety of settings, not in a single one where the situation might be tying them to a mode that was not their real preference.

And there is the matter of *mixed* Sensory Modes. If you ask people whether they ever use sentences like "I see what you're saying," which mixes eye and ear (except for the deaf, who do in fact see speech rather than hear it), they will ordinarily say that they don't. They will tell you that such sentences aren't logical, and that they'd never use them. But if you listen to them awhile you may find that they are wrong. Here are three examples of mixed Sensory Modes I heard on television news broadcasts:

"They haven't left a good feeling in anybody's mouth." (A sportscaster talking of some football players.)

"You look at what an inmate says to you . . ." (From a prison official.)

"Let's take a listen now . . ." (A newscaster leading into a press conference in space with a group of astronauts.)

There hasn't been enough research on this topic to tell us whether people who use mixed sensory language in this way have a mixed preference as well—a double preference, perhaps. But if I heard someone consistently using mixed sets like those in the examples, I would try hard to observe their language in a situation of stress; if they still used mixed patterns, I would conclude that they had a double preference. I have never encountered that situation, because in my experience the influence of stress and anxiety has always caused the individual to fall back on a single Sensory Mode. But I have no reason to believe that it could not happen. And if you did identify someone's preference as including more than one of the modes, it would not change the rules for your response.

Using neutral language will not give you the same kind of communication advantage that comes with Sensory Mode matching. However, it will allow you to avoid the *dis*advantages of outright conflict. It will keep you in a neutral stance until the person you are talking with gives you enough information to let you make a choice among the modes.

## The Satir Modes: Recognizing Them and Responding to Them

Dr. Virginia Satir is a world-famous family therapist. In her work, she has noticed that people under stress tend to use one of five patterns of language behavior, which she calls *Blaming, Placating, Computing, Distracting,* and *Leveling.* Her set of categories, which she uses in therapy, is also very useful in syntonics. It gives you a large chunk of reliable information about the language you are hearing and seeing.

In the examples that follow, I will be using a special format to indicate how they would sound if they were spoken rather than written. Words and parts of words that would be heard as having higher pitch and louder volume than usual (called *heavy stress*) will be all in capital letters. Ordinary stress will be indicated by italics in the usual way.[2]

A Blamer[3] talks like this:

> "HOW could you POSSIBLY have DONE such a thing?"
> "WHY don't you ever *think* about MY feelings?"
> "You ALWAYS do whatEVER YOU WANT to do, and never MIND how it makes *other* people feel!"

Blamers pepper their speech with words like these: *always, never, nothing, nobody, everything, none, not once.* When they ask questions (and they ask far too many questions), they put an abnormally heavy stress on the question word. "WHY did you do that?" "WHAT is the MATTER with you?" "WHEN did you ever consider the feelings of ANYbody except your OWN self?"

Blamer body language is equally unpleasant. Blamers will loom over you, and shake their index finger or their fist at you. They scowl and frown and glare. They stare fiercely at you. Even when you can't be sure exactly why, there is something about the way they move and their tone of voice that makes you feel threatened and uneasy.

There are Blamers who are a bit less obvious. For every Blamer who says "You IDIOT, don't you EVER look where you're GOING?", there are probably several who say, "SWEETHEART, *couldn't* you be more CAREful where you put your FEET just ONCE IN A WHILE?" They are Blamers all the same, and their language gives them away.

A Placater is almost exactly the opposite of a Blamer. Placaters wiggle and fidget and lean; they hang on you, or cringe away from you. Satir has suggested that they will remind you of cocker spaniel puppies, desperate to please. This is the sort of thing Placaters say:

> "Oh, *you* know ME! Whatever YOU want is okay with ME!"
> "Would I MIND if you left me with the *kids* while you went

out to DINNER? Don't be SILLY, of COURSE not! I'd LOVE to stay with the kids! YOU know how I am . . . NOTHing bothers ME!"

Placaters are very easy to spot.

Computers don't bluster, as Blamers do, and they don't fawn on others, as Placaters do. Computers sound like this:

> "Sensible people are aware that planes are safer than cars."
> "There is clearly no reason for alarm."
> "It would appear that there is a minor problem."

Computers avoid the words *I, me, my, mine, you, your, yours.* They try to keep their language as divorced from the real-world situation as possible. They are determined to give the impression that they have no emotions, which means that they use as little body language as they can. Very few facial expressions. Very few gestures. Typically, they assume one posture and expression at the beginning of an interaction and do their best to maintain it without change.

Distracters are impossible to miss, because they give the impression of such linguistic chaos and panic. Under stress, Distracters cycle through the other patterns randomly. They may begin by Blaming, then switch to Placating, then back to Blaming, then a brief stretch of Computing followed by more Placating. And their body language is as disorganized as their words. This is how a Distracter sounds:

> "WHY don't you ever ask ME what I'D like to do on the weekends? Not that it matters . . . YOU know how I am, I don't CARE what we do, just as long as it makes YOU happy. But simple courtesy would seem to indicate that a choice of destination should take into account the tastes of each individual. But, shoot, whatEVER you want will be okay with ME, you KNOW?"

And so infuriatingly . . . distractingly . . . on.

Finally, we come to the Leveler. Levelers are *not* always easy to spot. The problem is that they may use exactly the same words as a Blamer or a Placater or a Computer, and this can cause you to be confused. *There is a striking difference.* The Leveler means exactly what the Leveler says. There is no mismatch among the Leveler's words, the Leveler's body language, and the Leveler's feelings. Each of the communication channels in the Leveler is syntonic with all the others. When the Placater says, "I don't care," it's false—the Placater usually cares very much indeed. When Levelers say they don't care, it's because that happens to be the truth. And they won't be using Placater body language as they speak.

When a Blamer says, "WHY do you AL*ways eat* SO MUCH JUNK food?", that is a verbal attack; a Leveler who uses the same words may be very impolite and unkind, but the question is not an attack. It's a simple request for information. You will be able to observe two unmistakable clues. First, the Leveler won't be using Blamer body language. Second, there will be no abnormal heavy stresses on words or parts of words in the Leveler's sentence.

All through this book I will be discussing stress patterns in language, because they are often the only clue you have to important language facts. Compare these two sentences, one from a Leveler and one from a Blamer.

> **A Leveler Talking:**
> "Why do you always smoke so much when you're driving?"
> **A Blamer Talking:**
> "WHY do you AL*ways* SMOKE so much when you're driving?"

Do you hear the difference? It's hard to make it clear in writing, because our writing system is not designed for the job. The fact that I haven't put any words in capital letters, or any underlined words, in the Leveler example doesn't mean that it would be spoken in a complete monotone; there would be slightly more stress on some parts of the sentence than on others. But the pattern I've indicated with capital letters in the Blamer sentence is unmistakably not just normal stress. Try reading the sentence aloud, really bearing down on the words that are in capitals, and listening carefully; you will hear yourself sounding like a Blamer.

You can tell a Leveler from a Computer, even if the words used are identical, because the Leveler will not maintain the rigid body language typical of the Computer. And no Leveler goes through the wild sequence of pattern changes that the Distracter uses.

It will have occurred to you that someone who can *pretend* to be a Leveler is a hazard to communication, and you are right. The Phony Leveler is dangerous. There are ways to spot Phony Levelers, and in a later chapter I'll discuss this in detail. For the moment, however, assume that you have to deal only with real ones. A real Leveler whose feeling is that she dislikes you, whose body language expresses that dislike, and who comes right out and *says* that she doesn't like you is challenge enough at this stage.

Whenever you find yourself involved in a language interaction that isn't just idle small talk, you should decide which of the five Satir Modes you are hearing from the other speaker. It shouldn't take you long to decide, and the signs will be easiest to recognize when they matter most—in confrontations. This is extremely valuable information, because there are clear rules in syntonics for the use of Satir Modes.

The first rule is a basic emergency kit item: IF YOU DON'T KNOW WHAT TO DO, GO TO COMPUTER MODE AND MAINTAIN IT. Always. When you don't have sufficient information to make a reasoned choice, Computer Mode is the proper strategy. It isn't very efficient for transmitting information, but it is the most *neutral* mode and therefore the safest. It may not be in tune, but it will clash less than any other choice.

The second rule is: EXCEPT FOR LEVELING AT A LEVELER, TRY *NOT* TO MATCH THE SATIR MODE COMING AT YOU. Blaming at a Blamer is useless, and will only result in verbal violence. Distracting at a Distracter is panic feeding panic. Computing at a Computer (which is how committee meetings are usually run) is slow and cumbersome, with the two speakers struggling to see who can convey the *least* information.

As for Placating at a Placater . . . this is what you will get:


DIALOGUE 3

TRACY: "Which movie shall we go to?"
BILL: "I don't know . . . YOU decide, okay?"
TRACY: "Hey, YOU know ME! I don't CARE which one we go to! It's up to YOU, Bill."
BILL: "But it doesn't make any DIFFerence to ME! No, I insist—YOU pick."
TRACY: "I wouldn't THINK of it. Because I really and truly don't CARE."

Those two people are never going to go anywhere together.

Feeding a Satir Mode by responding in the same mode intensifies it, you see. In the case of Leveling, that may be a good thing. Leveling at a Leveler means that the information coming at you is the simple truth and so is the information going back. If the situation allows that, it's hard to improve on it. Using Computer Mode at a Computer, which reduces the amount of information going in both directions and pares information about feelings to the absolute minimum, is not necessarily a bad thing. There are times when that is exactly the effect you want, and when the efficient transmissions of the simple truth would not be a good idea at all.

What matters most is that you choose the Satir Mode for your response consciously and systematically. Base your choice on three factors: (1) your own communication goals; (2) the real-world situation in which the interaction takes place; and (3) the language behavior of the other person involved.

There are two final points that I want to mention before I leave this topic and move on to the third technique. First, there will be times when you will notice a mismatch between the *words* used by the person you are talking with and the body language that accompanies them. You may hear Placater words but see Blamer body language, for example. In such a situation, your best strategy is to assume that the body language is more reliable than the words, unless you have an excellent reason to believe otherwise.

Second, there is a reliable principle that holds for both the Sensory Modes and the Satir Modes: Although people have clear mode preferences, and will tend to rely on the preferred mode in difficult situations, they will ordinarily be able to switch from one mode to another without much difficulty. Some people find this easier than others do, and the larger English vocabulary for sight makes it easier to switch from Touch to Sight Mode than to go in the opposite direction. But someone who is literally locked into any one of the modes—for example, a person who cannot seem to talk other than as a Placater, or a person who seems able to use only Touch Mode—has a problem that goes far beyond the scope of this book, and that needs the attention of an expert.

If you find it hard to switch among the modes at first, don't assume that this means *you* have a serious problem. Especially if you have fallen into the habit of using a particular mode all the time, even when it's not very appropriate, other modes may feel artificial and strained and unnatural to you. This is to be expected, and it will go away with time and practice. If you almost never use touch vocabulary, and you find yourself talking to someone who is clearly touch-dominant, look upon it as a valuable opportunity to try out something new—don't decide that the other person will have to switch to your preferred mode or that the two of you will just have to go on using different modes. The words and phrases that sound so bizarre to you as you say them, because you are self-conscious about them, will not be as obviously awkward to your listener. And each time you use a Sensory Mode or a Satir Mode that is the right one for the occasion but not the most natural one for you, you will be sharpening your verbal skills. Practice when the outcome of the interaction is *not* critical, and you will then feel confident with the technique when a situation comes along that really matters to you. If you wait until you are involved in a confrontation where your promotion or your marriage or your final grade depends on the result before you start mode switching, you will have chosen a very poor strategy.

# Verbal Attack Patterns: Recognizing Them and Responding to Them

There are undoubtedly thousands of different ways to put a verbal attack pattern together, ranging from the crudest and most obvious ("You worthless creep!") to the most subtle and ingenious. No one book could ever list all those possibilities, and this book won't try. However, there are certain types of verbal attacks that are so common, and so typical, that they make up a very large proportion of the linguistic pollution that you have to deal with in your daily life. It's well worth learning to recognize those and respond to them. You will then have not only an efficient mechanism for handling a common problem, but also a solid foundation from which you can deal with less common ones. Many attacks that don't fall into the set of patterns described below will be variations of members of the set, or combinations of them; your knowledge of the basic twelve will help you spot them and respond appropriately.

There is one term that has to be defined before we go on—not because it's difficult or rare, but because it is used in so many different ways by people working in different fields. It's important to define it for this book, and for syntonics, so that other definitions won't cause confusion. The term is *presupposition,* and is defined for us as follows:

A PRESUPPOSITION IS ANYTHING THAT A NATIVE SPEAKER OF A LANGUAGE KNOWS IS PART OF THE MEANING OF A SEQUENCE OF THAT LANGUAGE, EVEN IF IT DOESN'T APPEAR ANYWHERE IN THE SURFACE STRUCTURE OF THE SEQUENCE.

For example, consider the sentence "Even *John* could get an A in *that* class." If you are a native speaker of English, you know that the meaning of that sentence includes (among other things not relevant here) these two other sentences:

"John's not worth much."
"That class is not much of a challenge."

Notice, however, that neither one of those sentences is "there" anywhere. Both John and the class have been severely criticized, but not a word on the surface contains either of the insults. That is because the criticisms are both *presuppositions* of the sentence. Because English is your language, you know that those two chunks are presupposed. (There is no reason to assume that someone who is not a native speaker *would* know, and you should keep that in mind in cross-cultural communication situations.)

In the attack patterns we're going to examine now, the important material is usually hidden away as a presupposition. This is a major difference between the relatively skilled verbal attack and such crudities as obscenities and ethnic slurs. It takes *no* skill to call someone names.

I'll discuss the first two patterns in detail, for clarity's sake; the remaining ones will be given only brief comments. As always in this book, words or part of words that have abnormally strong stress will be written all in capital letters.

## Attack Pattern 1

"If you REALLY loved me, you wouldn't waste MONEY the way you do!"
—or—
"If you really LOVED me, you wouldn't waste MONEY the way you do!"

Please take a long and careful look at that sentence. Read it out loud, bearing down hard on the words in capital letters. What does it mean? What does it presuppose?

Right! It presupposes "You don't really love me." That claim, and not the part about wasting money, is the real attack. We can divide it into two parts, like this:

| Presupposed Attack | Bait |
|---|---|
| "If you REALLY loved me . . . }<br>"If you really LOVED me . . . } | you wouldn't waste MONEY the way you do!" |

The person using this pattern expects you to take the bait, because that is what usually happens. If you do, this is what you can expect:

DIALOGUE 4

> TOM:   "If you REALLY loved me, you wouldn't waste MONEY
> the way you do!"
>
> SUE:   "What do you MEAN, waste money? I DO NOT waste
> money! I am VERY CAREful with our money!"
>
> TOM:   "Oh, YEAH? Well, then EXPLAIN to me, please, why we
> are already BROKE and it's NOT even the fifteenth of
> the MONTH yet, genius!"
>
> SUE:   "Look, it's NOT MY fault that you can't earn a decent
> living!"

You'll have no trouble predicting the rest of the lines. Tom has
set Sue up for a fight, she has taken the bait, and nothing good
is going to come of this.

This is an excellent example of the phenomenon called "os-
cillation," completely out of control. You have verbal abuse
being matched by verbal abuse that is matched in turn by more
verbal abuse; the whole system is going into wild overload. It's
like what happens when you are pushing someone in a swing,
and instead of adjusting the force of your push to the information you have about how high it's going each time, you *always* push harder when it returns to you. The language in
Dialogue 4 is Blamer language; Tom's "you wouldn't waste
MONEY the way you do" clearly means "always," and so does
Sue's "I am VERY CAREful with our money!" The intonation, the
open insults, all are straight Blamer Mode; this is what happens when you use Blamer language at a Blamer.

What Sue should have done was ignore the bait—no matter
how outrageous it was, no matter how unfair, no matter how
infuriating—and reply straight to the presupposed attack, like
this:

> TOM:   "If you REALLY loved me, you wouldn't waste MONEY
> the way you do!"
>
> SUE:   "When did you start thinking that I don't really love
> you?"

Notice what Sue has done, now. She has replied straight to the presupposed attack, ignoring the bait. She has used a neutral reply; all that is presupposed by her question is "At some time you started thinking that I don't really love you," and Tom has already told her that himself. It's important to use the neutral "when" and not "why," because "Why do you think I don't really love you?" is asking for a reason. Notice what happens in that case:

> TOM: "If you REALLY loved me, you wouldn't waste MONEY the way you do!"
>
> SUE: "Why do you think I don't really love you?"
>
> TOM: "I just TOLD you why—don't you ever LISTEN? Because you throw our money around like it grows on TREES, THAT'S why!"

For Sue to use the neutral "when" question is a way of applying Miller's Law; she has stepped into the world that Tom is speaking from, the world in which he claims that she doesn't really love him, and she is asking—neutrally—when he first noticed that to be true in that world. Tom will be very surprised by this, because it isn't the script he is expecting. And that surprise will make it difficult for him to move smoothly into his tirade about Sue's extravagance.

Right here and now, while we have this excellent example before us, I want to make an important distinction. Syntonics is a system for verbal self-defense and for improvement of the language environment; it is *not* a system for verbal aggression. You will occasionally read books or articles on the subject of verbal self-defense that provide you with counterattacks (often called *put-downs*) to use in response to verbal abuse. For example:

> TOM: "If you REALLY loved me, you wouldn't waste MONEY the way you do!"
>
> SUE: "It's amazing that so many men—when they get to be YOUR age—start thinking their wives don't love them!"

What Sue has done here is a kind of tuning, unquestionably.

Tom is coming at her in the key of Vicious, and she is tuning up to use the key of Vicious right back at him. This is *not* syntonics, just as boxing is not karate. The goal of syntonics is harmony, and counterattacking will never produce anything but discord. Sue's response above is not verbal self-defense; she has simply moved in to do her own version of head-bashing. If this is the sort of thing you're interested in doing, you are reading the wrong book.

### Attack Pattern 2

"If you REALLY loved me, you wouldn't WANT to smoke."
—or—
"If you really LOVED me, you wouldn't WANT to smoke."

This pattern is much like the first one, but more subtle and more skilled. You still have the presupposed "You don't really love me," but there is another chunk of presupposed attack hidden inside the bait. "You wouldn't WANT to smoke" presupposes that you can voluntarily keep from wanting to; it presupposes that you have voluntary control over your own desires. This is nonsense. You may have excellent willpower and be able to refrain from doing lots of things you want to do; but you cannot by an effort of will choose not to *want* them.

This attack is particularly nasty because it puts you in the situation Gregory Bateson named "the double bind." Suppose that you aren't able to stop smoking—then you've proved that you don't really love this person, and you lose. On the other hand, suppose you *do* stop smoking—you still lose, because you aren't able to stop wanting to. Damned if you do and damned if you don't, you see.

| Presupposed Attack | Bait |
|---|---|
| "If you REALLY loved me, <br> "If you really LOVED me, | you wouldn't WANT to smoke." |

When you respond to this attack pattern you continue to follow the syntonics strategy: IGNORE THE BAIT AND RESPOND NEU-

TRALLY TO THE PRESUPPOSED ATTACK. But this time you have two presuppositions to choose from, and therefore two possible responses. For example:

"When did you start thinking I don't really love you?"
"When did you start thinking that I can just choose not to want things?"

Or you may want to reply to the second presupposed attack in Computer Mode, like this:

"The idea that people can voluntarily control their desires is a very interesting one."

By switching to Computer Mode you have moved the focus of the interaction to an abstract question: Can people control their desires by force of will alone? And you have moved it away from you personally. This is a way to surprise your opponent, both by failing to respond as expected and by defusing the confrontation in taking the personal focus out of it. If you prefer to stress the personal angle, but still want to defuse the hostility, here is one more possible response:

"You are very kind to suggest that I can stop wanting something just by deciding that I *will* stop."

This response acknowledges the presupposition, ignores the bait completely, and turns the attack into a compliment. Your opponent will look very foolish responding to this with "I am *not!*"

The principles of this technique should now be clear:

1. Identify the presupposed attack and the bait.
2. Ignore the bait.
3. Respond directly to the presupposed attack, as neutrally as possible.

Now I am going to list the rest of the attack patterns to be presented in this chapter, without the detailed discussion. I'll sort them out into the Satir Mode that is most typical of each one—but understand that any one of them can be reworded to fit into a different Satir Mode. The mode chosen is just the most likely one, not the only possibility.

The two patterns above were both in Blamer Mode. Here are six more that are most typically Blaming, with the suggested responses.

### Attack Pattern 3

"Don't you even CARE about (your children, the rest of the people in this department, your grades, world hunger, etc.)?"

The presupposed attack here is very clear: You don't care about *x*, and you are a worthless, despicable creep because you don't care—any decent person *would* care. The abnormal heavy stress in this pattern may continue from the word "about" all the way to the end of the sentence; that is the most typical form. For example, "Don't you even CARE ABOUT THE WAY YOUR COOKING IS DESTROYING OUR MARRIAGE?"

One of the best responses to an attack of this kind is just to say a firm and uncompromising "No," in the classic tradition of the martial arts. This is like using an attacker's own strength, plus the advantage of surprise, to send that attacker flying across the room. You are expected to say, "Of COURSE I care about *x*!", and sail right into a fight. Don't do it. This may be enough in itself to stop the attacker cold, because it's such a shock. Or it may lead to a dialogue like this one:

DIALOGUE 5

A: "Don't you even CARE ABOUT NUCLEAR DISARMAMENT?"
B: "No."
A: "NO??? I don't believe you SAID that! Only a CREEP would say a thing like that!"
B: "I'm sorry—are we talking about disarmament or are we talking about creeps?"

An alternative way to respond to one of these "Don't you even CARE" attacks is to go to Computer Mode and shock your opponent in a rather different way. Like this:


DIALOGUE 6

    A: "Don't you even CARE ABOUT WORLD HUNGER?"

    B: "Indeed I *do!* Especially since the publication of the Whackelfinger Task Force Report."

Now your opponent must choose. He can pretend that he too has read the report—which you have of course made up on the spot—and make a fool of himself. Or he can make a fool of himself like this, instead:


DIALOGUE 7

    A: "Don't you even CARE ABOUT WORLD HUNGER?"

    B: "Indeed I DO! Especially since the publication of the Whackelfinger Task Force Report."

    A: "Whadda you MEAN, the Whackelfinger Task Force Report?"

    B: (Say nothing. Just raise your eyebrows and look surprised.)

    A: "You made it up. I don't believe it. There's no such report."

It is now safe for you to smile at this person; you have won.

The more obviously absurd the name of the study you make up, the better; it is your way of saying "Your ridiculous question deserves a ridiculous answer, and here it is."

## Attack Pattern 4

"EVEN a WOMAN should be able to understand THAT book!"

The presupposed attacks are that women are inferior and

that the book doesn't require much intelligence to understand. The proper response is this one:

> "The idea that women are somehow inferior is very common, but I'm surprised to hear it from *you*."

The very last thing your attacker is expecting as a response is a sentence that first lays the attack right out on the table, to be looked at by one and all, and then is followed by a compliment. The ball is in your opponent's court, and none of the choices are going to be much fun. The sophisticated attacker will thank you and withdraw from the fray as quickly as possible, before more face is lost.

If you feel that you cannot bring yourself to compliment this person, or that it would be totally dishonest to do so, fall back on the reliable neutral question, and ask:

> "When did you start thinking that women are inferior?"

But under no circumstances do you acknowledge that *you personally* are the woman referred to in the attack. Your opponent has chosen to talk of hypothetical women, on the surface; take full advantage of that fact and talk of hypothetical women yourself.

In this all-purpose workhorse of a pattern, anything at all that is named after the stressed "EVEN" is presupposed to be second-rate. In its crudest form, it turns up like this:

> "EVEN YOU could pass THAT class!"

The proper response when the attack is made openly personal in that way is to use the neutral "When did you start thinking that I . . ." question, tailored to the occasion.

Notice that not every sentence that begins with "even" and a noun phrase is an attack. If, for example, you say, "EVEN JOHN attended THAT class!", you are expressing surprise about John's actions, but there is no automatic presupposition that either John or the class is in any way inferior. The pattern has to include one of the *modal auxiliaries* of English, or one of their variants, or it collapses. Here's the list of auxiliaries: *may, might, can* (or *be able*), *could, shall, should* (or *ought to*), *will, would, must* (or *have to*).

### Attack Pattern 5

"EVERYONE underSTANDS why you can't get along with other PEOPle, dear."

Don't let the "dear" at the end confuse you. A Blamer utterance is no less a Blamer utterance because it comes decked out with "dear," "sweetheart," "you poor thing," or "my dearest love." You wouldn't have any trouble recognizing "You're a worthless CREEP, sweetheart" as an attack.

The claim that you can't get along with other people is the bait in the example; as always, it should be ignored. And what is presupposed is a very clever and often very cruel trick. In one case, there really is something about you that might interfere with your relationships with other people, which your attacker is aware of—perhaps something about your appearance, perhaps a physical disability, perhaps something in your past. Much of the time, however, the attacker is relying on the fact that every single one of us has *something* that we don't want other people to know or are afraid that others will notice. It may be trivial; it may be serious; it may be only our imagination. But when you hear "EVERYONE underSTANDS why . . .", your attacker is counting on you to think, "Oh *no!* Oh no, they've found out!" Or "Oh no—they've *noticed!*" And most of the time that is what the victim *does* think, which feeds the attacker's bad habit.

Don't fall for this, please. Your proper response is the following:

"I'm sure they do understand. And I want you to know that I appreciate it."

With body language to match. Look confident, charming, and politely appreciative. This is not what the attacker is expecting you to do; you are not being fun to pick on. The abuser is now, linguistically speaking, flat on the mat. Good move!

### Attack Pattern 6

"YOU'RE only PRETENDing to be sick to get ATTENtion, you know!"

The bait in this attack can be summed up as "You'll stoop to anything to get attention." The act you're stooping to may be specified on the surface, as in the example; or it may be left unexpressed because it's clear in the real-world context of the situation, like this:

"YOU'RE only DOing that to get ATTENtion, you know!"

Whether the attention-getting activity is openly stated or must be reconstructed from the situation, your proper response is to ignore it. *Do not take the bait.* To say "I am *not* pretending! I *really am sick!*" only gives your attacker a chance to say "Oh, you *are not* sick!", followed by a steadily more demeaning wrangle over your symptoms, their reality, the competence of your doctor, etc. In this confrontation, the only proper move is to defend yourself by simply stepping out of the way and allowing your attacker to fall down naturally. You say something like this:

"It's kind of you to be so understanding."

This will not work if it sounds like sarcasm. It must be said with neutral politeness and well-bred intonation. If you prefer, you can shift into Computer Mode and say:

"One so rarely meets people capable of clear perceptions."

When I teach this move, it often happens that my students or clients reject it instantly. They say, "I couldn't do it. I see what you mean, but I just couldn't let anybody get away with something like that."

And I see what *they* mean. Of course. But I try to make them understand that the reason verbal abusers say these things is because it's important to them to see their victims distressed. The explanation for that need will vary from abuser to abuser. Some verbal abusers just enjoy seeing people miserable. Some are frightened and insecure and need the victim's discomfort as a way to reassure themselves that they do have some power in this world. Some abusers are victims all day long at work and have stored up so much anger and frustration by the time they get home that they have to take it out on someone—and they do it by verbally abusing those they live with. (Or they are abused at home and take it out on the people they work with.) Whatever their motivation, so long as the attack results in the expected response, the victim is giving the attacker *exactly* what is wanted. To my mind, that is far more a case of letting someone "get away with it" than failing to argue about an ugly chunk of bait.

We tell children who come home crying because they've been teased that the only way to stop the teasing is never to let the teasers know that you mind—because *then it's no fun for them.* This is just as true of adult verbal abuse. So long as it works, the attacker will keep right on doing it. So long as it works, the victim is training the attacker—by positive reinforcement and reward—to be a chronic abuser.

Women in our culture are pressured to fill the role of peacemaker, to always be the one who pours oil on troubled waters, to constantly soothe and nurture and comfort. It is extremely difficult for many women to defend themselves even when they are entirely justified in doing so. The fact that verbal abuse is not taken as seriously in America as physical abuse doesn't help matters; I have had a number of women among my clients who say to me, "At least he doesn't *hit* me," as if that excused the verbal abuse they were subjected to. To such women, I point out that they are not being "nice," or nurturing or loyal or any of those good things, when they devote their lives to training others to be verbal bullies. This usually goes a long way toward eliminating the guilt they feel about verbal self-defense.

Notice that when you are accused of being desperate for attention, and you respond to that by declining to participate in an argument that would provide you with *lots* of attention, you are responding directly to the presupposition and denying it on the spot. Your refusal to take the bait makes the presupposition false.

### Attack Pattern 7

> "*You're* not the ONLY person who has PROBLEMS, you know!"
> "*You're* not the ONLY patient I HAVE, you know!"

And so on. This is one of the easiest of all attacks to handle, and is typically used only by people who are so accustomed to being powerful that they don't feel any need to do their verbal abusing skillfully. The chances that the attacker is wrong, and that you really *are* the only whatever-it-is named in the attack, are so small that they're not worth considering. The only proper move in response is a hearty "You're absolutely right!" That should put an end to the confrontation. Never under any circumstances should you play this particular silly game by answering with something like this:

> "Why do you say *that*? Do you mean that I act like I don't *know* you have other patients? Did I *do something* to make you *feel that way*? What did I *do*?"

That's Placating of the very worst kind. It's a way of saying "Oh dear, if I've made somebody as important and powerful and perfect as *you* are annoyed with me, I *must* have done something *awful* to deserve it! It would be so kind and generous and wonderful of you to explain to me what I did, so that I won't do it again!" And you'll be one very lucky Placater if your abuser doesn't hand you a sucker punch by looking disgusted and snapping, "Don't be ridiculous!" at you. That is precisely what you're asking for.

**Attack Pattern 8**

This is the last of the typically Blamer Mode attacks. Like this:

> "WHY do you always act like you're the only person in the ROOM?"
> "WHY do you always have to spoil everything for everybody ELSE?"
> "WHY don't you ever think about anybody but yourSELF?"

All the ugly verbiage after the stressed "WHY" is the bait, of course; the presupposition is that you do whatever follows, and that you have a reason for doing it that your attacker has the right to demand from you. This is a crude attack, and usually comes at you from people who know you very well, who know how to hurt you because they know what things you are sensitive about, and who don't feel that they have to *bother* being subtle. It is also a favorite technique of trial lawyers; to ask a witness "WHY did you throw the bag of marijuana out of your car?" presupposes that the witness had the marijuana and threw it, and asks only for the reason behind the action.

If you provide the requested reason, you have admitted by default the truth of what you've been accused of. Never respond to "WHY don't you ever consider anybody ELSE's feelings?" with "Because nobody ever thinks about MY feelings, THAT's why!" Furthermore, don't respond to the bait by challenging your attacker like this:

DIALOGUE 8

A: "WHY do you spend every single minute you're awake EATING?"

B: "Whaddayou MEAN? I DO NOT spend all my time eating!"

A: "REALly! Well, tell me what you've DONE since you got up this morning, then."

B: "I don't have to tell you *any*thing!"

A: "Yeah . . . You CAN'T tell me, because you'd have to say you've been stuffing your face ever since you got out of BED this morning!"

B: "I WOULD NOT!"

This is a waste of time and energy, a great deal of fun for the verbal abuser, and entirely without honor or dignity.

There are three possible ways to respond to this type of attack; your choice among them will depend on your personal situation.

1. Take your opponent's ball and run with it, as fast and as blatantly as you can.

A: "WHY do you always act like you're the MOST important PERSON in the ROOM?"

B: "I think it must be because I'm so egotistical. I really don't think about anyone but myself, you know, and so it's natural for me to behave that way. People who are concerned about others *think* of others, and that's very interesting. But personally, I am only concerned about myself."

This response leaves little for your attacker to say. You've spoiled the whole thing. Be extremely careful not to use any abnormally heavy stress patterns, and to maintain a relaxed and serene body language pattern, however, because if this response sounds sarcastic, it will fail.

2. Provide a reason that is completely ridiculous, as a way of demonstrating that you don't intend to play this silly game.

A: "WHY don't you ever consider anybody ELSE's feelings?"

B: "Because it rains so much in the South, especially on the railroad tracks."

3. If it can be done, and if the relationship is worth the trouble, prove the presupposed accusation false on the spot, as in the following dialogue.

DIALOGUE 9

> JANE: "WHY don't you ever do anything to make me HAPPY?"
>
> BOB: "Okay, let's go spend the weekend at your cousin *Tracy*'s place."
>
> JANE: "Good grief! I don't WANT to go visit Tracy!"
>
> BOB: "That wouldn't make you happy? Okay, we won't do it."

Twice, in only four conversational turns, this man has disproved the claim that he NEVER does anything to make his wife happy—first by offering to take her somewhere (presumably somewhere he knows she isn't likely to want to go, but always somewhere that he is willing and able to go if she accepts), and then by agreeing *not* to go when she tells him that she doesn't want to. If she had said, "Hey, that sounds like fun!", he would have accomplished the same thing by finishing off the dialogue with "Good! If you'd like to do that, we will." Not every attack of this kind is set up in a way that will allow you to carry out an Instant Falsification move, but when it can be done it is extremely effective.

Now we can move on to two attack patterns that most frequently occur in Computer Mode.

**Attack Pattern 9**

"A person who REALLY wanted to keep his job would make an EFfort to get the reports in on TIME."

This is nothing but a Computer Mode variation on the "If you REALLY . . ." pattern that we started with. And certainly, if your boss says to you, "If you REALLY wanted to keep your job, you'd make an EFFORT to get your reports in on TIME!", your proper response is "When did you start thinking I don't want to keep my job?" But when the attacker shifts to Computer Mode, that's not safe; this is what you're risking:

A:   "A person who REALLY wanted to keep his job (etc.) . . ."

B:   "When did you start thinking I don't want to keep my job?"

A:   "I wasn't aware that anyone had MENtioned YOU, Throckle."

Ah, yes. What are you going to do now? Say "You MEANT me!" and hand your boss the chance to explain to you what paranoia is and ask if you've ever considered seeing a counselor? I don't recommend it.

Instead, take advantage of the way your opponent has set this up for you; use the attacker's own strength and momentum as part of your defense. Ignore **the bait**—which is the claim that *you* don't get *your* reports in on time—and word your response in Computer Mode. Say:

"You're absolutely right. Promptness is one of the most important factors in the efficient functioning of a business."

Now your boss has a choice. She can continue in Computer Mode, discussing the abstract issue of promptness in the workplace. Or she can ask, "If that's how you feel, why are your reports always *late?*" You will then have forced her to shift either to Blamer Mode or to Leveling, to make her complaint specific, and to give up the lofty and uninvolved Computer stance. She isn't likely to do this unless it's *true* that you always turn your work in late, in which case your problem is not a linguistic one. And she's not likely to waste much time in the abstract discussion, if she chooses that way out of the confrontation.

**Attack Pattern 10**

"SOME professors would really get MAD if their students didn't listen to a single word they SAID, you know!"

This has a long list of presuppositions attached to it, including:

"You don't listen to a single word I say."
"I'm not like other professors; I'm very special and unique."
"You should be grateful to have a special professor like me."
"You should feel guilty about not listening to what I say, when I'm so very wonderful and different from other professors."

You handle this in the same way that you handled Attack Pattern 9. You ignore the bait and match the attacker's Computer Mode. With confident and courteous body language, you say, "I'm sure they would, and I wouldn't blame them a bit." Just as in the previous pattern, the attacker must now either drop the lofty Computer stance and make it clear that *you* are the one being accused—meanwhile giving up the claim to being unique and special and a gift to all students—or drop the attack and join you in an abstract discussion of hypothetical students listening or not listening to hypothetical professors. Do not become involved in anything like this:

DIALOGUE 10

PROF: "SOME professors (etc.) . . ."
YOU: "I DO TOO listen! I ALWAYS listen!"
PROF: (Icily) "I don't recall having mentioned your *name*, Ms. Jones. But since you have chosen to bring it up yourself . . ."

The primary purpose of putting an attack into Computer Mode is to leave the verbal abuser the option of claiming not to have intended the attack in the first place. When you know that, it becomes a weapon for your defense; use it.

At this point you may be wondering why I have been advising you to respond to these two Computer Mode attacks with Computer Mode responses. After all, the rule I gave you told you *not* to match Satir Modes.

I haven't changed my mind. And I would be the first to say that the best response of all to Attack Patterns 9 and 10 would be to *Level*. Something along the line of "Never mind trying to pretend that you're talking about some hypothetical person. It won't work. Let's just get the problem right out in the open and save ourselves some time." If you're able to carry that off, it is unquestionably the right way to go. But in examples like those I've provided, when the attacker outranks the victim substantially, that option may not be one open to you. When that's the situation, the only possible response to Computer Mode is more of the same. Blaming, Placating, and Distracting are out of the question.

Finally, we have two attacks that usually are in Placater Mode.

### Attack Pattern 11

"Even if you DO lose your job, I'll never say it was YOUR fault!"

Hear that dart whiz by your ear? "I'm *so* nice!" this person says. "I'm *so* marvelous and wonderful! No matter how stupid you are, even if you do go and lose your job like the ninny we all know you are, don't you worry—you've still got wonderful me to stand by lucky stupid you." The part about losing your job is the bait; ignore it. Say:

"It's unfortunate that everyone can't have your good sense and sound judgment."

This is no fun at all for the Placater, who wants you to grovel awhile about your incompetence and then add some rhapsodies about the saintliness of the Placater, but it's an excellent move.

### Attack Pattern 12

> "You KNOW I'd never tell you what to DO, Harold—but if you marry that woman, you'll REGRET IT for the REST OF YOUR life."
> "I KNOW it's none of my BUSINESS, Marian—but if you keep feeding those children too much candy, you'll RUIN THEIR teeth."

This pattern includes a linguistic device called a *Hedge*, which Placaters use as a way to deny that they're saying what they're saying. It's a little more subtle than the device of that same kind that I hate most, in which the speaker says most of what he or she is going to say (and shouldn't say) and then tries to cancel it with *"Oh, never mind!"* But it's just as infuriating.

Don't take the bait. Don't discuss the person you plan to marry, or the way you feed your child, or any of the other things that your attacker has already acknowledged are your business and yours alone. Look the Placater firmly in the eye, smile politely, and say this:

> "I want you to know that I appreciate the way you resist the temptation to interfere. Not everyone has your good manners."

This will either silence the Placater immediately or result in a swift change of the subject.

And no matter what attack pattern you're facing, never let yourself be misled by the fact that your attacker does not fit the typical physical image of an abuser. When a small child says any of the following things, they are true verbal attacks and should be handled just as if they came from adults:

"If you REALLY wanted me to get good grades, YOU'D buy me a computer like all the OTHER kids have!"
"SOME kids would feel like they were NEGLECTED if their mother was always working *late* at the OFFICE!"
"EVEN if you DO make me stay home, I'LL still forgive you!"

Physically unintimidating people of any age may have astonishingly powerful verbal skills. And children are often formidable verbal opponents.

## A Final Note about Stress Patterns

I want to close this chapter with a few words about abnormal stress patterns. One of the things that distresses me most about books and articles I read on improving communication, on being more "assertive," etc., is that they give so little attention to stress patterns. They offer example sentences and dialogues in abundance—but with no stress marking indicated, as if each such sentence had only one possible melody that could go with it. There is a classic pair of sentences that linguists use to demonstrate how unsafe that practice is:

"John called Mary a Republican, and then she insulted him."
"John called Mary a Republican, and then *she* insulted *him.*"

Those two sentences mean very different things; only in the second sentence do you know that when John said to Mary, "You're a Republican," the speaker considered that an insult. The words are identical in the two sentences—only the stress accounts for the difference in meaning.

When you hear someone use a sequence of words that matches the words in one of the verbal attack patterns, please remember that the words alone are not enough to identify them as attacks. Only if abnormally heavy stress is also present in the sequence can you be sure—without additional information—that you are hearing a verbal attack. Some speakers may include more abnormal stresses than others, or place them a little differently in the sentence than others; nevertheless, the fact that those abnormal stresses are present is the single most important clue you have that you are under attack. And no matter *what* sequence of words you are hearing, if the speaker is fluent in English and is using abnormal stresses, *you should be wary.*

To talk sensibly about "abnormal" stresses, we need some information about normal ones, because every English sentence, normally spoken, has some portions that are given more stress than others. Only robots give each word in a sentence an identical amount of stress. We'll discuss this in more detail in chapter 7; for now, there are a few general things that can be said.

First, every normal English sentence has at least one stress peak—one word or part of a word that has more stress than the rest of the sentence. If the sentence contains other sentences, each of them will have one such peak. For example: in "As we walked through the forest, we saw a bear," there are two sentences, and each has a stress peak; a probable reading would have a peak at "walked" or at "forest" and at "bear."

Second, the English sound system has something called "emphatic stress"; we use it to indicate that a part of an utterance is important and should be given extra attention. It is a heavier stress than the normal stress peak, and is usually indicated in writing by underlining. For example, "As we walked through the forest, we saw a *bear*" is likely, and normal, unless seeing bears is not an unusual event for the speaker.

Third, English has what is called "contrastive stress." This is a heavy stress, also indicated in writing by underlining, given to one item to contrast it with something else. For example, you might say, "As we walked through the forest, we *heard* a bear," if you wanted to disagree with the other person's claim that you had actually seen the animal.

All of these stress patterns represent *normal* stress. When you go beyond them, you are entering the domain of abnormal stress. Have you ever heard a small child talk like this?

"DADDY? GUESS what WE saw? It was the BIGGEST, most ENORMOUS old BEAR you EVER EVER IMAGined! And it was RIGHT on the ROAD where we were WALKING, and . . ."

Children can go on like that for a very long time, and in children it is both normal and—within reason—charming. In adults, it is neither of those; the adult who talks that way will be perceived as childish or worse, no matter what words are used. Trust your ears—when you hear stress patterns in adult speech that are not like any of the three patterns outlined above as normal for the English sound system, and the adult using them is a native speaker, you are hearing *abnormal stress*. Abnormal stress, plus any one of the sequences of words from the twelve attack patterns presented in this chapter, means that you should be prepared to defend yourself. Abnormal stress together with Blamer speech, no matter what the words, probably represents a verbal attack. And *any* instance of abnormal stress patterns should cause you to pay careful attention until you are certain that you understand why those patterns are being used. The speaker may just be very happy and excited, for example. Listen carefully, so that you will know that is the explanation.

## Notes

1. It may well be that this is true only for English and for languages with vocabularies like that of English. (Japanese, for example, appears to have many more words for the perception of taste and what is called "mouth-feel" than English does.) And there are of course more senses in human beings than the traditional five. But if people have strong preferences for other senses beyond sight, hearing, touch, smell, and taste, they probably have no way to make their preferences clear in English.

2. It's unfortunate that a single word—*stress*—is used in English to refer both to unusual pressure on human beings in their daily lives and to unusual emphasis on parts of utterances when they are spoken. We talk of people "suffering from stress" and learning "stress management" and the like; we also use the term *stress* to refer to the difference between the verb *convert* and the noun *convert*. In both cases, it is a technical term. I can't just decide to substitute *anxiety*

or *pressure* for one usage and *emphasis* for the other, although I might prefer to do so. The context should make it easy to tell which meaning is intended in this book.

3.    The Satir Modes are not categories of personality types; that is, it is inaccurate to say that someone "is" a Blamer, Distracer, or Placater. Whenever I refer to "a Blamer" or "a Placater," it should be understood to be a shorthand for the cumbersome—but more accurate—sequence "a person who is using Blamer Mode" or "a person who is using Placater Mode."

# 5
# *Syntonic Listening*

Remember Miller's Law? It is directed first of all to the *listener*—because before you can assume that what someone is saying is true, and try to imagine what it could be true of, you obviously have to listen to that person's words. If you understand only English, you will have great difficulty applying Miller's Law to a speech by someone who speaks only Thai. But listening to a language you know and understand should *not* be hard for you. Listening is one activity for which your own biology is structured to favor the application of Miller's Law.

Listening syntonically is not only a natural thing to do, it is beneficial for you, in the same way that clean air and a healthy diet are. And yet, until quite recently, all the attention was given to speaking, reading, and writing; listening was ignored. Even now, despite the existence of a thriving International Listening Association and a great deal of new information from researchers, many books and classes that claim to be about listening are really about such things as taking accurate notes.

I am certain that this situation is going to change very rapidly, especially with the publication of the work of Dr. James J. Lynch. We're going to take a look now at some of the things that are known about listening (including those reported by Lynch); you will see that the information is useful for far more than just passing lecture courses.

You will not be surprised to hear that people tend to change their posture, and to move their bodies and their features, in a rhythm that matches the rhythm of their own speech. This synchrony between the verbal and nonverbal streams of a speaker's language behavior—called *self-synchronization*—seems intuitively right and reasonable. But this is just the tip of the synchronization iceberg; there is something more than self-synchrony. There is also an almost identical matching between the movements of a speaker and the movements of a listener, called *interactional synchrony*. It happens so quickly that we are not consciously aware of it; in fact, it is only with modern photography that it has been possible to demonstrate its existence.

When you listen to someone talking, your body moves in synchrony with what you hear. You don't match the speaker's movements exactly, of course. (If you did that, it would be perceived as *mocking* the speaker, and it would cause anger and distress.) What happens is that when the speaker changes position, so does the listener; when the speaker gestures, so does the listener. It is the rate of change and its timing that match.

The delay between the speaker's movement and the corresponding listener movement is about twenty *milliseconds*, a fraction of time so tiny that the two seem to be simultaneous.

This activity is so fundamentally a part of being human that it is present in infants during the first day of their lives. At any age, the absence of this body syncing, or an unusual delay during body syncing, is a signal that something is wrong; autistic children, for example, often do not show normal interactional synchrony. To keep *from* participating in this shared rhythm, normal persons have to make a deliberate effort—either by forcing themselves to maintain a single posture and facial expression or by "tuning out" the speaker completely, or both. On page 73 of *Beyond Culture* (New York: Anchor Books, 1977), Edward T. Hall says that "it appears that synchrony is perhaps the most basic element of speech and the foundation on which all subsequent speech behavior rests."

And it's not only your body that is doing things along with the speaker as you listen. Your mind is also actively involved, far more deeply than just as a source of direction for the motor activity. One of the most miraculous of all the matching operations that the human mind is capable of goes on while you listen to someone speaking a language that you understand.

People talk at various speeds, with 150 to 200 words a minute about the average. But the brain cannot process language by listening at that speed. It is physiologically impossible to understand what you hear if you have to listen to all of each sentence, then determine that sentence's meaning (for example, by determining what each word means and then putting them all together into larger units), then listen to the next sentence, and so on. That cannot be done, and you cannot learn to do it, any more than you could learn to run at a speed of sixty miles an hour if you just practiced hard enough. What you do when you listen goes like this:

**1.**   From the very beginning of the utterance you hear, you start generating in your own mind a set of possible meanings to match the meaning the speaker is trying to express. You do this by using your knowledge of the language, of the speaker, of the particular situation, and of the real world.

**2.**   The instant you have what you perceive as a meaning match, you move on to the next sequence being spoken. Only if you suddenly discover that you have what can only be a serious *mis*match do you slow down and consider each and every word separately—and you do that only until you are satisfied that you have eliminated the problem.

Notice that this is *not* a passive process! This is an *active* process, in which you use your own language skills to create meanings that are syntonic with the meanings intended. Hearing is a passive process in much the same way that smelling is—but hearing is not the same thing as listening.[1]

If you are only hearing, and not listening, you will not be moving in full synchrony with the speaker. True listening—syntonic listening—requires you to be in tune with the speaker both in body and in mind. It is a great deal more than simply hearing.

This is of course the reason why you as a speaker are able to tell if another person is really listening to *you* or not. When you say that someone's eyes were "glazed over" or that a listener was "a million miles away" or that you "might as well have been talking to a wall," you are demonstrating that we are perfectly able to notice the *absence* of normal body syncing, even if we aren't consciously aware that it exists. It is not really possible for you to fool yourself into thinking that people find you fascinating to listen to, if in fact they don't.

As is true for many issues in contemporary science, there are scholars who agree with the evidence for interactional synchrony and scholars who don't. There are experts on both sides of the question. But you don't have to wait for the final results of the scholarly debate to come in (something that has been known to take hundreds of years). To find out whether it's worth *behaving* as if you agreed, try the following experiments while you are listening to someone.

**1.** TRY NOT TO MOVE AT ALL. Assume a position that's comfortable for you, and a facial expression that you can maintain easily, and stay like that. As far as possible, don't change your expression, don't raise your eyebrows, don't smile, don't lean forward or backward, don't tilt your head. Behave as if someone were taking your picture with a timed exposure and your moving would ruin it. Keep this up for at least five minutes.

**2.** TRY TO MOVE *OUT* OF SYNCHRONY WITH THE SPEAKER. Work at it; be actively asynchronic. When the speaker moves, hold still. After the speaker has completed a gesture or a change of posture, make some motion of your own. Move as much as you like, change your facial expression as much as you like, but only when the speaker is not moving.

Can you listen—not just hear, but listen—while you are doing either of those two things? Can you understand what you are listening to?

You might also try the first of those experiments when you are the speaker. Try talking without moving *at all*. Do people listen to you when you do that? Do they seem to understand what you are saying? Do they pay attention?

These are informal experiments, but they are not insignificant. And I am quite willing to predict that the results you get will tend to increase the confidence you feel in the existence of interactional synchrony and its usefulness in your own language environment.

At the beginning of this chapter I mentioned the work of James J. Lynch. What Lynch and his research associates have done is prove that syntonic listening is *good for your health*. His experiments demonstrate that when people are speaking— no matter how seemingly trivial or dull the subject—their blood pressure rises; when people are listening, really listening and not just hearing, their blood pressure falls. Proper listening is a relaxation for the body. People who are busy doing what Lynch calls "defensive" listening—waiting on the edge of their chair for a chance to break into the conversation and grab the floor, rehearsing in their head what they are going to say when they get a chance, struggling to interrupt—do not show the normal drop in blood pressure. Their blood pressure stays elevated, just as if they were doing the talking. And a person who suffers from high blood pressure can be helped significantly if he or she can just be taught to truly listen.

And that is not all. There is yet one more fringe benefit that comes to those who listen syntonically. One of life's most constant irritations is the speaker who bores you frantic, going on and on and on about some subject that seems to you an awful waste of time and energy. If you firmly believe that there is no such thing as telepathy (or auras, evolution, or whatever), the speaker who insists on telling you all about that subject can make you miserable. Unless you listen syntonically!

Begin at the beginning. Apply Miller's Law. Assume that what the person is saying is true, no matter how outrageous you would ordinarily think it is. Just arbitrarily assume that it's true. Now try to imagine what it could be true of. You will find that this turns otherwise maddening conversations into the linguistic equivalent of really good crossword puzzles; it has carried me through many an interminable ride on the Greyhound bus. Only by listening with total attention can you get the information you need about the sort of world in which what the speaker is saying to you could be true. Each little detail becomes one more piece of the puzzle.

Syntonic listening is going to be very good for you, you see. You will have the benefit of a shared rhythmic activity that is essential to your normal functioning as a human being. And your blood pressure will stay healthily down, because (a) that is one of the normal physiological effects of proper listening and (b) you will have a way to escape a great deal of what has previously been perceived by you as boring or infuriating conversation.

The next question is, of course, how is syntonic listening done? What do you have to do? What series of steps must you follow?

We are all in luck—this is another of those situations in which your body knows how, even if you don't know it knows. If I were to ask you "how" you run, talk, climb stairs, or do any of a thousand other activities you do every day, you wouldn't be able to tell me. The odds against your being able to tell me how you tie a bow are enormous. You don't "know" which muscles move, or in what sequence, or how the central nervous system starts and stops those movements, or what chemical substances must flow through your body to keep it all going; none of that information is likely to be part of your conscious knowledge. But your body *does* know how all this is done, and you would be able to demonstrate that for me by just doing whatever I'd asked you to tell me about.

In the same way, your body (more accurately, your "body-mind") knows how to listen syntonically. It may be lazy about doing it, or selfish about it, but that's a different issue. It knows how to synchronize its movements with those of the speaker. All you have to do to get that process under way is *listen*. Really listen. Don't take notes! Don't think about what you would like to say when your turn comes. Don't think of how much more you know about what is being said than the speaker does, or how much better you would be able to express it. Don't watch for a pause, some spot where you could seize the chance and start talking yourself. Don't think about where you're going after the language interaction is over. Don't stare at the ceiling or the clock or out the window. Give the speaker your full attention. Regardless of the situation, pretend that you are absolutely gripped by every word that is being said. If you do that, your body will automatically move into syntonic listening, with no further effort on your part. You don't even need to know that it's happening.

What if you are one of those people I mentioned a moment ago, who thinks that this is too much bother, too much work? What if you don't *want* to give your attention in this way? If that is true, even if you are convinced that syntonic listening would be sufficiently good for you to make it worth a try, you're going to have trouble at first. You'll start with the best of intentions, listen carefully to a few sentences—and then suddenly you'll realize that you haven't heard a word the speaker was saying for quite some time.

This will happen no matter what the subject of conversation is. If it's something that genuinely interests you, you'll stop listening because you want to be the one who is talking about it; if it's something that doesn't interest you, you'll stop listening because you're bored. This is to be expected, but you'll have to make an effort to break yourself of the habit. When you catch your mind wandering, grab it, drag it back, and *listen*. When you catch yourself interrupting, stop, apologize, ask the speaker to continue, and *listen*.

Practicing this with real speakers, present and aware, may not be easy. They may decide that talking to you is more trouble than it's worth and refuse to participate. But you have an alternative way to practice: Listen to a speaker on television. You need to watch someone who is talking over a reasonably long period of time and who is not trying to be funny. Ideally, you need someone who is not reading from a TelePrompTer, but is actually talking. Television preachers are extremely useful for this purpose; much of educational television is suitable. It won't matter to your televised speaker how many times your mind wanders and you have to drag it back and try again. Your "partner" in this interaction will go right on talking until literally turned off. And after you've done this awhile, you will be able to interact more comfortably with speakers who are there in the flesh.

An important question is, can you *fake* syntonic listening? Robert Bolton, whose book *People Skills* (Englewood Cliffs, N.J.: Prentice-Hall, 1979), has excellent material on listening, says you can't, because the speaker will always catch you. I agree with him. It's possible for you to set up a good starting pose for yourself—sitting relaxed but alert, leaning slightly toward the speaker, looking intently at the speaker's face as if it had your total attention. You can do that. But there is no sequence of body movements that you can memorize and carry out as you pretend to listen, because *your movements are completely dependent on the speaker's body language, which is in turn dependent on the speaker's words.* Speakers match their own body language to what they are saying, and neither the verbal stream nor the nonverbal can be predicted, except for sequences so trivial that they are not relevant. If you're not really listening, you won't be body syncing. And the speaker will notice that, even if his or her only conscious sign of awareness is a feeling of irritation or disappointment or uneasiness. Adult speakers may be too polite to do what a little child would do and say, *"Hey! You're not listening to me!"* But they will know.

It's true that the world is full of people who spend a great deal of time together, for whom language interactions may have become little more than rituals. One or the other may talk, but neither listens, and the one speaking doesn't really mind that. What is involved is a kind of metamessage that says "I'm here with you, and I'm glad to be here with you, and you matter to me." In that case, the only "listening" skill needed is staying awake and saying "Mmhmmm" and "Really?" once in a while in the pauses. That's communication; that's interaction; but it's a type of language behavior quite different from what we've been discussing. It's not appropriate for other situations.

Even for people like those just described, the mismatch detector is still on duty. A change in the speaker's usual behavior—some signal that what is being said *requires* attention—will ordinarily be noticed and reacted to appropriately. When one member of such a pair can say to the other, "You know, that bull elephant there in the hall shouldn't be in the house," and get no response except "Mmhmmm" or "Really?", the metamessage is "I may be physically here with you, but that's as far as it goes." There's nothing in that metamessage that tells the speaker that he matters to the listener in any way.

We have now identified one very important difference between speaking and listening. Remember our brief discussion of the Satir Modes, and the dangerousness of the Phony Leveler? It *is* possible for a skillful speaker to do a great deal of faking. Levelers are supposed to be people whose *internal* state is syntonic, because every one of their channels of communication is in perfect tune with the others; the Phony Leveler is, by definition, faking that state of self-syntonicity. But there's no such thing as a person who can skillfully fake real listening, not if the speaker is paying any attention at all to what is happening. By knowing this, we are able to simplify our lives considerably.

If you're wondering whether you are listened to properly, there are two clues you can actively watch for. Both represent a failure of the listener to synchronize with your body language. Watch for the listener who doesn't seem to move at all (unless that's what *you* are doing, in which case it does demonstrate synchrony). And watch for body language that is totally out of sync with yours, such as staring out the window, gestures made when you aren't moving, eyes that are "looking right through you," and so on. If you're close enough to see the pupils of your listener's eyes, watch them—they should get larger when something you say is perceived as worth attention. If that never happens, there is a good chance that you are only being heard, not listened to. You'll find that it isn't hard to spot the listener who is not body syncing with you at all, and you will get very good at spotting those who are only partly in sync.

# Listening Styles

In the previous chapter, we looked at two ways to classify the language behavior of speakers. We learned that by observing what people say and their body language we can obtain useful immediate feedback information during language interactions, using techniques for recognizing and responding to their use of the Sensory Modes and the Satir Modes.

There is a similar process for the observation and analysis of listening behavior, using as data the responses the listener makes to your speech.[2] Once you've determined that a person *is* listening to you, you can move on to find out *how* the listening is being done. Here are five common listening styles, with examples of typical responses that identify them.

1.  **Evaluating**
    POSITIVE: "That's a very kind thing to say."
    NEGATIVE: "That's a completely ridiculous thing to say."
2.  **Interpreting**
    POSITIVE: "You're only saying that because you're so upset about your grades."
    NEGATIVE: "You're only saying that because you want to make me feel guilty."
3.  **Emotional**
    POSITIVE: "I'm so sorry you feel that way . . . I wish I could help."
    NEGATIVE: "It makes me feel awful to hear you talk like that . . . I wish you'd just be quiet about it."
4.  **Probing**
    POSITIVE: "Maybe things aren't really as bad as they seem. What were the *exact* words that your boss said to you?"
    NEGATIVE: "Either give me an exact concrete example or don't bother me about it."
5.  **Summarizing**
    POSITIVE: "It seems to me that you're saying you don't think your solution will work. Am I understanding you properly?"

NEGATIVE:    "What you mean is, you made such a mess of
it that the situation is hopeless. That's what
you're really saying."

Each of these listening styles can produce either positive or
negative responses, and can include utterances using any of
the Satir Modes or Sensory Modes. Obviously, any of them can
occur in the attack patterns that we have identified. For example, suppose you've talked to your boss for a few minutes
and this is the response you get:

"EVEN somebody that's only been in this department a
MONTH should be able to see that that's a STUPID way to set
up a vacATION schedule!"

Your boss has listened to the schedule you were proposing,
and is responding. What he says tells you that he has been
using the Evaluating style of listening, judging what you were
saying and then stating that judgment. He's doing this as an
obvious Blamer—notice the open attack pattern, the abnormal
use of stress, and the words "only" and "stupid." The Sensory
Mode preference appears to be Sight Mode—you should be
able to *see* how wrong you are. What do you do next?

First, you apply the rules for responding to Sensory Modes
and Satir Modes. You do not start Blaming back at your boss;
that would be a waste of time, as you know. You will try using
sight vocabulary items yourself, matching the Sensory Mode
you identified. You might decide to speak in Computer Mode—
because it isn't Blaming, and it is neutral, and the boss outranks you—adding Satir Mode strategy as a way of adjusting
to this listener. Your goal is to change the situation, so that
the *next* response to your speech will indicate a more successful communication. You want to hear a response something
like this:

"In other words, you were trying to say that if we gave
your plan a try for a while it might help us work out a
system that would *really* be what we need. I guess I didn't

see what you were saying before . . . it doesn't look as bad as I thought it did at first."

That's better. Now your listener has switched to a Summarizing listening style, has stopped Blaming and started Leveling, is still using visual Sensory Mode, and seems to be willing to discuss matters. A response like that would confirm for you that your own linguistic adjustments had been the correct ones.

Each time that a listener responds to you, analyze it this way before you go on. Body language alone can give you clues to the Satir Mode being used; a simple "I see" or "I hear you" or "I get it" may be enough to let you identify the Sensory Mode. Longer responses will give you more information, but even the briefest ones can be valuable indicators of your proper strategy. This is precisely the information you need in order to make adjustments in your language behavior *while the interaction is going on.*

## What if You Have to Do *All* the Talking?

I am forever running into people who claim to have this problem. They tell me that there is very little conversation in their lives, and that they are forced to do all the work of communication themselves. If you are one of these people—if you either do all the talking or feel obligated to *try* to do all the talking—you need to answer a question for me. *Why do you do that?* Answers I usually get include the familiar "I don't know" as an opening line, followed after a bit of coaxing by one of these:

"Because I'm interesting, and other people are boring."

Maybe. I've been lucky—I come from a family of lawyers, musicians, teachers, and preachers. I've traveled a lot. I've been a university professor and a writer and a linguist. I've spent most of my life with people who had plenty of interesting things to talk about. But in all these years, I've known at most two people who were so interesting that I could literally listen to them for hours without ever growing bored.

Are you really a person like that? *Find out.* Do people hang on your every word? Do they become unaware of anything else but your voice? When they see you coming, do they hurry to join you? If you try to turn over the floor to someone else, do they press you to go on talking instead? Does it seem to you, if you watch them closely, that they are body syncing with you, and enjoying that? Do you have their full and total and delighted attention?

If so, then I congratulate you, and I am sorry I haven't had the pleasure of your company. But if that is your situation, you don't have a problem. If you get tired of doing all the talking, just be still.

> "Because I'm the *boss* (parent, teacher, doctor, husband, officer, etc.) and they damn well BETTER let me do the talking!"

Fine. You have no illusions. If you don't care whether your audience is only pretending to listen, you still have no problem. If you do care, however, read on.

> "Because nobody ever listens to me, so I *have* to keep talking."

Aha! This is the most usual situation. Even when the talk glutton is the dominant person in the interaction, this is usually it.

People who were always hungry as children often overeat as adults, even when they have a secure food supply and an adequate income. This is a fear reaction: "I'd better eat now, because I can't be sure there'll be any food tomorrow." If you grew up stifled, never being allowed to talk or never being really listened to when you did talk, you may be carrying a similar fear around with you: "I'd better talk now, because I may never get another listener."

People starved for food or water will overindulge horribly

when they get a chance, but the body will wisely reject the excess. Unfortunately, people starved for listening have no such internal reflex to protect them. Instead, what happens is that others do the rejecting. And that makes things worse. Now these people will grow even more frightened. If they have established a reputation as one who always hogs the floor, people will make an excuse and walk away when they start to talk. When they try to catch somebody's eye to get a turn to talk, the speaker will pretend not to see them. When their hand goes up in an audience, it will be ignored. If they *force* their conversation on people, they may be heard but they will not be listened to. And they will have produced exactly the famine that they were so afraid of. Are you one of these people?

If you are, there is a clear goal for you. You will have to become a speaker who is at least not a torment to listen to; and you will have to talk interestingly and pleasantly and *patiently* until people begin to realize that you have changed. Most of all, you will have to force yourself to listen, in spite of the distress it causes you to do so. There is no other solution except that of paying someone the standard therapist's fee of $75 an hour and up to listen to you.

It may be a great deal of trouble to follow the instructions in this book, but it will not cost you $75 an hour, and it will not hurt you the way that spending your life being someone people flee from will hurt.

## Telephone Listening

Life is filled with things that are assumed to be true because they are "obvious" or "self-evident." It's always a shock to learn that one of those things is not true at all. It gives you a chance to imagine what it was like to hear from the town crier that the world was round rather than, as was obvious and self-evident, flat.

Among the set of self-evident myths is the idea that if you want to lie you're better off doing it on the phone, where people can't see you and you are therefore more likely to get away with it. That happens to be false; it is in fact easier for people to spot a lie when they hear it on the phone than when they hear it from a person present at the time.

The research studies suggest a number of reasons for this. For example:

1.  There is less distraction in telephone speech, so the listener can concentrate more easily.
2.  There is less emotional involvement in telephone conversation, which eliminates yet another sort of distraction.
3.  Pitch changes, which are important to the detection of deceit, are easier to hear when attention is focused entirely on the voice.

I agree with all three of these proposed explanations; they are surely accurate. But I think that the generalization we can draw from them is this: *Without body language feedback, a person who lies cannot obtain the necessary data for the constant fine-tuning required to make lies work.* The auditory (ear) channel of communication alone does not provide enough information for this purpose. The speaker who would like to deceive can't even watch for body syncing or other obvious clues to attention. Which means that on the phone you *can* fake listening!

In person, it's easier for speakers to deceive and very difficult for listeners to do so. On the telephone, this is reversed—it is the listener who can deceive more easily, and the speaker who has difficulty. The ear is a much better judge of lying than the eye is, contrary to what is often assumed—and the very best channel of all for lying is the *face*, which is of course invisible in telephone communication. (It's interesting to consider what this may mean for people who do teleconferencing with video and can see one another as they talk, but we don't yet have enough data on that to come to any firm conclusions about it.)

Knowing this gives you crucial strategic information about the method you choose for carrying on language interactions when you suspect that you might be dealing with a Phony Leveler. You are better off having your conversation by telephone. The telephone will keep you from being influenced by the perfect match between the Phony Leveler's speech and body language, which is so convincing when you can see it. And it will keep the Phony Leveler from being able to observe your reactions and make constant linguistic adjustments based on them. That gives you a much better chance in such an interaction than you would have if it were carried on face-to-face.

Used properly, this is a major advantage for the listener. But unless you listen with your full attention, the advantage will be canceled. Half-listening on the phone, while you read a magazine or watch television or daydream, will be no more effective than half-listening in person. Listen carefully for changes in the pitch of the voice; research indicates that when people are trying to deliberately deceive others the pitch of their voices will rise.

This does not mean that high pitch is a clue to the detection of deception, however. A rise in pitch in the speech of someone who has a naturally low-pitched voice is just as significant. It is the deviation from the pitch level established by the speaker as the norm—the *mismatch* between what has been established as typical and the higher pitch—that warns the listener to be wary.

Your best strategy as a listener, when you're not certain that you can trust a speaker with whom you plan some sort of interaction, is to have at least one discussion of the issues by telephone before you have the face-to-face meeting. That will give you an opportunity to listen for deception in a situation where the speaker can't use body language and associated feedback skills as tools to influence your perceptions.

## Notes

1.  Notice that—as is typical for the impoverished vocabulary of this sense in English—the single word *smell* has to serve for both the passive and the active meanings of the term.

2.  See Eastwood Atwater's book, *"I Hear You": Listening Skills to Make You a Better Manager* (Englewood Cliffs, N.J.: Prentice-Hall, 1981), for a discussion. The classification of listening styles is based on the work of psychologist Carl Rogers; I have used a slightly different terminology from Atwater's or Rogers's.

# 6
# *Language Choices: Part One*

Books on language often seem to imply that it's possible to separate verbal communication (VC) from nonverbal communication (NVC). I understand why, but in fact that separation cannot be made. Verbal communications gets its meaning from nonverbal communication, and vice versa; each serves as the other's context. Consider the gesture of a fist smashing hard into an upturned palm. Is that a violent or aggressive gesture? Does it mean that the speaker is angry?

It might; and then again, it might not. Look at the two sentences below.

> "When you hammer these skinny little nails, you've got to hit 'em smack on the head the first time (FIST SMACKS INTO PALM), or they'll bend on you for sure!"
> "It makes me furious (FIST SMACKS INTO PALM) just to have to be in the same *room* with him!"

The gesture is the same in both examples, but its meaning depends upon the words that are used with it; you can't separate the two.

Every human language contains gestures called *emblems,*[1]

which have an independent meaning of sorts—just as words have an independent meaning of sorts. The V sign made with the index and middle fingers is an emblem that meant "victory" to a previous generation of Americans and now is used to mean "peace." But look at these examples:

> "You are so *naïve*, always jabbering about PEACE!"
> "To me, the most important issue of all is peace."

In both examples, the emblem-gesture may be used by the speaker simultaneously with the pronouncing of the word "peace," and listeners would understand that the emblem *meant* "peace." But both the word and the gesture have rather different meanings in those two sentences! Nor can we tell, from looking at just the printed words, whether the sentences are spoken jokingly, sarcastically, bitterly, or in any of a multitude of other possible ways. We just don't have enough information available to us.

The printed word doesn't allow the luxury of complete truth, because it doesn't allow the presentation of simultaneous information, and because we have no symbol system that accurately conveys nonverbal information, simultaneous or not. This can be extremely frustrating to linguists and people in related disciplines—and it is frustrating to me. Because the only way that I can present a useful discussion of the two interdependent components of oral communication in writing is to do just what I complained about in the first sentence of this chapter: I have to resort to the traditional artificial separation.

It's like the artificial separation in a book on tennis that has a section on "the forearm" and another on "the wrist," as if they functioned in isolation from each other. Or a medical text, with its sections on "the heart," "the kidney," and "the brain," all treated as independent entities in isolation. If there were some other way to do it—if writers could combine the written word with the equivalent of a videotape and sound track—this separation could be avoided. No doubt the time will come when our technology will make that possible, and when the fiction writer will be forced to choose between the old-fashioned book that leaves the reader free to use the imagination and the new-fashioned book in which that freedom is gone. For now, however, there is no choice.

What we're going to do, therefore, is begin at one end of the continuum that stretches from "verbal" to "nonverbal," with the question of specific word choices. Then in Chapter 7 we'll move on to areas where VC and NVC overlap very closely, such as tone of voice and intonation. We'll end with the most nonverbal portion of all, which is commonly called "body language." But please remember as you read that these divisions are an artificial structure imposed by the format of the written word, and that it is all really one simultaneous process; words PLUS intonation PLUS body language, all happening together at the same time, and all interdependent. The separation is only a convenience for the writer and the reader.

## Lexical Choices—The Words You Say

Theoretically, the choice of words to say is infinite. Formally, any sequence of language whatsoever might be used at any time whatsoever. Even if you reduce the number of possible choices by excluding all fully ungrammatical sequences such as "Elephant the by walked" and all meaningless sequences such as "Pleatless purple concepts sparkle effortlessly," the number of possibilities is still—formally—infinite. For any sentence whatsoever, no matter how long, it is always theoretically possible to say "and" and go on with more words, so that every individual sentence of English could be infinitely long. (This is why we could never list all the possible sentences of any human language, even with the most powerful computer.)

But we don't *live* in the formal theoretical world. No real sentence can be infinitely long, because the speaker would collapse with exhaustion or lose his voice or fall asleep . . . the sentence would end relatively quickly. And in the real world , of all the infinite number of possible things to say, the vast majority can be eliminated by the speaker in advance. You know in advance, when you state your rules for talking to strangers in elevators, that you don't have to consider the color of the elevator walls; in the same way, in choosing things to say, you know in advance that many millions of possibilities don't even have to be considered.

The point at which a discussion of lexical choices becomes worthwhile is when that theoretical infinity of choice has been reduced to a manageable real-world number, and that is where we will begin. It's crucial for you to realize that you do *have* choices, and that you have more control over them than you may have realized.

The choice of words can be a life-or-death matter. If you are a law enforcement officer, or you serve on a crisis hotline, or you answer the phones for a hospital emergency room, the words you choose may literally mean the difference between life and death for others. People who choose the words for evacuation instructions during fires or safety preparations in airplane crashes have an awesome responsibility. Even those who ordinarily don't have to think of such things may have the experience of needing to speak carefully when someone talks to them about suicide. In such situations, we know that every word counts.

If we face every language interaction as if it were a crisis, it will cause a troublesome self-consciousness that will make communication almost impossible. But we should abandon the opposite extreme, in which we behave as if any old word will do if it makes approximate sense. There is a middle ground.

In this section we're going to look at a group of techniques for choosing your words systematically. All of them can be added to your language skills without an unreasonable investment of time and energy; all are easily used by fluent speakers of English (and can of course be adapted to other human languages).

## The Power of Presupposition

The first technique is: USE WORDS THAT HELP YOU PRESUPPOSE WHAT YOU WANT YOUR LISTENER TO ACCEPT.

## Time Words

Many of the time words of English presuppose that what accompanies them in an utterance exists in time. When you use such words to link two propositions together, this can be very useful. For example:

> "Until we find the cure for cancer, we should keep on giving our support to research."

The word *until* in the sentence lets us presuppose "we will find the cure for cancer"; putting the proposition headed by *until* first in the sentence gives it additional importance. This is less likely to provoke argument than saying "We have to find the cure for cancer before we can stop giving our support to research." (Notice that in *that* sentence the time word *before* presupposes that we can stop supporting the research; this effect should not be accidental on the part of the speaker.)

> "After you pass the history exam, we'll go to the beach."

In this sentence, the word *after* lets us presuppose that you will pass the history test, as if that could be taken for granted. It's very different from "If you pass the history exam, we'll go to the beach," which expresses no confidence that the exam will be passed.

## Time Words plus Illusion of Choice

You can make this handy property of time words even more effective if you combine it with an illusion of choice that distracts the listener from what is being presupposed.[2] Suppose that you want your son to wash the dishes, and you anticipate a natural reluctance on his part. Choose your words like this:

> "While you're doing the dishes, would you rather listen to 'Band A' or 'Band B'?"

The word *while* presupposes "you will be doing the dishes," and the offered choice serves to distract your son from the unpalatable fact that you're offering *no* choice about whether to do the dishes. You could, of course, say, "If you'll do the dishes, I'll let you listen to 'Band A' or 'Band B', whichever you like," and make a more blatant demonstration of your power over your child; the gratification that would provide to your ego is not worth the automatic resistance it would provoke.

Do you want your PTA or Kiwanis Club or church group to have a Spring Festival, and know that you can expect some of the members to object to the idea? Then choose a time word that presupposes the event and offer an illusory choice with it, like this:

"During our Spring Festival, would you rather have an indoor banquet or just a picnic in the city park?"

This will not stop people strongly opposed to a Spring Festival from expressing their objections. But people who haven't given the matter much thought, or who don't particularly care one way or the other, will tend to let the presupposition pass and give their attention to the question of banquet versus picnic. If there are enough such people, you will have an advantage over your opposition. This strategy is just as effective at a board meeting, or in any other negotiation, as it is in the two examples given. What it does is make it easier for your *listener* to apply Miller's Law, you see. Your choice of words makes it easy for the listener to imagine the reality in which your Spring Festival is the obvious correct choice; furthermore, it helps to exclude from your listener's mind the set of other possible events your group could sponsor.

If you are a salesperson, say, "Until we agree on the final price, would you rather see samples in powder blue or foam green?" This presupposes that the final price will be agreed on, and thus that the sale will take place, and distracts the buyer's attention toward the matter of color choice.

No doubt you are thinking that this technique is verbal manipulation; you are right, that's exactly what it is. But there is *no way* that you can avoid verbal manipulation. Every verbal attempt that you make to persuade someone else to do anything at all—even the bare-bones goal of persuading someone to listen to the words you are saying—is a form of verbal manipulation. Even silence is a form of verbal manipulation.[3] Since you cannot communicate without manipulating, and you cannot not communicate and survive, it is better for you to have some idea what you are doing. And it is absolutely vital for you to know what people who are speaking and writing *to* you are doing! This is not a case in which ignorance is bliss, unless the role of victim appeals to you.

## Nominalization

Every human language has a process called "nominalization," which is a way of turning predicates into nouns. (For present purposes, consider predicates to be verbs and adjectives.) The nice thing about a noun, in terms of using words to presuppose content, is that when you put certain other words in front of the noun you presuppose that the thing named *exists*. Consider the following pair of sentences:

"The sign on the lawn was destroyed."
"The destruction of the sign on the lawn was a surprise."

The first sentence claims that someone or something destroyed the sign, and that claim has to be supported. The second sentence, however, has taken the verb *destroy* and turned it into the noun *destruction*; putting "the" before "destruction" then presupposes "the sign was destroyed," and all that is being claimed is that the event was a surprise.

You can nominalize any verb of English by adding *-ing* to it (this is, in fact, how you test a word to see if it *is* a verb); you can nominalize any adjective by adding *-ing* to the form of the word *be* that comes before it. Like this:

"Swimming is good exercise."
"Being happy is not always easy."

In addition, many English predicates have special noun forms that end with *-tion* or *-ness* or a similar suffix. Like this:

"Carelessness can be fatal."
"Abandonment is difficult to prove."
"Confusion often results from poor planning."

To use a nominalization as a way of presupposing something, follow this sequence of steps: Make it the subject of your sentence; put a definite article or demonstrative (*the, this, that, these, those*) in front of it; finish your sentence with a predicate. That's the basic technique, without frills.

Adding frills will make it considerably more powerful, however, and we can now move on to examine some of the possibilities. The effect of the frills is to make the presupposition you're offering even stronger.

## Nominalization plus Possessive

The presupposition of existence that is created by a sequence of possessive plus noun is so strong in English that it's hard to override. Navajo has sentences that can be translated literally as "My horse does not exist"; such sequences sound very strange to the English speaker's ear. You can use this as a way to make your presuppositions more powerful, as in the examples below.

"The student's destruction of the sign surprised us all."
**Presupposed**: The student destroyed the sign.
"Molly's abandonment of the child was a mystery to everyone."
**Presupposed**: Molly abandoned the child.
"Your arrogance is very interesting."
**Presupposed**: You are arrogant.

## Nominalization plus Possessive plus Description

The final step in providing nominalized presuppositions with verbal armor is to add a descriptive chunk or two to the noun phrase you're constructing. The English speaker would find a sentence such as "My beautiful white Arabian horse with the flowing mane and the gorgeous tail does not exist" to be nonsensical—if it doesn't exist, how can you describe it in such detail? And why bother? Look at the following sentence.

> "Your constant extravagance must be a real nuisance for you."

This presupposes first of all that you are extravagant, and then goes on to presuppose that your extravagance is constant—that is, that you are *always* extravagant. However, both claims are tucked away in a sentence that is structured as a kind of sympathetic comment; and all that's openly up for proof is the observation that your taken-for-granted constant extravagance must interfere with your happiness.

This technique is one of the most popular of all weapons for the public speaker. There's no opportunity at the time for someone to deny the presupposed material, and as it piles up during the speech it tends to become overwhelmingly convincing. That's why a politician likes sentences such as "The unbridled and uncontrolled and unprecedented extravagance of the present administration is a source of astonishment to the public." Get a dozen or two of those into a twenty-minute speech and you stand a good chance of bringing people to believe that that's what they thought in the first place. And if you have only thirty seconds available to you, this pattern allows you to pack a tremendous amount of content into those few seconds—very useful in the "paid political announcement" or the television commercial, especially if it is to be repeated a number of times.

Suppose you must discuss with someone the fact that he or she is always late, and you would rather not waste your time in a long wrangle over whether that is true or not. In such a case, it's much better to approach the interaction by presupposing the existence of the problem with "Your constant lateness" and then adding an innocuous predicate such as "is a curious phenomenon." It is harder, given the rules of conversation, for the person you're speaking to to say, "Whaddaya mean, I'm always late?" when you have carefully tucked that claim away in a presupposition. The only proper sequence of that type is the lame "Whaddaya mean, it's curious?", and with that response the person has admitted the constant lateness.

Similarly, when you need to compliment someone and then move on, without becoming tangled in a struggle over whether the compliment is deserved or not, it's best to presuppose the words of praise. If you know that you must deal with a Placater, for example, you want to avoid an exchange like this one:


DIALOGUE 11

    A: "You are *really good* at drawing caricatures!"

    B: "Oh, I am not! Shoot . . . *I* can hardly *draw* at ALL!"

    A: "No, I *mean* it! You're better at it than anybody I know."

    B: "Oh, *you* know *me*! I do the best I *can*—but *I* know it's not very *good*!"

    A: "Listen, I wouldn't say it if it wasn't true."

    B: "Oh, of COURSE you wouldn't! Oh goodness, did I *sound* like I was ac*cus*ing *you* of not TELLING the TRUTH? Oh, I didn't mean to say anything of the *kind*! I swear, I am ALWays putting my *foot* in my mouth!"

    A: "Now, that's not so! I mean . . ."

Uhuh. This could take the rest of the week to get out of. It's much better to presuppose the Placater's artistic skill and give him or her something else to Placate with, preferably something unimportant. Like this:

"Because of your incredible skill at drawing caricatures, we're asking you to be our featured artist at the bazaar— would you rather sit by the entrance door or the exit?"

Now the artistic skill is tucked into the presupposition, heavily reinforced by a possessive and a word of description, and there is an illusion of choice at the end to distract the Placater's attention. This is much better.

## Factive Predicates

English has a set of predicates that are called "factive" predicates.[4] This means that when they are followed immediately by an embedded sentence, that sentence is presupposed to be a fact—*even when the predicates are used in the negative.* This sounds complicated because the terms are unfamiliar, but it's very simple; the best way to make this clear is by example. For instance:

**Positive:**
"I'm sorry that the door was open."
**Negative:**
"I'm not sorry that the door was open."

You see? The *embedded* sentence—"the door was open"— continues to be presupposed as true in both complete sentences. It makes no difference whether the speaker is sorry about it or not. This tells us that the predicate "be sorry" is factive. Contrast that with this pair:

**Positive:**
"I think that the door was open."
**Negative:**
"I don't think that the door was open."

It's clear that "think" is *not* a factive predicate, because the negative sentence no longer presupposes an open door.

The effect of this pattern is partially responsible for the incessant use of the word *regret* in announcements about things that aren't regretted at all, as in these examples:

> "The management regrets that all the tickets for this event have been sold."
> "The State Department regrets that this information was somehow leaked to the press."
> "The company regrets that the terms of the contract do not allow overtime wages to be paid."

*Regret* is factive; whether you say "I regret that Harry left" or "I don't regret that Harry left," Harry is still gone.

When you want to make sure that a particular statement will be perceived by your listeners as *true*, use this characteristic of English to help you. Fit the statement into a sentence with a factive predicate.[4]

## Miscellaneous Trojan Horses

I call these Trojan Horses because they have unpleasant surprises hidden in them. The famous incriminating question pattern of the trial lawyer, as in "Have you stopped smoking marijuana?", is an excellent example. If the witness says yes, he has admitted that he used to smoke marijuana before he stopped; if the witness says no, she has admitted that she still smokes marijuana because she hasn't stopped. That works for the lawyer because the predicate "stop VERBing" presupposes the predicate "start VERBing," regardless of the response.

Look at the following three sentences:

> "I am delighted that you won the prize."
> "I am delighted that you happened to win the prize."
> "I am delighted that you managed to win the prize."

The first sentence is a compliment and a pleasant thing to say, but the others contain Trojan Horses. The second presupposes that your winning the prize was only an accident; the third presupposes that although you won you had a dickens of a time doing it. Both are ways to avoid a wholehearted compliment.

Trojan Horses are primary causes of two kinds of communication breakdown: the one that leaves the speaker bewildered, asking, "But what did I *say*, for crying out loud?"; and the one that leaves the listener deeply hurt but unable to figure out why.

It's important for you to become conscious of the presuppositions of words that you use so that you can avoid using them when they have negative meanings embedded in them that you may not have intended and so that you can use them deliberately when their effect (whether positive or negative) is part of your communication goal. If you are a native speaker of the language you are using, this takes no special training, just careful attention. But if you're not used to paying attention to such things, it will require extra effort on your part for a while.

At which point we come to the "But that wasn't what I MEANT!" issue. Whenever I talk about language behavior of this kind, someone in the audience is sure to say, "But if the person said it without realizing it had that other stuff in it, it doesn't count!" Or "It's not fair to get mad at him!" Or "It's not her fault and she can't help it!"

*Once in a while*, this is true. Everybody makes speech errors from time to time. Slips of the tongue are part of being human. If people who ordinarily give you no cause to think of them as verbal opponents or abusers say something like "I'm so glad you managed to pass the course," and then deny that they intended to be insulting, I think you should believe them. *Once*. But not when it happens over and over again! It's not possible for a native speaker of a language to be consistently unaware of its presuppositions. It *is* possible for someone to have bad verbal habits that have become automatic, because everyone has allowed that to happen and perhaps helped it along; but once those bad habits are pointed out, the automatic quality disappears, and so does the excuse. It is as typical for verbal abusers to hide insults in Trojan Horses and then deny any intention to be abusive as it is for them to use the verbal attack patterns and deny knowing that was what they were doing. Their denials should not impress you.

A common practice in the workplace is for males in competition with females to use Trojan Horses that hide presuppositions about childishness, excessive emotion, and the like. This lets them take advantage of the common belief that the speech and behavior of women are characterized by those qualities. The male administrator who says, "The company was only too happy to humor Ms. Smith in this matter," is not unaware that only children and irrational persons are ordinarily "humored." And that administrator knows quite well that if the woman he claims to have "humored" objects to his use of the word, she will be perceived as *being* childish and irrational. This is dirty pool, and the shots are deliberate; the woman who doesn't understand the game is in for trouble. Here are a few more examples of this type of cutesipation:

> "We are very pleased with the way Ms. Smith always manages to get her reports in on time."
> "We are all grateful to Ms. Smith for this valuable piece of gossip."
> "Every man in the company was pleased to allow Ms. Smith to be promoted to her present position."
> "We all appreciate Ms. Smith's willingness to chat with our customers at such length."

Skillful men do not say these things with sarcastic intonation or body language. They will steadfastly insist that they have no negative intentions, if challenged. But you could spend twenty years in a corporate boardroom without ever hearing anyone claim to have "humored" a male executive. (If you do hear such a thing, you can be certain that he is respected by no one.)

You usually cannot counter these items on the spot; that is one of the reasons why they are so useful to the attacker. But there is one thing that you *must* do, while you are learning the game: Be absolutely certain nobody sees that the Trojan Horses have caused you distress. If they don't appear to bother you, your attacker may interpret that to mean that you *do* know how to play, and decide not to take chances. After all, if you were able to respond effectively to one of these attacks, he would be in the position of having lost points to a woman (or to a man viewed by the others present as powerless). He won't risk that. Your strategy is to appear so impervious to the attacks—and so knowledgeable—that he'll suspect you are setting him up. The male sees all this as a sort of linguistic poker game—it's up to you to bluff. Note: Only two types of men will do this—those who would really *mind* losing a point to a woman, and those whose major interest is not in what happens in the long run but in playing the game. In neither case are the attacks accidental.

## The Power of Naming

The second technique for making systematic word choices is: USE THE POWER OF NAMING. Many cultures have an open and obvious component of respect for naming. In such societies the choice of a name is a deeply serious matter involving complex formal rituals; a person's true name may be known only to the immediate family. The lack of such an open structure in American culture obscures the fact that naming is as powerful an act in the United States as it is anywhere else. Our emphasis has shifted from the names of people to other sorts of naming; we should not let that give us a falsely limited idea of the power of names.[5] I know no better way to demonstrate this for you than to present the following examples.

1.   There is a fifty-one-foot cement cross on a hill overlooking Eugene, Oregon. When the Oregon Supreme Court (in response to a lawsuit) ordered the cross taken down, the city officials declared it to be a "War Memorial." A dedication ceremony was held, and a tasteful sign identifying the "memorial" was added. The court reversed itself and withdrew the order. (This is like attaching a sign reading "Farm Family History Exhibit" to a municipal nativity scene.)[6]

2.   In San Francisco there is a firm headed by linguist Ira

N. Bachrach, called NameLab. What NameLab does is provide companies and products with names; an example is Nissan Motor Company's "Sentra" automobile. The typical fee for this service is at least $35,000 per name.[7]

**3.** In the early 1970s, scientist David Rosenhan and eleven of his colleagues were able to get themselves admitted to twelve different mental hospitals in this country simply by claiming that they heard voices. The name given to their "illness" was usually "schizophrenia." Once in the hospital, they made no attempt whatsoever to behave like mentally ill persons. Nevertheless, their average stay was nineteen days and they were treated for schizophrenia during that entire time. They openly took notes to make a record of the experiment; this note-taking was entered in their medical files by hospital staff as yet one more symptom of their illnesses. (The real patients, not so impressed by the label's power, spotted them as fakes almost immediately.)[8]

**4.** A study done by E. J. Langer and R. A. Abelson found that well-trained psychologists and psychiatrists rated an interviewee as reasonably well-adjusted when told that the videotaped interview they were watching was a "job application." But they rated the same individuals as more than moderately disturbed when they were told that the tape was of a "psychiatric interview."[9]

**5.** It would be unpleasant for health care personnel to have to use either of the following two sentences in speaking to patients:

"Your doctor has caused you to become sick."
"Your hospital has caused you to become sick."

To avoid this awkward situation, patients with illnesses caused by a doctor are told that they have "iatrogenic" illnesses; those with illnesses resulting from hospital stays are told that their sickness is "nosocomial." The word root *iatro-* means "medical"; the root *nosocom-* means "hospital." (And I was once told quite solemnly that the problem I was experiencing—a painful leg vein—was a disorder called "ileofemoral phlebomyalgia"— which means "a painful leg vein.")

**6.** The traditional position of researchers on the sense of smell has been that most people are only able to identify about sixteen odors. But recent research has made it clear that the problem is not in the nose but in the name. When subjects in experiments are given smells with *names* attached to them, their ability to identify and remember odors improves remarkably.[10]

**7.** Much public attention is now being given to the naming device called the "euphemism." The National Council of Teachers of English deserves a great deal of credit for bringing unsavory euphemisms into the glaring light of media publicity with its annual Doublespeak Award. The following are typical examples of euphemisms:

| *Euphemism* | *Traditional Name* |
|---|---|
| mental hospital | insane asylum |
| senior citizen | old person |
| disadvantaged child | poor child |
| sanitation engineer | garbage collector |
| routine limited-duration protective reaction | air raid |
| to deliver ordnance | to drop bombs |

To name a missile intended specifically for the purpose of making war "The Peacemaker" is an extension of the euphemism process into proper naming.

Two points unite all of these examples, and should be kept firmly in mind. First, *be very careful when you name things.* Second, *think before accepting other people's names for things.* The effects of naming can be miraculous—or catastrophic. Never look upon the choice of a name as a casual matter.

Once children have been labeled "slow learners" and the label has been entered in their school files, every learning difficulty they have thereafter will be viewed as evidence for the label; and every new teacher will listen to their language and watch their behavior with that label in mind. Once medical patients have been labeled "hysterical" or "hypochondriac" (or, as shown above, "schizophrenic"), every aspect of their behavior tends to be seen as a confirmation of the diagnostic name.

We *need* names, to help us remember and to help us talk about what we remember. But names are so powerful, and so difficult to get rid of once established, that it is almost better to have no name for something than to have the wrong name.

## Avoiding Communication Barriers

The third technique for choosing words is: AVOID COMMUNICATION BARRIERS, EXCEPT WHEN YOUR DELIBERATE GOAL IS TO BLOCK COMMUNICATION—IN WHICH CASE, LEARN TO USE THEM WISELY.

The list of communication barriers below was first put together by Thomas Gordon.[11] (I have added two items to Gordon's original twelve.) None of them is inherently bad, but each of them—for one reason or another—is likely to bring a language interaction to a halt. Because this remains true no matter which of the possible stress patterns is used, I have not indicated any stresses in the example sentences.

### *Communication Barriers*

1. **Criticizing**
   "You failed that test because you're too lazy to study."
2. **Name-calling**
   "You sexist pig!" "You loudmouth!" "Creep!"
3. **Diagnosing**
   "I know why you're doing that . . . you're doing it because you want to impress your mother-in-law."
4. **Praising Evaluatively**
   "You're always so good to everybody; you never think about yourself at all."
5. **Ordering**
   "Stop that right this minute!"
6. **Threatening**
   "If you don't change your mind, you'll regret it for the rest of your life."

7. **Moralizing**
   "It's wicked for you to treat your sister that way."

8. **Excessive/Inappropriate Questioning**
   "Why did you do that, for heaven's sakes? Did you stop to think about it, or did you just go right ahead without engaging your brain?"

9. **Advising**
   "Let me tell you what I'd do if I were in your place."

10. **Diverting**
    "You think that's bad? Shoot, let me tell you what happened to me this afternoon!"

11. **Logical Argument**
    "If you spend more money than you earn, there's no way you can keep from getting in debt. That's obvious."

12. **Reassuring**
    "It will all work out; you'll see. You don't have to worry about it anymore."

13. **Cutesipation**
    "You're so cute when you're mad, you know that?"

14. **Contradiction**
    "You are not cold; you couldn't possibly be!"

These barriers can be either positive or negative; all have the effect of cutting off communication and ending the language interaction. It's just as difficult to go on talking after someone has called you an angel or a genius as after the uglier names in example 2 above. Consider this example:

"You are the sweetest, kindest person I ever met—you're an absolute saint!"

Certainly that is a positive thing to say, and no one could take offense at it. But how on earth is the person you say it to supposed to respond?

Or look at this one:

"Everything will be all right—really. There's no reason in the world for you to worry about being sick at your age."

This is meant to be comforting and helpful, but it's an example of the twelfth barrier, Reassuring. Unfortunately, once you've said this the person you are talking to may no longer feel free to talk about a health problem, and that could mean serious trouble. The person may badly need the information or advice that you could give.

Remember, however, that there are times when your goal *is* to block communication and bring an interaction to a halt. It may be an inappropriate time for the subject of conversation to be discussed; it may be that the interaction would require more knowledge or skill than you have available at the time; it may be that someone present is using the interaction as a way to achieve a goal of verbal manipulation or abuse, and you feel obligated to step in and protect the intended victim. Whatever the reason for derailing the communication, some one of the fourteen barriers will be just what you need.

But be careful—be sure that you're using a barrier for that purpose, and not just through ignorance or carelessness. If you have the feeling that people "never tell you anything," it may be because—with the best of intentions—you keep setting up these barriers and making it impossible for them to feel comfortable talking to you.

## The Three-Part Assertion Method

The fourth, and last, word-choice technique I will describe in this section is the use of a pattern called "The Three-Part Assertion Message."[12] These messages are a technique for expressing your discomfort, displeasure, or other negative reaction to someone else's behavior. They are a bit tricky to get exactly right at first, and those who work with them recommend that you write them down before saying them aloud, until the technique comes naturally to you. Here's the pattern to be followed:

"When you *x*, I feel *y*, because *z*."

For example:

"When you fix yourself a snack after school and leave all your food and dishes sitting out, I feel angry, because I can't start cooking supper until I clean up the kitchen."

Your complaint, which is $x$ in the pattern, should be *absolutely specific* and contain no extra pieces. Not "When you don't do your fair share of the work around here . . ." Not "When you you are too lazy to clean up after yourself . . ." Just "when" followed by the specific and precise action that you object to.

There should be nothing extra in the $y$ or $z$ sections of your message, either. Don't say "I feel like a slave in my own house" instead of the simple "I feel angry." Don't fill in the $z$ section with "because I know it means you don't love me" or "because I already do more than my own share of the work." Be sure that the reason you offer for objecting is something that can be directly demonstrated and observed.

It's very important that you always set up these messages as "When you . . ." followed by "I" and never by "you." For example, this is a very bad idea:

"When you don't load the dishwasher, you make me sad, because then I have more work to do."

If you want to complain that someone "makes you sad," that is a *separate* complaint; it is something that person does, in your opinion, and something you object to. It has no place in the middle of a complaint about not loading the dishwasher. "You make me sad" presupposes "you have the power to cause me to become sad," and that is an issue for discussion all by itself; it has no place in your statement. Instead, say "When you don't load the dishwasher, I feel sad, because then I have more work to do."

You will have noticed that these messages bear a suspicious resemblance to the Logical Argument communication barrier on page 100. That may be all right; it may be that you don't want to discuss your complaint, only to get it out in the open where the other person can think about it. If you *do* want to have a discussion, you should plan to follow up your three-part message with an open request for one, and to help the other person overcome the difficulties you have created by beginning the discussion in this way.

There is no question but that this pattern is valuable as a way of stating complaints effectively. Absolutely. But I suspect that its greatest value often comes not from *using* the messages but from constructing them and writing them down. If you put them together honestly, you may be astonished at the way they evaporate. There you are, furious with your child for not cleaning up his room. Very carefully, you work out your message. Like this:

> "When you don't clean your room . . ."
> ". . . I feel very angry . . ."
> ". . . because ?????. . ."

Now what?

> ". . . because I always had to clean my room when *I* was a kid."
> ". . . because somebody might go in there accidentally and see the dirt."
> ". . . because only rotten kids don't clean their rooms."
> ". . . because my mother would be *shocked* if she saw your room."
> ". . . because I don't let *my* room get dirty."

And so on . . .

The careful construction of these messages forces you to isolate precisely what the other person does that you object to, precisely how you feel when it happens, and precisely why it bothers you. The construction of the message may prevent a silly argument, just because it makes it obvious that the issue isn't really worth arguing about.

All of us would be reluctant to open a discussion with this sentence:

> "When you do whatever it is that you do that is so infurating, I feel like hitting you over the head with a brick,

because for some reason I can't explain, whatever it is that you do drives me crazy."

If you find that something of that sort is as close as you are able to get to stating your complaint, it's a reliable indication that you need to pay more attention to what the person who distresses you is doing, and how it makes you feel, so that you'll have a running chance at discovering the reason for your emotion.

There is yet another excellent use for these messages. If you are a person whose perception of daily life is that you are always in trouble and that everyone is always angry with you, but you don't know why, try to convince the people around you to construct three-part messages for you. Messages that will tell you *specifically* what you do that is so annoying, how it makes them feel, and why. It's awful to have the conviction that you can't do anything right no matter how hard you try and to be completely in the dark about it.

I remember very well living in a house with a number of older women who spoke French, a language they assumed I understood because I could say a few easy sentences. As the months went by, they treated me more and more coldly, and by the time I left I felt like a pariah. Years went by before I finally learned what had happened. Every morning they had been sitting down near me and saying, for my benefit, "Well, why don't we go pick some tomatoes?" (Or cook lunch, or wash the sheets, or do some other household task.) Then they would look at me, and I would look back and smile, and they would wait for me to offer to help. When I didn't, they'd look at the ceiling and go off by themselves to do whatever the task was. They never suspected that the reason I didn't offer to help was that I didn't understand what they were saying. And I was so frightened by the contempt on their faces that I not only didn't dare ask them to explain, I was afraid to try to join them—I thought they didn't want me to. Eventually they avoided me altogether, since they considered me a lazy spoiled brat.

Most of the time, your communication problems will not be due to the fact that a foreign language is being spoken. It might work wonders, therefore, for you to ask the people who are obviously annoyed with you to put together some clarifying three-part assertion messages.

On the other side of the fence: Don't take it for granted that the person you are upset with knows why. I have talked to many youngsters who, when asked *why* their parents are angry, say, "Because I'm no *good*, that's why!" It is quite possible for them not to be aware that there is a small list of specific things they could do that would turn them from no-goods into ordinary members of the family once again. And if you don't tell them (perhaps because you "know in advance that it wouldn't do any good") they will grow up and leave home without ever realizing what the problems were.

## A Few Words on the Language of Acute Crisis

It would not be appropriate in this book to discuss in detail the problem of choosing your words in situations of acute crisis. There are good books available on this subject, for both the specialist and the layperson. (For example, see Everstine and Everstine 1983.)

What I will do here, therefore, is make a few general statements about the use of language in that acute crisis the average person is most likely to encounter: *having to talk to a person who appears to be irrational or out of control.* Ordinarily you will need to do this only until the experts (doctors, psychiatrists, law enforcement personnel, clergy, etc.) arrive to take over; but those brief moments while you're waiting can be critical.

First, remember that people will cling more intensely to their private version of reality in an acute crisis than in any other situation. They may be literally incapable of perceiving any other version, no matter how reasonable they would be under normal circumstances. THIS IS NOT THE TIME TO TRY TO "REASON" WITH SUCH A PERSON. When the reality an individual perceives is one of terror—perhaps to the extent of appearing life-threatening—it is not helpful for you to say, "You're all right; everything is fine." You intend that as reassurance, but your intention is not relevant; the message that will be understood is that you are challenging the other person's view of reality and denying it.

Second, understand that no matter how bizarre the language and behavior of the person in acute crisis may seem to you, there is a system of logic behind it. Within that person's reality, that logic holds. During the time that you are obliged to interact with such a person, apply Miller's Law rigorously— assume for the moment that what the person is saying is true. What, then, could it be true of? Do your listening from within that framework.

Third, don't make the mistake of appearing to have *power* over the situation. Your instinct may be to take charge, to promise that you'll make things better, and then—at any sign of improvement—to say, "See? Didn't I tell you I'd take care of it?" This can be very hazardous, because the person in distress may accept the idea that you have power to change the situation and begin making demands of you based on that assumption. When, as is often the case, you aren't able to comply with the demands, the level of disorder will rise sharply; you will be perceived by the person in crisis as having lied, or as being unwilling to help.

Finally, in such a situation you should use what you know about Satir Modes, Sensory Modes, and verbal attack patterns. If you are trying to talk with someone whose dominant Sensory Mode appears to be touch, and who is under great stress, never use any of the following sequences or anything remotely resembling them:

"See here . . ."
"Look . . ."
"Listen . . ."
"Listen to me . . ."
"I know everything looks really bad right now . . ."
"You're not seeing things clearly right now . . ."
"You're not hearing what I'm saying to you . . ."

If you're sure the dominant mode is touch, say things like this:

"Will you tell me how you feel . . ."
"I'm not sure I'm in touch with the problem . . ."
"I'm trying to put my finger on what's wrong . . ."
"I'm not sure I get it . . ."

And if you aren't sure that's the right move, avoid *all* sensory language if you can. Ask what the person is thinking, not what she is feeling or seeing or hearing. Use the most neutral speech you can manage, and stay in Computer Mode. Remember that your goal is simply to avoid making matters worse until the experts can reach you.

## Notes

1.   P. Ekman and W. V. Friesen, "The Repertoire of Nonverbal Behavior: Categories, Origins, Usage, and Coding," *Semiotica* 1 (1969): 49–98.

2.   This technique of illusory choice was first proposed in print by J. H. Weakland and D. D. Jackson, and was much favored by Milton Erickson.

3.   There is a dangerous trend in medical writing to behave as if there were some entirely neutral way to communicate, which can be opposed to the "manipulative patient's" way of communicating. There is no such thing.

4.   This term comes from the work of linguists Carol Kiparsky and Paul Kiparsky; the most accessible reference is their article "Fact," in the book *Progress in Linguistics*, edited by M. Bierwisch and K. E. Heidolph (The Hague: Mouton, 1970.)

5.   There is, however, quite a lot of research to indicate that the given name an individual has can have significant social consequences in America.

6.   This example is discussed in J. Dan Rothwell's excellent book, *Telling It Like It Isn't* (Englewood Cliffs, NJ: Prentice-Hall, 1982), p. 12.

7.   For more about NameLab, see Robert A. Mamis, "Name-Calling," *INC.*, July 1984, pp. 67–74.

8.   This experiment has had a vast amount of publicity. A good brief account is D. L. Rosenhan, "On Being Sane in Insane Places," *Science* 179 (1973): 250–58.

9.   This study was reported in Langer and Abelson's article "A Pa-

tient by Any Other Name: Clinician Group Differences in Labeling Bias," *Journal of Consulting and Clinical Psychology* 42 (1974): 4–9.

10.   See William S. Cain, "Educating Your Nose," *Psychology Today*, July 1981, pp. 48–56.

11.   See Gordon's book *Parent Effectiveness Training* (New York: Peter H. Wyden, 1970). Also see Robert Bolton, *People Skills: How to Assert Yourself, Listen to Others and Resolve Conflicts* (Englewood Cliffs, N.J.: Prentice-Hall, 1979), pp. 15–18.

12.   For a very fine discussion of this technique and the construction of the messages, take a look at *People Skills*, pp. 139–59.

# 7

# *Language Choices: Part Two*

Nonverbal communication (NVC) is a vast and unwieldy subject. Books and articles on "body language" sometimes give the impression that NVC is only facial expression, body posture, and gestures; if that were true, it would be a lot easier to deal with. But NVC can only be accurately defined as *everything* that is part of oral communication except the actual words used. That means that it includes not just expressions and postures and gestures, but also voice quality and intonation. It includes the clothes you wear and the way you wear your hair and how far you stand from other people when you speak to them. It includes your silences just as surely as your utterances. I'm not going to try to cover all that territory. But I will provide you with general information, and some useful techniques that relate to areas of NVC about which—unlike your clothing and your hairstyle—you may not be aware that you have choices.

We will begin with *intonation*, which Sally McConnell-Ginet defines as "the tune to which we set the text of our talk."[1] It is the *melody* of our speech. Intonation is the first substantial part of language that a baby learns, and it's the hardest part of any foreign language for adults to learn—it's ordinarily intonation that gives a fluent speaker of a language away as not a *native* speaker. There is much research proving that a frequent reason for real-world rejection (such as the refusal to hire someone for a job) is intonation perceived as unpleasant. This is manifestly unfair—if you are well qualified, your intonation should have nothing to do with whether you are hired—but it is the way things are in the real world, and it cannot be ignored. We will look at three aspects of intonation: voice quality, stress, and pauses.

## Voice Quality

There is no "right" or "wrong" quality of the voice, no set of perfect standards that you can check your voice against to find out if it is everything it should be. If there *were*, it would be a false set of standards, because it depends upon the varying perceptions of listeners. Whether a voice is judged as pleasant or unpleasant is entirely a matter of the way it is perceived by the person who hears it. Certain types of voice quality go in and out of fashion, as do certain styles of dress. There are, however, a few stable principles that we can rely on with regard to American English today.

**1.** A high-pitched voice in an adult is perceived negatively. We associate high voices with small children, and we find a high adult voice as offensive as any other sort of childish behavior. The adult speaker with a high voice will almost inevitably be treated like a child by others—ignored, fussed at, bossed around, "humored," set aside. And the adult, unlike the child, is not perceived as someone whose voice is only *temporarily* high-pitched.

**2.** The combination of high pitch plus *nasality* is the most negatively perceived of all voice qualities. A low-pitched nasal voice, particularly in men, is often perceived as very acceptable. But the *high*-pitched nasal voice is a serious barrier to communication.

**3.** A voice that deviates toward the extremes of volume—either too loud or too soft—will be perceived as unpleasant.

**4.** A voice that deviates toward the extremes of dynamism—either too monotonous or the nameless opposite of too monotonous—will be perceived as unpleasant. (Common terms for the latter, although far from precise, are "melodramatic" and "overdone." And abnormal stress patterns are probably the factor most often responsible for this characteristic.)

There are, of course, persons whose voices have these negatively perceived characteristics for medical reasons. If you have a speech disorder, if you are hearing-impaired, if you have an illness that causes extreme physical weakness—any problem of this sort—the achievement of a more pleasant quality of voice may be difficult or impossible for you. If it is possible, it may require the assistance of a medical expert. In such a situation, the appropriate thing for you to do is consult a doctor, who will determine what can be done and refer you to expert help. It is not my intention in this book to interfere in this process; I will, however, come back later to the topic and suggest strategies you can use to offset the problem and minimize its effects.

If your problem is not a medical one—and usually it is not—you should do two things. First, check your voice to find out if it has the negatively perceived characteristics listed above. Second, if it does, *fix* it. This doesn't require the services of an expert, or years of training with a voice coach. You are not trying to develop the voice of an opera star or a great Shakespearean actor; you are trying to develop a voice that will not be a barrier to effective communication with others. Furthermore, you are working to develop some *control* over this aspect of your language behavior, so that you can make deliberate choices about the sort of voice quality you use in a given situation. Your voice is a musical instrument that belongs to you; there is no reason why you should be unable to play it.

First, you need to determine whether your voice is already fine just as it is. The best way to do this, especially to check for high pitch and nasality, is to record your speech and listen to the result. A tape recorder that sells for $30 or less will do the job. (A machine of this kind is one of the most useful tools you can have in learning to be syntonic, in any case, and is an investment that you should make if you can.) If purchasing a tape recorder is beyond your budget, check your local schools, your public library, your church, and your friends—somewhere among those sources you will find a machine that you can rent or borrow for a while.[2]

You need a recording of your voice that is as much like your natural speech as possible. It should be at least thirty minutes long, so that there will be time for you to get over being self-conscious. If it will take you two hours to get over that, fine; record for two hours and a half, and keep only the thirty-minute sequence after the self-consciousness has worn off. Don't *read* aloud, because your reading voice may be radically different from your speaking voice. The most reliable way to get natural speech is to leave the recorder running while you are having an ordinary conversation with someone who lets you do a fair share of the talking. If you'd feel uncomfortable doing that, or you don't have a friend who is willing to be taped along with you, you can work alone. Pretend that you're talking to someone else, and talk about something that is easy to talk about. Your pet peeve will do. Talk about things you liked to do, or hated to do, when you were a child. You want a subject that will let you hear how you sound when you have some emotional involvement in what you are saying.

Once you have your tape, sit down and listen to it. Carefully. Is your voice high-pitched? Is it nasal? It is too loud or too soft? Is it a monotone—or a monotone's nameless opposite? How does it sound?

At this point it is customary to provide a comforting little paragraph explaining that the shock you feel when you hear your own voice on tape is nothing to worry about, that everybody sounds awful to their own ears when taped, plus a few soothing words on the difference between sound conducted by air and sound conducted by bone. I am not going to conform with that custom. It's polite, but it's not helpful. The truth is: IF YOU SOUND TERRIBLE TO YOURSELF, YOU PROBABLY SOUND TERRIBLE TO OTHERS AS WELL. Trust your ears and your brain; they know what they are doing. If you're really not sure, or suspect that there's something wrong with the tape recorder, get a second opinion. Ask someone who often hears you talk to listen to five minutes of the tape and tell you if it sounds like your ordinary voice. If it does, then that is likely to be the way you actually *do* sound, no matter how strange it seems to you.

Note: If you sound *wonderful* to yourself, you absolutely must get not only a second opinion, but a third and a fourth, because this is very unusual. If other people agree with your own assessment that your voice quality is pleasant and satisfactory, then you should relax and read the rest of this section only for informational purposes.

## Working with the Tape Recorder to Improve Voice Quality

Through this whole procedure, keep one thing in mind: *Your goal is to sound like your own self with better voice quality.* Your goal is to improve your own natural speech, not to learn to do a flawless imitation of someone else.

Begin by finding a friend or acquaintance whose speech you perceive as pleasant, someone whom you enjoy listening to and whom others enjoy listening to. Have your friend make a tape about thirty minutes long, talking on a subject such as "The Teacher I Hated Most," "My First Day at School," or "Foods I Can't Stand"—a topic that will produce natural speech. Choose someone of your own gender and age group, and your own ethnic background.

Once you have your practice tape, you will work with it at your own convenience, at your own speed, and in privacy. There is no "correct" amount of time for you to spend at this task; it's up to you and will depend on your personal situation. The *way* that you do it, however, is a different matter; for it to be successful, you must proceed as follows:

**1.** Listen several times to a brief section of the tape—a single average sentence, or two very short ones, at most—until you are familiar with that chunk. Don't write the material down, because reading with the tape is not helpful; just become familiar with it.

**2.** Now rewind the tape, and say aloud the sequence you've been listening to, WITH THE TAPE. Do not repeat *after* the tape; speak with it.

**3.** Repeat step 2 several times—not so many times that you get bored, but at least three times. A dozen times is not too many.

**4.** Move on to a new stretch of the tape, and repeat steps 1 through 3.

**5.** Continue this until you've worked through the whole tape.

The reason I'm being so dogmatic about this is because the chances are so strong that any commercial language tape you've ever used consisted of sentences followed by pauses during which you were instructed to repeat what you'd heard. This is the time-honored traditional method, but it will not work for our present purpose. What you need to do is speak *with* the tape and free your mind to do what it is superbly equipped to do: MATCH your voice to the taped model.[3] If you repeat after the speech, this can't happen, because (a) you have to remember how the model sounded, and that is an extra and distracting task; and (b) that memory will be filtered through your personal perceptions. Repeating after the tape is a fine way to train yourself thoroughly in your own mistakes; speaking with the tape is a way to achieve a syntonic match by letting your own language skills function as they are intended to do.

It's important not to go too far with this technique. You don't want to achieve a *perfect* match with the tape, because you would then have trained yourself to do a perfect imitation of your friend's voice. That's not what you are trying to do.

Assume that you're spending half an hour to an hour working with the tape each time, and that you've done that over the course of a week. Now—before working with the model any longer—make a tape of your own speech on some subject that is natural to you. Listen to your tape and judge it for voice quality just as you did at the beginning of the project. If you feel that you've become too accustomed to the sound of your recorded voice to judge it accurately, get a second opinion.

Carry out this checkup procedure after roughly every half-dozen practice hours. And when you have altered your own voice quality enough to be pleased with the result, it is time to *stop*. After that, you might want to record your voice again every six months or so, to be certain that your former bad habits haven't returned, and that should be sufficient. (And if you become desperately bored with your practice tape before you reach your goal, don't hesitate to have the person who recorded it for you make you a substitute tape, for variety.)

Remember, please, that it took you years to achieve your original voice quality; don't expect to change it significantly in only a few weeks. Be prepared for this project to take a while. How long will ordinarily depend on three factors: (a) how far your voice deviates from a positively perceived quality in the first place; (b) how much time and energy you have to spend working with the tape; and (c) how much talent you have for languages, a matter that is probably determined more by your chronological age than by anything else. The natural ability to learn human languages with ease begins to decay in human beings around puberty; the rate at which that decay occurs, and its extent, will vary from one person to another. Very roughly speaking, the older you are, the longer it will take you to accomplish the change in voice quality that you want, all other factors being equal.[4] You are not in a contest, and you have no deadline to meet; don't place artificial pressures on yourself.

Finally, I would not want you to think that the technique of working in unison with a model to learn a skill is some radical innovation on my part. It is the technique used in the language-learning laboratories at the University of California, San Diego; it is a primary method for professional dance teaching. And it has a venerable tradition—it is, for example, the way that the exercise patterns called "T'ai Chi" are learned. In unison with the teacher.

What happens as you do this is that your body and mind take over your consciousness to do things you could not do deliberately. As you are speaking with the tape, your mind checks constantly for mismatch. It notes that your voice is just a little bit different from the model; it makes minute adjustments in your rate of speech, in its volume and dynamics, in the tension of your vocal cords, in the quantity of air that you breathe. Then it checks again to see if a closer match has been achieved. This will happen over and over again until your brain is satisfied that no further mismatch exists (which is the reason you should stop the process *before* that state of perfect syntonicity), despite the fact that you could not even begin to carry out the task deliberately. This cognitive skill that you have is one of your greatest resources, and it's a shame that it is so little used.

It's relatively easy to decide from a recording whether your voice is high or nasal; it's not too hard to hear whether your voice is monotonous. It may be extremely difficult, however, to hear whether you speak too softly or too loudly, since you'll tend to compensate for this by adjusting the volume control on the tape recorder. For this characteristic, you may need to ask others who talk with you frequently for help in making your judgment. To some extent you should have clues readily available. When you talk to people, do they suddenly step back away from you? Do they frown as if they were uncomfortable when you speak? Then you may be talking too loudly. Alternatively, do people ask you to repeat yourself when you talk? Do they learn toward you and frown as if they were straining to understand your words? Then you may be speaking too softly. If your voice quality is sufficiently overloud or oversoft that it matters, the chances are that it will provoke these listening behaviors; if it doesn't, you probably don't need to worry about volume.

It's hard to say too *much* about the importance of good voice quality. People who have it have an enormous (and unfair) advantage in every aspect of communication; Ronald Reagan is one of the best examples of this phenomenon. People love to hear them talk because they enjoy the sound of their voices, and because the sort of attentive listening their voices evoke makes them feel relaxed and comfortable. (Remember, the effect of that sort of listening is to lower the blood pressure and slow the heart rate; it is physically good for you.) It takes very bad linguistic habits indeed to cancel out that advantage.

If you are someone who is unable to achieve good voice quality for medical reasons, I cannot emphasize too strongly how important the other techniques discussed in this book are for you. You need them as a way of offsetting the disadvantage and making the communication odds more equal for you. Furthermore, if you are able to hear recorded speech, you may find that working with a tape recorder as described in the preceding section *will* be of some help to you. It's an inexpensive experiment and one that doesn't require an expert's assistance; it might be worth trying it briefly to see what happens. You might find that although you cannot lower the pitch of your voice, you can make it less nasal, or vice versa; it's possible that if you can't change either pitch or nasality, you can still make your voice less monotonous. A change for the better in any of the characteristics that trigger negative perceptions in listeners is worth making, I promise you, even if you must settle for a total voice quality that is less satisfactory than you would have chosen.

## Phonological Stress

I discussed stress patterns in chapter 3, as part of the description of English verbal attack patterns. I want to return to the subject here, as well as elsewhere in the book, because it is very important.

The system of rules that governs the sounds of a language—which sounds are used, and how they are combined—is called its *phonology*. In English, the stress that is added to sounds, and to sequences of sounds, is important not only for voice quality but because it literally can change the meaning of what you say. Far too little attention is given to this matter in books on communication. The writing system of English is so poorly designed for indicating intonation that it's almost useless for the purpose, and writers facing that fact usually decide not to take on an impossible task. I understand the problem, but I feel that they should at least provide a warning.

Let me give you a typical example. In *Nursing '81* (January 1981), there was an article titled "The Manipulative Patient

Spells Trouble," written by Jamie I. Richardson. Richardson, who is a nurse, lists twelve "manipulative cues" that will help other nurses identify patients as manipulative. One of the cues is illustrated with the following example sentence, which I reproduce here just as it was in the nursing journal:

> "The doctor told me I could have a pain shot whenever I needed it."

Just like that! Without any indication as to where the stresses might fall or a warning that it might matter. (And I want to emphasize that this is not unique to Richardson; this is the typical practice.) Please read the following sentences aloud, giving the sequences that are all in capital letters strong emphasis and more volume, and listen carefully.

> "The DOCTOR told me I could have a pain shot whenever I NEEDed it."
> "The doctor TOLD me I could have a pain shot whenever I needed it."
> "The doctor told ME I could have a pain shot whenever I NEEDed it."
> "The doctor told me I COULD have a pain shot whenever I needed it."
> "The doctor told me I could have a pain shot whenever I needed it."

I am quite sure you will agree that all those sentences mean different things and would be said in different situations. Worst of all, the example with *no* strong stresses indicated—the one used in the article to illustrate manipulative language—is in fact the one most likely to be nothing more than a neutral report of information. It is what a patient would say if the doctor had given him or her instructions to tell the nurse that a pain shot should be available on request. There is not the slightest reason to believe that it is a clue to identifying the manipulative patient, and the idea that nurses all over the country might think it is and act accordingly is alarming. It's not trivial.

This kind of thing happens in two situations. In one case, the writer is aware of the problem but the editors of the publication won't allow the use of frequent underlining or words all in capital letters. When this happens, writers should do their best to convince the editors to allow an exception to be made; if that fails, they should add a line something like this one: "This sentence should only be viewed as a clue to identifying the manipulative patient if it is spoken with unusually heavy emphasis on the words . . ." (followed by the words most likely to get abnormal stress).

In the second case, the writer simply takes it for granted that the stress pattern he or she has in mind for the sentence is the one that the reader will have in mind. This is either ignorance or arrogance, and is valid only when the writer has provided a lengthy context to support the chosen intonation, as in a short story or novel. It is never safe, and never excusable, when what the writer offers the reader is example sentences in isolation.

One of the things we know about the way people process language is that even when they seem unaware of a particular linguistic feature, if it is brought to their conscious attention they will be able to demonstrate that they *are* aware of it. For example, people who hear the sentence "Visiting relatives can be unpleasant" may claim to be unaware that it has more than one possible meaning. But if you point out that it can mean either that relatives who are visiting can be unpleasant or that going to visit relatives can be unpleasant, they will have no trouble constructing many other examples of the same kind.

In the same way, people will often tell me that they "can't hear differences in stress patterns" and therefore can't use that sort of information in their language behavior. But when I have them consider pairs of sequences differentiated only by stress, such as those below, they immediately acknowledge that they can perceive such differences after all.

> "the convert" versus "to convert"
> "a RUSSIAN teacher" versus "a Russian TEACHer"
> "Mary has plans to LEAVE" versus "Mary has PLANS to leave"

"What are we having for lunch, Bob?" versus "What are we having for lunch—BOB?"

They also find it strikingly easy to identify abnormal stresses if I say to them, "Even YOU should be able to hear THIS abnormal stress pattern!"[5]

Phonological stress in English is technically a complex matter involving many details about vocal cord tension, subglottal pressure, and so on. We don't need all those details in order to work with stress in syntonics, however, because from the point of view of the speaker of English, phonological stress is reliably perceived as higher pitch and louder volume. The higher the pitch and the louder the volume, the heavier the stress is perceived to be.

A major function of phonological stress is to indicate what part of the utterance the speaker wants to call the most attention to. In many sentences, no one part has unusual importance for the speaker, and no stress will be very heavy; nevertheless, there will be one stress peak in that sentence, typically toward the end. The reason that too many strong stresses in a single utterance constitute poor communication strategy is that they make it impossible for the listener to understand you. You are indicating *all* of the stressed items as the part of the utterance that matters most to you—how is the listener supposed to choose among them?

You can often hear very strange examples of misplaced stress from television newscasters. They are reading written language from their TelePrompTers, and will make a decision early in a sentence that the stress should go on some particular portion; when they discover later, as they read, that they've put it in the wrong place, it's too late to fix it. Why no one in the world of journalism feels that it would be a good idea to develop some system for indicating those stresses I do not know.

Be careful with phonological stress. It carries a great deal of meaning—use it wisely. And pay close attention to the way that others use it in speaking to you. When you are trying to understand written language, remember that sentences with no stress indicated often could mean a number of different things, and don't leap to conclusions. If you receive a letter or a memo that contains language that might be insulting, stop by the writer's desk or call the writer on the phone and ask casually to have the dubious sequence read aloud to you. (Blame it on the handwriting, or say that you've spilled coffee on the item and can't read it.) Then listen to the stresses the writer gives to the sequence. Never, under any circumstances, accept someone else's spoken presentation of another person's written speech if the stress patterns would be crucial; it's not safe, and can lead to much misunderstanding and confusion.

## Pauses

It may not be obvious that it matters much when and where you pause in your speech, or that pauses have any real importance. The idea that a linguist might devote an entire lifetime of research to the investigation of pauses may strike you as ridiculous. But research shows that 40 to 50 percent of all spontaneous speech *is* pauses. Do those pauses have any purpose, or are they just evidence of inefficiency?

Psychologist Geoffrey Beattie carried out one of the major experiments done to answer this question. He had his subjects talk at length while forbidden to pause, and recorded the resulting speech. He found that people not allowed to pause had to use repetition of words or sequences as a way of keeping their speech from breaking down. He concludes of pauses that "subjects cannot produce spontaneous speech without them, although speakers do seem to be able to substitute repetition in speech for unfilled pauses, when required."[6] (A "filled" pause is one in which the speaker uses "uh" or "mmmm" or something of the kind to fill the silence.)

Beattie's research showed that although some pauses are accidental, most fill one of two functions. Either they are *cognitive* pauses—which allow the speaker time to plan speech that is upcoming—or they are *social* pauses, which help in the management of speech. Social pauses are used to regulate turn-taking, to prevent interruptions, to give the listener time to think about what is being said, to check to see if the listener is paying attention, and so on. Visual clues are important in getting the turn to speak passed along in an orderly way in face-to-face interactions, but such cues cannot be the only ones, or telephone conversations would be impossible. Pauses are clearly responsible for much of this "traffic control" function.

The primary reason you need to be concerned about pauses when you consider verbal self-defense is because of the connection between pauses and interruptions. Under ordinary circumstances, a pause *at the end of a sentence* is a signal that the speaker is ready to give up the floor and let someone else have a turn, if only to answer a question before the first speaker continues. People who are following the rules of conversation won't grab the turn if a pause occurs at what is obviously not a stopping point.[7] But even the most courteous listeners will interpret the combination of end-of-sentence *plus* a pause to mean that the speaker is through, and they will begin talking. People who give this set of cues without intending to yield the floor are going to be interrupted a lot. The most currently cited example is England's Prime Minister Margaret Thatcher, who is constantly being interrupted in spite of her political power and prestige and the fact that she is a dominating and articulate woman. She apparently gives unintentional clues indicating that she's ready to give up the turn when she really isn't.

I have mentioned before that the world is full of falsehoods that are accepted by almost everyone as "obviously and self-evidently true." In that set is the common assumption that women are always interrupting. This has been checked many times, by both male and female researchers, and it has been proved false. It is men who do most of the interrupting, by a wide margin, especially when the speaker they interrupt is female. In the *Village Voice* (August 18, 1984), Geoffrey Stokes ("Lesser Miscreants") noted that "the historic fact of being nominated for vice-president is apparently not enough to protect a woman from the widely documented fate of being interrupted more often than similarly situated men." He then pointed out that on "This Week with David Brinkley", the television show, the three male participants interrupted Geraldine Ferraro *thirty-two times* in less than thirty minutes.

Presumably this male interruption pattern is due to a number of factors, such as the fact that men tend to outrank women in language interactions, and the stereotyped preconception that women's speech is not important. But the way it happens to women in high positions and prestigious situations makes it clear that those can't be the only reasons. It is probable that both women and men who are frequently interrupted are giving unintentional signals that they're ready to let someone else talk.

In Gary S. Goodman's excellent book on doing business by telephone, *Winning by Telephone* (Englewood Cliffs, N.J.: Prentice-Hall, 1982), he recommends as a defense against this problem a technique he credits to actor John Wayne. Goodman says that of course you have to pause for breath now and then, but he says to do it in the middle of your sentences rather than at the end. And he suggests that you practice doing this with a tape recorder until you can carry it off without sounding artificial. If people are forever interrupting you, this is a good idea and should not be restricted to telephone conversation. In face-to-face interactions, follow the mid-sentence pause procedure, and don't let the person you are talking to catch your eye; the combination will either eliminate the interruptions or force the other person to take the speaking turn in a way that is openly rude. You may not be able to keep people from interrupting you, but there's no reason why you should make it *easy* for them. There are also people who talk on and on and on, helplessly, wishing that someone else *would* take a turn, and baffled as to why it doesn't happen. They become painfully aware that everyone present is bored and annoyed, but they don't know what to do about it. (They may have spent most of their lives with overtly rude speakers who charge right into the middle of sentences and get the turn by drowning others out.) If this happens to you, you need to learn to give clear signals that you are ready to yield the floor. If you've asked a direct question, people will know that you want them to answer. But if you are at the end of a sentence that isn't a question, and are ready for someone else to talk, do this: Let your voice pitch drop; look at the person most likely to speak next; and pause *in complete silence*. I have had clients who insisted that this was exactly what they did, but who—when they demonstrated for me—filled their end-of-sentence pauses with "uh" or "mmmm," or ended sentences with a rise in pitch, or both, often while staring off at some vague point in space. You must make it unambiguously clear that you *mean* to pause.

To see what happens when pauses are neglected, observe a child of about three or four who is determined not to let anyone stop her until she gets to the end of her story. Such a child does not pause at all, even to breathe; she will grab a breath between words, no matter how odd the result. In a small child this may be amusing, and it can always be stopped by a firm word or two; in an adult, it is *not* amusing, and it may be exceedingly awkward to break into.

To get some feeling for your own use of pauses, try Beattie's experiment—try to talk without them. Remember that *filled* pauses are not allowed either. Can you do it? For how long? Pay attention to what happens to your speech as you try to keep this going.

## Body Language

The literature on body language is so large that reading it all is a staggering task. It doesn't help matters that it's also full of controversy and contradiction. Publications range from popular treatments such as *How to Read a Person Like a Book* to highly technical materials filled with terms such as *kinesics, proxemics, paralanguage, chronemics*, and many more. The popular publications are often misleading, giving the impression that memorizing lists of gestures and postures will enable you to know exactly what other people are thinking and feeling. The scholarly literature makes it clear that neither units of body language, nor clusters of such units, have any inherent meaning in isolation from the context and the culture in which they are used. But often this material is written in such impenetrable academic language that the general public has little access to the information. Almost every area of the field is in dispute to some degree, and the points of controversy vary from one scientific discipline to another. This is normal for an area of scientific research as new as nonverbal communication, but it makes it hard for the nonspecialist to decide what to believe.

I will try to be neutral in what I say here, and I will provide references at the end of the chapter so that you can explore the issues further if you wish. However, there is no way to avoid controversy in a field that is in such a state of turbulent activity, and that is so important to every single one of us.

The *importance* of body language is not one of the areas in dispute. Estimates of the exact amount of information carried by NVC (which includes voice quality, intonation, and pauses) in a typical conversation range from a low of 65 percent to a high of 95 percent. No matter what percentage you accept, however, there is full agreement that NVC carries more than half of the information in any language interaction. *More than half.*

There also appears to be no argument with the proposition that when the verbal channel and the nonverbal channel are in conflict it is the nonverbal that should be relied on unless you have specific information to the contrary. All over the country, executives, politicians, and professionals of every kind are participating in expensive workshops and seminars intended to train them to achieve a match (often called *congruence*) between their verbal and their nonverbal communication.

Except in the most simplistic popular treatments of the subject, there is also full agreement that body language units and clusters can be assigned meanings only within their real-world context, and only for a specific culture. We do not read in responsible sources that "scratching your nose" *means* a specific thing, straight across the board. Most information of that kind in print is valid—when it *is* valid—only for middle- or upper-class American white native speakers of English. Furthermore, even within that very narrow range, much of it is valid only for adult males.

Given this situation, it is fortunate that we can assemble our own data bases, our own collections of information, valid for our own lives and within our own cultures. Each of us knows our own nonverbal grammar very well, although much of what we know is below the level of our conscious awareness. We can therefore use syntonics techniques to become aware of what we already know; we don't have to begin from scratch. Let's look briefly at some general information from a number of sources, and then I will describe some techniques for use in improving your NVC skills.

Here's a typical scholarly quotation (to give you the flavor of the material), from the work of Adam Kendon.

> Gesticulation and speech work together in an intimate relation of great flexibility and subtlety. However ... the mode of encoding of context is quite different in gesture from the mode of encoding in speech. Whereas in language highly conventionalized forms from an already established vocabulary are used, which are organized sequentially according to grammatical rules, in gesticulation encoding is presentational. Though conventionalized forms may be used, the utterer has considerable freedom to create new enactments which do not then pass into any established vocabulary. As far as can be seen at the moment, gesticulation is not composed of elements which are formed into constructions according to a syntax. They occur, rather, as a succession of enactments whose sequencing is governed by the order of ideas in the discourse.[8]

There's a thicket of academic prose to be waded through with linguistic hip boots and machete! Kendon is saying that although VC and NVC are interdependent, there are basic differences between them. NVC units don't have an obligatory order in the way that words do; the sort of explicit rule that causes you to reject "boy the left" does not exist for NVC. What you *would* reject would be body language that was completely unsynchronized with the rest of the communication—for example, if someone were to talk about hammering small nails while waving a farewell, although nobody was leaving. Kendon is saying that the order in which we use units of body language is not based on independent rules; rather, it is based on a metarule that says it must match the order of the ideas in our spoken language. He is saying that you are much more free to make up body language units on the spur of the moment than you are to make up words, and that there is no dictionary you can go to to look such units up.

Suppose that the part of your speech you want to encode in

body language is a sequence like this: "The first thing I do is cut out a square of silk about this big, with a pair of sharp scissors." There is no gesture list you can turn to to find one which encodes that specific sequence of words. There is no rule that requires you to add *any* gesture to the utterance. If you want to add one, any of a large number of "cutting out an item of such-and-such a size with scissors" gestures would be appropriate; you are free to make it as elaborate or as unobtrusive as you like. You may use a gesture that illustrates the size of the square and doesn't mention the scissors, or one that shows the act of cutting with scissors and ignores the matter of the size of what is cut. The gesture you choose may be one that is never used again except coincidentally, that is unique with you in that situation and then abandoned.

But there *are* rules. There are things you could not do and expect to be understood, and the set of such things is infinite. You could not use a gesture of beating cake batter, or driving a car with a steering wheel; you could not whirl on the toes of one foot in a pirouette. And you continue to be subject to the rules that govern parts of NVC other than "gesticulation," such as the rules for intonation and for the utilization of personal space.

Kendon also says that gesture units aren't just extra trimming added to the words spoken; he claims that they are an alternative channel for the communication of ideas, and that it is reasonable to expect one gesture unit for each idea expressed. (Not everyone agrees with him on this point, by the way, but I am convinced that he is right. I suspect the controversy comes primarily from the fact that not everyone defines the concept "gesture" in the same way.)

There are numerous proposals for sorting and classifying body language. Ray L. Birdwhistell, a pioneer researcher in the subject, proposed for middle-class American English speakers a descriptive set of thirty-three specific units he called "kinemes," including four eyebrow motions, four eyelid motions, three types of head nod, and so on.[9] P. Ekman and W. V. Friesen proposed the following system of classification by functional types:[10]

1. **Emblems.** Nonverbal acts that are conscious and deliberate and have an exact "translation" into words.
2. **Illustrators.** Nonverbal acts that are conscious and deliberate, and that "act out" what is being said.
3. **Affect Displays.** Facial expressions that show emotions, and that may or may not be conscious and deliberate.
4. **Regulators.** Nonverbal acts used to manage the "traffic" of language interactions, such as nodding your head to show that you're listening; people are usually aware of these, but they are essentially automatic.
5. **Adaptors.** Nonverbal acts that are not conscious or deliberate, and that we are usually unaware of, but that represent a connection between what we're saying and some action— for example, jabbing at the air with a pencil as you talk of being angry.

Sets like these (and the Satir Modes are another such set, with which you will be familiar) are known as "taxonomies." They begin with the most basic division of all: body language that is related to what is being said, like the five types listed above; and body language that has no connection with what is being said, such as swatting a mosquito during a sentence having nothing to do with insects of any kind. With the exception of the term *emblem*, which seems to have wide acceptance as a name for body language units or clusters with reliable word-like meanings, most of these systems are of interest only to the specialist.

Beattie's research shows that complex NVC units start during pauses in the stream of speech and seem to be related to the selection of what is to be said next. He says that they are not associated with social pauses intended to indicate the end of a speaker turn, and that the listener who sees them is being given information about the status of the interaction as well as information that may relate to the actual content. The complex gestures begin just before the part of the utterance that they refer to and continue during some part of that utterance; they do not usually *follow* it. They often help the speaker maintain control of the floor—and Beattie mentions that the much-interrupted Margaret Thatcher has a habit of not getting her complex gestures started until after the interruption has already begun, at which point it's too late for it to hold her listeners' attention. He is saying, among other things, that it's as hard to interrupt a complicated gesture as it is to interrupt a sentence, but that the gesture must *accompany* the sentence if it's to be useful in this way.

This is all very intricate, to be sure. But it is crucial to verbal self-defense and to effective communication. The question we have to ask ourselves is: How are we to make any sense of it all for use in the real world of language interactions? How are we to get beyond considering it as only interesting information, of no practical use?

One thing we can do is realize that since interactional synchrony—the synchronization of listener body language with speaker body language—is important to effective communication, we must see to it that our body language is something people can synchronize *with*. If you are constantly jerking and jabbing with your body language, if you are constantly switching from one sort of body language to another, as the Distracter does, if you are given to wildly elaborate acting-out of your speech, it may be almost impossible to body sync with you. If it is, it's also going to be hard *work* to listen to you. You're going to be perceived as "hard to follow," and many listeners will tune you out because it's too much trouble not to.

It's not as easy to get a clear perception of your body language as of your voice. If you have access to a video camera or movie camera that will allow you to watch a good film of yourself involved in thirty minutes or so of spontaneous conversation, by all means take advantage of the opportunity. That sort of equipment is not as inexpensive, or as easy to rent or borrow, as an audio tape recorder; however, if you can manage to arrange for it, it will be well worth your trouble. You might try this as a group project with several friends, sharing the cost of tape and rental and filming all of you talking together. Then sit down and watch yourself, just as you listened to yourself on the audio recording.

Even if you aren't able to watch yourself on film or tape, however, you can still accomplish a great deal just by making the effort to be more *aware* of your own body language. Pay attention, to the extent that that's possible. Ask people you trust, and who talk with you frequently, to tell you what they notice about your NVC. Ask them if there are particular facial expressions, postures, or gestures that people associate with you. Do they think that you move *enough* when you talk? Or that you move too much? Make a note of the information you are given, until you begin to have sufficient data from which to make some solid judgments. Pay special attention to discovering which of the Satir Modes you tend to use as a body language mode when you are excited or under stress. And the techniques that are described below will help.

### Techniques for Improving Your Body Language Skills

Like artificial division of language into "verbal" and "nonverbal," there is traditionally an artificial division of the human being into "body" and "mind." We have no English word that we can use to express the verbal-nonverbal whole; the word *language* is as useful for that purpose as a brick wall is for looking through. Please keep in mind, as you read, that when I refer to either body *or* mind I am referring to both and to their constant interdependency and interaction. The techniques described in this section are designed for the body and mind, and are intended to help you learn at least the following:

**1.**  To be so good at observing the body language of others that you have it available to you as feedback information in every language interaction—immediately, on the spot, and while you are yourself involved in the interaction.

**2.**  To be so good at using body language that you have control over the feedback information you are providing to your listeners.

**3.**  To make your words and your body language syntonic, so that there is no mismatch between them unless you specifically *intend* to provide a mismatch.

**4.**  To use body language, with conscious awareness, to achieve your own linguistic goals.

**5.**  To rid yourself of body language that triggers negative perceptions in your listeners that have nothing to do with what you are saying, or that cause others to perceive you as a likely verbal victim.

*USING YOUR TELEVISION SET.* Cars are magnificient de-vices for learning to drive, because they provide immediate feedback—for all senses—at all times; they also respond in-stantly to the information provided by the driver. We don't have an equally perfect device for learning body language, un-fortunately. But we have a moderately good one, in the ordi-nary television set. All day long, and much of the night, you can observe body language on your television. You can do that when it's convenient for you, and for only so long as it is con-venient for you; you can do it in privacy, without having to pass any entrance requirements; and it is as close to being free instruction as you are going to find anywhere. I have already mentioned some ways to use the television for honing your verbal skills; here are four more.

### *Vocabulary Building*

1.  Turn on the set, preferably to a show that presents ap-proximately normal communication; but almost any-thing will serve in a pinch, if it involves language. (A sports event won't do, because people who are playing football or driving stock cars aren't involved in language interactions.) DO NOT TURN ON THE SOUND, JUST THE PICTURE.
2.  Choose one of the persons talking on the screen and watch that person until you spot a body language *clus-ter*—that is, a recognizable whole made up of a position of the body plus an expression of the face plus any ac-companying gesture or gestures.
3.  Now, turn away from the set, and do your best to copy the cluster that you just saw. Arrange your body in the same way that the speaker on television arranged his or hers, to the extent that you can remember it. NOW HOLD IT—DON'T MOVE.
4.  Without changing the arrangement of your body, ask yourself: "What am I feeling? What kind of situation would I be involved in if I assumed this particular ar-rangement of my body? What kinds of things would I be talking about?"
5.  When you've decided on a situation that could be a con-

text for that cluster in your own language and dialect, think about it until you can imagine it very clearly. As you are doing that, *notice what happens:* You will discover that although you may have remembered only one or two units of a cluster, your "bodymind" knows what the rest of the units are and will make the necessary adjustments to complete the set. When you feel that no further adjustments are necessary, pay careful attention to what you're doing. How are you holding your head? Where are your hands? What are your feet doing? What are your eyebrows doing? Gather as much information as you can.

6. Make some sort of notes, while this is clear in your mind. Write them down, or dictate them to your tape recorder. Dictation is the most accurate, because you can do that while maintaining your position, but writing will serve. You are building a data base, an informational record that will be valid for you personally within your own culture; you can't do that from memory alone.

7. When you've done all you can with this cluster, look at your television set and go back to step 2. Repeat for as long as you are interested and not tired of the activity.

NOTE: If you get stuck at step 3, don't force it. Either you didn't get enough information from what you saw to remember it, or the cluster isn't part of your personal grammar. Just go back to step 2 and start again.

## Decoding

This technique is less systematic; it's also not such hard work.

1. Watch the body language on your television screen, WITH THE SOUND OFF, and try to determine what is being talked about.

2. When you think you know, turn up the sound and check to see if you were correct.

3. Turn the sound back off, and begin again.

VARIATIONS: Try watching only hands, or only feet, or only the area between the shoulders and the hips. Watching only the face is less useful, because you may have spent much of your life doing that, especially if you are male; try something new, from which you can learn new things.

If you find this extremely difficult to do, back up one step and watch with the goal of simply determining from the body language what emotional context you are seeing. Do you think the person you are watching is angry? Sad? Happy?

In both situations, you may be surprised to find that there seems to be a marked difference between the verbal and nonverbal channels. Assume that you have watched for a while and have decided that the body language you're seeing indicates anger, and then when you turn on the sound the words being spoken are entirely *free* of anger. What does that mean? It may mean that you've just made a mistake, and that the NVC you isolated didn't indicate anger at all; on the other hand, you may have made an accurate observation of someone who is showing a marked *mismatch* between speech and body language.

With this technique, taking notes is probably not a good idea. You are far too likely to write down information that isn't accurate—not because you aren't doing things properly but because the technique itself is too imprecise. Its goal is primarily to increase your *awareness*, and to help you become accustomed to observing body language with this sort of careful attention. That's much more important than being "right" about what you see.

## Using a Model

1. Choose a person who appears frequently on television or in movies, and whose personality you find especially appealing, and spend some time watching that individual with the sound turned off.

2. Try to identify body language units and clusters that your model uses consistently—it is safe to assume that they are responsible to a significant extent for your positive reaction to the person.

3.  Make notes, as you did for the Vocabulary Building technique. Include as much detail as possible.

VARIATIONS: Try the Decoding technique, using your model. Watch carefully for examples of *mismatch* between body language and speech; if you find some, try to determine what is responsible for the lack of congruence. In a professional media personality, mismatch ought to be very rare; it should take a substantial amount of stress or surprise to create it, and it should disappear very quickly.

Choose someone whose personality you find extremely *un*pleasant, perhaps infuriating, and go through the steps listed above. Try to determine what it is about the individual's body language that is bothering you—being very careful not to watch so long and so intensely that you start *learning* that behavior! Acquiring the body language of William F. Buckley, Jr., for example, without also having his money and power, could wreak havoc in your life.

And any time that you have a chance to watch a mime on television, grab it and watch *very* closely—but still keep the sound turned off. Even though the mime is not talking, the music that is played along with the pantomime will interfere with your observation of the body language. You want as few distractions as possible.

### Mismatch Detection

1.  For this technique, leave the sound turned *on*. Your goal is to spot mismatch between verbal and nonverbal communication, while you are observing both.
2.  Choose one of the game shows on which you see whole bodies rather than just heads and chests. Now listen to what people are saying, but don't look at their faces; look at the rest of their bodies, watching for conflict.
3.  When you've become skilled at this, move on to more challenging contexts, if you can find them. Watch some politicians, for example, if you can find a broadcast that doesn't hide their bodies behind a podium or a thicket of microphones and cords. Watch the very pleasant anchorpersons on morning news shows. Does their body

language indicate to you that they are really as relaxed and pleasant and fascinated by what they're doing as their speech would claim?

With all the techniques and variations above, it will be obvious to you that using a videocassette recorder would make them far more powerful. If you have a videotape of a body language model and can play it many times, until you are familiar enough with it to try "pronouncing" some of it simultaneously with the model, in the same way that you pronounced words simultaneously with the audio tape, you have access to very valuable training. (Be careful, just as you were with voice alone, not to overdo this practice. Your goal is *not* to learn to do a flawless imitation of the celebrity you're observing.) And of course the ability to see a given stretch of body language over and over again will make it possible for you to do a much more detailed and thorough analysis than if you see it only once. It will give you a chance to check your notes, correct them or add to them, etc. This is sure to increase your skill and speed your progress.

*IMPROVING BODY LANGUAGE FROM WITHIN.* Not all techniques require you to have electronic gadgets available. For example, here are two that can be done even during a power failure.

### Visualization

This technique works in the opposite direction, with the context for the body language coming from inside you rather than from an external source. It is a technique much used by actors, whose effectiveness in their roles depends in many ways on their ability to match their body language to the words they are expected to say.

1.  Imagine a situation, a language interaction, in which you might be involved. Think about it until it is vivid in your mind—imagine the physical setting, the other person or persons who would be present, and any other details that will make it real to you. Involve as many of your senses as you can. HOLD THAT IMAGE.

2. Turn your attention to your body, without changing its arrangement in any way. What are your arms doing? Your legs? How are you holding your mouth? What is your chin up to? Get as much information as you can before changing your position and expression.
3. Make notes of what you have learned.
4. Repeat at will ... perhaps taking the role of the other person in the setting you have already imagined so vividly, or moving to an entirely new one if you prefer.

### *Working with Written Body Language*

1. Choose a short story or article, or a book, that contains detailed descriptions of body language—a detective story, story of adventure, "thriller," anything that isn't just bare dialogue or dialogue accompanied only by "he said" and "she said."
2. Find a section of speech that has a reasonably extensive sequence of body language with it. Best of all is a section in which the character is described carrying out body language simultaneously with the words spoken. This sort of thing: "Shrugging his shoulders and scratching his left eyebrow with one ragged fingernail, he said, 'Well, ma'am, I don't believe I'm willing to do that.'"
3. Act out the sequence you've chosen. Does it work? Can you in fact reasonably do what the character is alleged to be doing while you say aloud the words that the character is alleged to be saying?
4. Make notes of anything useful you learn, and then move on to a new written sequence.

You may be very surprised at the frequency with which the answer to "Does it work?" is negative. And you will notice that your body language includes a good deal more than what was written, much of the time. This is one of the few language-related activities for which it may be that the worse the writing is, the more you will learn from it.

*WORKING WITH OTHERS.* Finally, we can move on to techniques to be practiced with real people instead of images. You could of course begin with these, but it would be a painful process for your partners. It's not at all unusual for the identification and note-taking process for a single body language cluster to take thirty minutes or longer; this is not intensely interesting for the others involved. Furthermore, it's not necessarily pleasant for others to be subjected to the kind of peering and staring required when you first begin working on your NVC skills. It's probably best for you to practice with televised or imaginary partners until you're a bit more expert.

### Working with a Friend

1. Have a friend join you in conversation, and talk awhile until you both begin to lose your self-consciousness about the situation.
2. When you see your friend assume a body language cluster that you can identify, say *"Freeze!"*
3. Make a note of the cluster's characteristics; then ask your friend, "What are you feeling? What are you thinking about?" If she's not sure, tell her to relax, and then ask her to assume that cluster again, based on your notes, and to try to decide what significance it has for her.
4. Tell your friend to relax, and *you* assume the body language cluster. How do you feel? Do you and your friend appear to share the same general "meaning" for that cluster? If there are specific differences, make a note of them.
5. Switch roles. You talk, and let your friend carry out the other steps. As always, keep a record of what you learn.

If you can find someone to do this with you who is from a different culture or subculture, you can acquire much valuable information—not only about the other group, but about your own. For both of you, being able to observe from *outside* will give you new insight. In my linguistics classes, I often compared the English "I was riding a horse" with its Navajo equivalent, which translates literally as "The horse was animaling about with me." The English structure is ME, MASTER: YOU, HORSE. The Navajo structure has nothing at all being done *to* the horse, and if there is any dominance relationship, it is in the horse's favor. This was instructive for both groups of students, but not exactly as you might have expected. It was by looking at the Navajo structure that the English speakers suddenly understood the *English* structure; similarly, the Navajo students were not particularly aware of the way their language encoded the sequence until they had a chance to look at the way it is done in English. It was a way of stepping outside the forest long enough to look at the trees. The same phenomenon will occur if you work on body language with someone from another culture; your goal is not to learn the other culture's nonverbal grammar—although it would be a bonus if you did so, of course—but to get a clearer look at your own.

Another excellent technique to practice with a friend is the kind of body syncing that you can't do under ordinary circumstances. Try to match your every movement *perfectly* to your friend's, so that the two of you are moving simultaneously. If you do this in real conversation, you will appear to be mocking your partner, and that will cause anger—don't do it. But if it is a shared activity, with a friend who has agreed to participate, it is one of the best; because the more skilled you are at this exact matching, the more easily you will be able to do ordinary body syncing in the real world. Switch roles from time to time, so that your friend will have an opportunity to acquire the same skill.

## One Last Controversy

I want to close this chapter with a brief introduction to the work of Manfred Clynes and its implications for the study of body language.[11]

Manfred Clynes was intrigued, and puzzled, by the question of why it should be true that a succession of musical tones in a particular arrangement could reliably produce in thousands of listeners the same emotional experience. Music has no "meaning" that you can point to; there is no content there. But people have quite reliable and uniform judgments as to what given sequences of music are "about." Clynes was not satisfied with just theorizing about the question, and he was a distinguished scholar in a number of fields, as well as a Juilliard-trained concert pianist. He had the necessary training to investigate the question in the most rigorous scientific manner. He wanted to find out how the brain associates musical sound sequences with particular emotional states when no obvious clue from language (in the title, for example) is present. He turned to something that music and emotional states have in common—a wave form: brain waves in one case, and sound waves in the other.

Through a series of intricate experiments using sophisticated electronic equipment, Clynes was able to identify a set of wave forms, each associated with a specific emotional state such as joy, grief, hate, and the like. Tests of many hundreds of subjects, from environments and populations as different as the undergraduate classes at M.I.T. and the Walbiri of Australia, showed that people with no prior information at all were able easily to tell researchers which wave form should be assigned to which emotional state. And this was true no matter what sensory modality was used to represent the wave forms themselves. Since one of the ways that a wave form can be traced in the environment is by a musical melody, he proposed that the reason a particular musical sequence reliably makes listeners think of a particular emotional state is that the musical wave form produces in the listening brain the corresponding *emotional* wave form. And although his original research question had been confined to music, the results convinced him that the same thing was true for the shapes of these waves when they were seen by the eye (as lines in a painting, for example) or when they were perceived by the sense of touch, as in a caress.

If Clynes is right, we have the beginning of an explanation for such puzzles as why some people just "have a way with" cranky babies and fretful invalids and fractious students, while others must resort to open mechanisms of control and punishment; why hearing some people talk just puts your back up, no matter what they're saying; why some law enforcement people can "talk down" a potential suicide or abuser, while others are helpless or actually make matters worse. If he is right, a substantial part of the explanation lies in the fact that such people are using the melodic lines of their voices and the visual forms of their body language to correspond to the emotional wave forms that are associated with positive rather than negative emotions. And other people respond with those emotions, although they are not consciously aware of what it is they are responding to.

As with any other scientific dispute, it may be a long time before the jury is in on Clynes's work. (And it may go in and out a number of times before the issue is finally settled.) But we don't have to wait for that, because we can make use of Clynes's research to carry out a very simple experiment of our own. If you examine the set of wave forms that Clynes has identified, you can see immediately that those corresponding to rage and hate contain sharp jogs and dips and deviations, while those corresponding to emotions such as reverence and love are smooth unbroken curves. For use in communication, we can reduce the data to two elegantly simple basic rules:

1.   Avoid all angular body language units.
2.   Emphasize all smoothly curved body language units.

Following these two rules would eliminate from your body language at once such things as shaking your index finger at people, jabbing at the air with the edge of your hand, pounding with your fist, and so on. The only exception would be when a body language unit of that kind was unmistakably being used to illustrate an action being discussed; even then, it might be well to minimize the angular body language.

Furthermore, you might try to incorporate the two rules into the intonation of your voice. Intonation that leaps sharply up and down in pitch, that cuts words off choppily, that punches at certain words and phrases, that clings to a straight monotonous line—all of these are linear and angular rather than curved. Imagine that, when you speak, your words become visible in the air on a line that represents your intonation—try to keep that line curving and smooth. *See what happens.*

If the technique is of no use to you, give it up, of course. In my personal experience, it is one of the most effective tools in the NVC skills inventory.

# Notes

1.  Sally McConnell-Ginet, "Intonation in a Man's World," in *Language, Gender, and Society*, edited by B. Thorne, C. Kramarae, and N. Henley (Rowley, Mass.: Newbury House, 1983), p. 70.

2.  Because communication skills are crucial to the success of a business and to the well-being of its employees, every business should consider buying at least one inexpensive tape recorder for the use of those employees. It's a small investment for potentially large returns.

3.  There is, of course, no reason why you cannot use commercial language tapes very successfully, since the flaw is not in the tapes (or records) but in the instructions that come with them. Just speak *with* the recorded utterances instead of repeating them after they are spoken on the recording.

4.  This doesn't mean that if you are an older person you should conclude that you can't do this—not at all. Just be prepared for it to take a bit longer than it would if you were younger. Your age will be an advantage to you in many other ways.

5.  This is an example of what linguists call "the cocktail party phenomenon." Think of how the sound of someone pronouncing *your* name will leap out at you from an otherwise undifferentiated blur of sound at a noisy party. Similarly, when an insult that is carried by abnormal stress patterns is directed at you personally, you will hear it; you may be mystified because you can't understand *why* you feel insulted, but you'll hear it nonetheless.

6.  Geoffrey Beattie, *Talk: An Analysis of Speech and Non-Verbal Behaviour in Conversation* (Open University Press, Milton Keynes, England, 1983), p. 65.

7.  This is one of the characteristics that clearly demonstrates the failure of doctors to follow the rules of conversation when "seeing" patients. They consistently use any pause at all (and sometimes do not even wait for a pause) as a way of taking the speaker turn away from the patient.

8.  Adam Kendon, "Gesticulation and Speech: Two Aspects of the Process of Utterance," in *The Relationship of Verbal and Nonverbal Communication: Student Edition*, edited by M. R. Key (The Hague: Mouton, 1980), p. 223.

9.  Ray L. Birdwhistell, *Kinesics and Context: Essays on Body Motion Communication* (Philadelphia: University of Pennsylvania Press, 1970).

10.  P. Ekman and W. V. Friesen, "The Repertoire of Nonverbal Behavior: Categories, Origins, Usage, and Coding," *Semiotica* 1 (1969): 49–98.

11.  The name Clynes has given to his work is *sentics*.

# 8
# The Twirk

It would be wonderful if we could feel reasonably certain that when we spoke to others, and when they listened to us, their reactions would be based upon the content of our speech. It would be wonderful if, no matter what the real-world outcome, we could always say, "*They reacted as they did because of what I said.*" Especially if we had been careful to make what we said interesting, rational, and compelling. It would be very nice indeed, but the world isn't like that. Unfortunately, no matter how admirable your words, you have to face the reality that I have named the *twirk*.[1]

Suppose you make an interesting, rational, and compelling speech, and you do that while wearing a purple velvet floppy hat with rabbit ears and scarlet satin roses. Then that hat is a *twirk*—and it will seriously interfere with the manner in which your speech is heard and understood by your audience. You could be the greatest orator since Demosthenes, and that hat would still undercut you and cancel out the power of your words and all the nonverbal communication that went with them.

A twirk on the order of that purple velvet hat is not a probable hazard in your life. We know better than to handicap ourselves in that way. And if you *did* make a mistake like that, getting rid of it forever would mean nothing more than taking the hat off and pitching it into the nearest garbage can. But there are countless other twirks that may pervade your language behavior, that you may be unaware of, and that may be extremely difficult for you to get any control over. This chapter will discuss a sampling of those.

Since the word *twirk* is one I've appropriated from the storehouse of obsolete lexical items of English, I will start by defining it for you. *A twirk is a feature of language behavior which attracts so much attention to itself that it outweighs both the content and the form of the speech it occurs with.* "It wasn't what she said, or how she said it—it was that purple velvet floppy hat with the rabbit ears and the roses!" No twirk is *in itself* either negative or positive; the very feature that wins approval in New York may offend and repulse in Los Angeles, and vice versa. The feature of your language behavior that elderly women find most appealing may provoke only irritation in young men, and vice versa. What distinguishes twirks is their power to ruin your efforts at effective communication—as well as their power to let you accomplish your communication goals using speech that has little or nothing to recommend it. In either case, what is absolutely essential is that you be *aware* of your own twirks so that you can take their effects into account when you speak, and—when possible—bring them under your conscious control.[2]

## Twirks in the Sound System

Let's begin with a very simple example. There is a vowel of English that linguists write like this: /ai/. It's the vowel in words like *sky, I, sigh,* and is called a "diphthong," meaning that it is a sound that starts like one vowel and ends like another. The diphthong /ai/ starts like the *a* in *father* and *calm* and ends like the *i* in *machine.* English has another of these changeable sounds (written /ɔi/), which starts like the vowel in *lawn* and ends like the *i* in *machine.* One of the most potent of twirks for the American English speaker is the pronunciation of /ai/ sounds as if they were /ɔi/ sounds. To speakers of other varieties of English, it sounds as if people who do this pronounce *buy* and *boy*, *sigh* and *soy*, exactly alike.

For many English speakers—the primary exception being native New Yorkers—this one twirky vowel is so attention-getting, and so negatively perceived, that each time you use it you lessen the effect of what you are saying. People stop *hearing* what you're saying, because so much of their attention is distracted by that one sound (like intermittent static on the line), and no sooner do they begin to forget about it than you remind them by doing it again. It has a positive potential, because using it while speaking to a group of native New Yorkers will make them feel comfortable with you. But for other speakers of American English it is the source of strongly negative reactions that can cancel out otherwise excellent language behavior. It goes without saying, I hope, that there's no logical reason for this whatsoever.

When I bring up this troublesome sound in workshops and seminars, there is usually someone who says, "Oh, you mean a New York accent causes negative reactions!" That is not what I mean. There are several features of the variety of English referred to as "a New York accent," and the vowel being discussed here is one of them. But it would make no difference *what* sort of accent you had—the /ɔi/ for /ai/ substitution would be a potential problem.

Everyone, without exception, speaks a dialect and has an accent. Native Californians, who are given to claiming that they have no accent, have distinct California accents. Television anchorpersons who have been trained in the elimination of every possible pronunciation feature that might be considered part of an "accent" end up with an unmistakable variety of English called "newscaster English." It's not the fact that you have an accent, or that you have some one particular accent, that creates most of the difficulty. It is specific features of pronunciation, word choice, sentence formation, and body language that cause negative perceptions, or positive ones, *associated with* various accents.

For the expert, an accent is a complex technical concept. To describe an accent with modest adequacy requires the space of a monograph, and ordinarily requires the assistance of tape recordings. We don't need that sort of detailed information here. For our purposes, what matters is the identification of those features of speech that listeners perceive negatively or positively, to a degree that has significant consequences for the speaker *independent of the content of the speech*. And it's important to remember that a twirk that is negative for one group of listeners will be positive for others, so that saying "Everybody hates to listen to a(n) _____ accent" is always an error. Reactions to accents will vary from one area of the country to another, from one subculture to another, and even from one speaker to another.

There are nine common pronunciation twirks of American English which (except when speaking to others who have them in their own speech) very frequently provoke negative perceptions that interfere with communication. Here is the list, including the substitution of /ɔi/ for /ai/. (If the symbols are unfamiliar, the words will make them clear for you.)

| | | |
|---|---|---|
| 1. | /ɔi/ for /ai/ | "boy" for "buy" |
| 2. | /ai/ for /e/ | "pint" for "paint" |
| 3. | /ɔi/ for /ər/ | "Boyd" for "bird" |
| 4. | /ah/ for /ar/ | "pock" for "park" |
| 5. | /ar/ for /air/ | "tar" for "tire" |
| 6. | /ah/ for /ɔ/ | "Don" for "Dawn" |
| 7. | /d/ for /th/ | "dare" for "there" |
| 8. | /t/ for /th/ | "tank" for "thank" |
| 9. | /ər/ for /ə/, at the end of a word before another word starting with a vowel | "a tuber is" for "a tuba is" |

This list does not include all the sound system twirks of American English, by any means; for example, in my own speech the rule that causes me to pronounce "war" as if it rhymed with "star" is a twirk. But it goes a long way, and includes the most *common* examples.

Now there are two questions to be considered. First: how do you find out if you have one or more of these twirks in your speech? Second: if you do, what do you do about it?

The first question is easily answered. For each of the twirks listed, I have given you a pair of test words, such as "boy" for "buy." If your reaction to any of those pairs is that their spelling is different but *they sound exactly alike,* you almost certainly have the twirk of pronunciation associated with them. You won't be able to hear it yourself, because the sound rules of your variety of English don't assign differing pronunciations to the two test words. That is the very fact that makes it simple to test for them.

The second question is much more difficult. You may not care to do *anything* about the situation, and that is your right. But if your attitude is that you don't intend to change and that if other people find you irritating that's *their* problem, please reconsider the matter in terms of your own self-interest, not theirs. If people find you irritating, it will interfere with your life: They won't do what you want them to do, and they won't help you (or let you) do what *you* want to do. Even if you have only contempt for the opinions of others, it is to your advantage, pure and simple, to learn to evoke more positive perceptions.

Assume that what you want to do is to be able to use the twirk *at will*—that is, use it when you choose to, and eliminate it from your speech when that is your preference. (There is nothing dishonorable about that goal.) You can proceed by taking lessons from voice coaches, speech consultants, or other experts. Or you can begin by using the same technique proposed on pages 110 to 117 for the improvement of voice quality. You can get a tape recording of the speech of someone who does not have the pronunciation twirk in question (or any of the others on the list of nine) and speak with that tape until your brain's mismatch detector straightens things out for you. If that fails, you can then fall back on the experts; if it doesn't, you will have saved yourself some money and annoyance.

You don't need an expensive commercial tape. Just have someone who does not have the twirk in his or her speech read a set of sentences that use words like the test words and tape them for your use. Consider the substitution of /ai/—as in "eye"—for /e/—as in "pay"—which is common in the speech of native Arkansans. If that is the sound you want to gain control of, you need a tape containing sentences like the following, prepared by someone whose speech doesn't include this twirk.

1. *"They* were *waiting* for us at the corner."
2. "I didn't *say* you had to *wait.*"
3. "The best *way* to do that is to *take* your time."
4. "If your *name* is *Jane,* you must be the *lady* from Little Rock."
5. "Please *pay* for your food at the usual *place.*"
6. "Those who *pray* there can see the *bay.*"
7. *"Say* what you mean or *they*'ll be confused."
8. "We have a *great* time at your Uncle *Jay*'s *place.*"

NOTE: The words that are italicized in the examples contain the sound involved in the twirk; the italics aren't indications of stress.

You could construct sentences containing many words with the troublesome sound, like the famous "The rain in Spain falls mainly on the plain," but I don't think it is a good idea. Two, perhaps three such words in one sentence is adequate, and is more likely to produce sentences that might actually occur in conversation. The more natural the taped speech is, the easier it will be for you to work with.

The replacement of a pronunciation twirk by its alternative doesn't mean that the alternative becomes a twirk. People who would have been distracted because you seemed to be talking to them about "boying a car" won't notice that you now talk of "buying a car." And that's exactly what you want to have happen—you want them not to be distracted.

During the student demonstrations of the sixties, quite a few people discovered that although ordinarily nobody paid much attention to what they said, if they just included one of a small set of obscenities in every sentence, at least once and preferably three or four times, they could be sure of an audience. This was absurd, but it worked. It got people's attention, even when the rest of what was said was drivel, and it was used for that specific purpose. However, nobody would listen to a speaker and remark on the astonishing absence of those obscenities from his or her speech unless there were a special reason to expect them. The absence of the distracting sound is not noticed, just as the absence of an offending silly hat is not noticed.

It will be obvious that if you have nothing useful or interesting to say, but are obliged to talk anyway, one way of getting through it is to use plenty of twirks, so that people's attention is diverted from the pitiful content of your speech. Do that well enough and the twirks will be the only thing anyone remembers. "I have no *idea* what she said! All I could hear was the awful way she kept dropping her *g*'s and saying *ain't*!" If that's your goal, it's easily accomplished. Any fourth-grade child knows that if the teacher calls on you to say what six times seven makes and you answer with "I ain't got no idea," there's a good chance the teacher will forget that you didn't know the arithmetic, while offering a few well-chosen remarks on the *right* way to say that.

It may be that your problem is not a characteristic of any dialect of American English, but rather a *foreign* accent, in its entirety. This is complicated by the fact that standards regarding foreign accents tend to be a matter of fashion, like standards of physical beauty. At the moment, a French or Hungarian accent is fashionable—and thus a twirk with positive effects much of the time—while any sort of Latin accent is the opposite. We hear, "Oh, she has the most gorgeous French accent!" We do not hear, "Oh, he has the most gorgeous Mexican accent!" No one has ever been able to demonstrate any logical reason for this, either, any more than they have been able to provide logical reasons for the perception of one particular body shape as more beautiful than another. The reed-thin woman living at a time when female beauty is defined as meaning ample hips and breasts and thighs will protest that it's ridiculous, and she will be right. Fashions in accents are equally ridiculous, but they have powerful real-world effects.

Other aspects of the problem cut across the boundaries of variation. Some accents are more nasal than others; but no matter what your accent, if you have a high nasal voice it will trigger negative perceptions. This means that the speaker with an unfashionable accent who also has a high nasal voice faces major barriers, *multiple* barriers, to effective communication. If you speak so loudly that you hurt people's ears, the fact that you bellow in "a charming French accent" won't make you much pleasanter to listen to. You will need to tackle both the problems of voice quality *and* problems associated with accent, and it's best to deal with the larger problem first, if possible.

If your accent is considered unfashionable, it would be worth your time to gain control of it and to be able to switch from the unfashionable accent to a more neutral one at will, by your own choice. This process is part of the skill called *code switching*, and it is valuable to you in the same way that being able to type or weld or drive a car is valuable. Get yourself a tape of a fashionable variety of American English, and practice speaking *with* the tape. A tape of Walter Cronkite or Diane Sawyer (or any newscaster of roughly your own age and gender) would be an excellent choice—just tape the material straight from your television set. To the extent that a "twirkless" variety of American English can be said to exist, it is the neutral English of the expert national newscaster. As always, be careful not to go so far with your use of the model that you train yourself to do a Walter Cronkite or Diane Sawyer *imitation*. And be very careful not to choose as a model an entertainment personality who has an unusual speech style as part of his or her stock in trade. The distinctive speech of a celebrity stand-up comic is an asset, because it sets that comic off from the hundreds of other stand-up comics; it would not be an asset to you unless you have similar goals.

Any competent linguist will tell you that the total elimination of a foreign accent from the speech of an adult is an extremely difficult matter; I agree. But what you are concerned with is not linguistic perfection as it might be measured scientifically—you are concerned with the perceptions of people who listen to you speak in ordinary conversation. The more closely your speech is tuned to theirs, the more they will perceive you as speaking *their* language, and the fewer artificial barriers you will erect between you and your listeners. Perfection would be nice, of course. But any decrease in the degree of mismatch that causes you to be heard as someone with an unfashionable foreign accent will be helpful and is worth working toward. The many different dialects and accents that are routinely learned and used by professional actors are far from flawlessly correct. But they are close enough to satisfy those who hear them in a world of extravagant linguistic diversity, and the fact that every drama department in the country assumes that its students can acquire them and use them at will is proof that the task is not as impossible as it is sometimes alleged to be.

Along with discouraging words, linguists can also offer some practical help from time to time. For example, if you have any one of the Latin accents (Mexican, Spanish, Cuban, etc.), there is something you can do immediately and deliberately to lessen the "Latinness" of your English. Whenever Latin speakers pronounce the sounds symbolized by the letters *t, d, l, n* at the beginning of a word, they put the tip of their tongue against the back of their upper teeth. Speakers of English making the same sounds put the tip of the tongue against the hard bony ridge just *behind* the upper teeth. If you pronounce the word *tea* first with your tongue tip against your upper teeth and then with it moved back against that bony ridge, you will have said it first with a Latin accent and then without. Do this aloud, please, and listen to the difference. (English speakers wishing to improve their accents in Spanish should do exactly the opposite.) Unlike such matters as whether your vocal cords are vibrating or not (which is what makes the difference between *s* and *z*), this tongue-tip maneuver is something you can do consciously and deliberately and without special training. And because this particular feature of speech comes along so often, it can do an astonishing amount to tune your English in the direction of native quality perceptually.

There is a minor movement in America today to "get rid of your Southern accent," as if a Southern accent—like a high nasal voice—were a guarantee of negative listener perceptions. You can even enroll in courses for this purpose. But people who are afraid that their "Southern accent" will hold them back in the world, despite the fact that Presidents John-

son and Carter both had strong Southern accents, should stop and think. For one thing, there are a number of different Southern accents, rather than just one; for another, the reaction to Southern accents is not uniformly negative. The Southern accents of Rosalynn Carter, Barbara Jordan, Ted Turner, and many others do not provoke negative reactions. It's not the "Southern accent" that is causing the negative reactions when they do occur; it is pronunciation twirks from the list on page 145, especially numbers 2 and 5. Eliminate those from your "Southern accent," and speak just a tad more quickly, and most people will find your speech perfectly acceptable.

## Twirks in the Vocabulary

Some twirks are nothing more than individual words or phrases that, for any of a number of reasons, trigger reactions in listeners with substantial effects independent of the content of the utterance. These reactions are rarely logical in even the most strained sense of the word, but they are as real as your elbow and can have severe social and economic consequences.

Word-choice twirks can be divided into six classes, as follows:

1. Grammar and Usage
2. Obscenities, Curses, and Epithets
3. Boundary Words and Phrases
4. Academic Regalian
5. Jargon
6. Miscellaneous

I want to give just a few examples from each class, with a very brief discussion. This is the easiest sort of twirk either to get rid of or to acquire. It takes much intensive effort and time to gain control of your pronunciation to an extent that lets you switch among accents at will, but very little effort is needed to eliminate a few dozen offending words from your vocabulary, or to add a dozen that will have positive effects. You don't need anything to accomplish this except determination.

## Grammar and Usage

It's unlikely that you have as a twirk the habit of saying things like "I shall endeavor to return before sunset" or "Were I but jocular, I'd laugh oftener." Grammar and usage twirks in your speech will probably be items like the following: *ain't* and its companion *ain't got no*; *hisself*, *theirselves* for *himself*, *themselves*; *leastwise*; *hopefully*. There is no logical reason why any of these should cause your listeners to shudder and make strange assumptions about the way you were brought up. In fact, *hisself* and *theirselves* are a good deal *more* logical than the "correct" forms, since they follow logically from *myself* and *yourself* and the rest. We don't say *meself*; why in the world should we say *himself*? But logic is irrelevant here; if you use these, learn to use them only when it is to your advantage to do so. The trial lawyer who leans toward the jury in a small rural Southern town and says soulfully, "Ladies and gentlemen, there ain't no reason—*not one*—to call my client a murderer," is using the system as it should be used. Linguistically speaking.

The objection to *leastwise* is completely arbitrary, as if purists had closed their eyes and stuck a pin in the word and declared it beyond the pale on no other grounds. There are quite a few of these, and they should simply be memorized and used only when appropriate. The word *hopefully* is a bit different, and an explanation would be probably be helpful. *Hopefully* is an example of language undergoing a normal process of change, while those opposed to change struggle to make a moral issue of a linguistic one.

English at this stage of history has two types of relevant *-ly* words. One type is the "manner adverbs," such as *patiently* and *carefully*. You can identify these because they are always paraphrasable (sometimes awkwardly) by "in a _____ manner"; thus, "He spoke patiently" and "He spoke in a patient manner" mean essentially the same thing. The other type is the "sentential adverbs," like *fortunately* which can be paraphrased with "it is _____ that" and a sentence. Thus, "Fortunately, cows can't fly" means essentially the same thing as "It is fortunate that cows can't fly." The only significant difference is that the "It is" version is in obvious Computer Mode and the other is not.

Now we come to poor *hopefully*, in a sentence like "Hopefully, I will pass the test." Look at the following sentences:

"In a hopeful manner, I will pass the test." NOT ACCEPTABLE
"It is hopeful that I will pass the test." NOT ACCEPTABLE

You see the problem. You can paraphrase "The patient smiled hopefully at the surgeon" as "The patient smiled in a hopeful manner at the surgeon," but that is not the *hopefully* that causes all the commotion. *That hopefully* can't be expanded as either a manner adverb or a sentential adverb, and it is clearly that dreaded entity, Something New. Unlike the sentential adverbs, which say "It is (whatever) that . . . ," this word says "I am hopeful that . . ." and takes the entire construction out of Computer Mode. "Hopefully, I will pass the test" means "I hope that I will pass the test" or "I am hopeful that I will pass the test," and real Computers don't say "I," right? I believe that *hopefully* will survive in English, because people quite clearly want it to, and because there are already some additional members of this new adverb class coming into use. (For example, I have heard students use *thankfully* in this same pattern.) But until it has been around so long that even the most scrupulous purists have grown accustomed to it, it is a twirk. And if you are talking to an audience of purists, or even just to one purist, and you start a sentence with "Hopefully . . . ," you have wasted the sentence; the purist won't hear it. It might be an excellent way to slip a sentence you don't *want* heard past a purist or two.

## Obscenities, Curses, and Epithets

I assume that I need to say very little about this group. You are free to construct your own examples of curses and obscenities. So far as I know, these have only two functions: (a) to serve as verbal abuse; and (b) to serve as a signal that you are part of a group when the use of curses and obscenities is a characteristic of that group. A useful rule, especially in cross-cultural situations, is this one: If you're not sure whether it is a curse or obscenity or not, assume that it *is* one. Then proceed as you would with any certified curse or obscenity.

An epithet differs from a curse or obscenity in being less formalized; you can make up epithets and be sure that they will be recognized as epithets, which is not always true of curses and obscenities. Epithets range from such basic uglies as "you idiot" and "you creep" to the most elaborate and fanciful uglies like "you intemperate and indecisive hypervegetarian excuse for a philosopher!" Both kinds will serve primarily to distract your listener from whatever else you say at the time.

## Boundary Words and Phrases

These are strange lexical items that come and go as slang words come and go. They are habit-forming, irritating, and highly contagious. Current examples are *like, you know, well, okay, I mean*. They are commonly described as useless, but they don't *start* useless. At first they serve as a way for the speaker to keep control of the floor without having to pause while he or she decides what to say next. If they continue to serve only this function, they may never become twirks in the speech of an individual; for example, President Reagan's opening "Well . . ." is used just enough to let it serve as a friendly opener. It says, "Well, just between you and me, and as we all know . . ." He doesn't start *every* sentence that way! Often, however, these little "fillers" take over someone's language the way a kudzu vine takes over a pasture, and then you get this sort of mess:

> "Well, okay, the first thing we ought to do, okay, is gas up the car. Okay? Like, if we run out of gas, you know, there aren't many stations along that road, okay? And if we get stranded halfway there in the middle of the night, you know, well, it won't be funny, okay?"

Of all the word-choice twirks, these are the peskiest. They are not only hard to get rid of when they've become habitual in your own speech, they are as contagious as the flu. If you spend more than an hour around someone who talks like that example, you will find—to your horror—that you have picked them up and that your speech is peppered with them. Grim determination is the only way to get rid of them—including such brute-force measures as fining yourself a nickel every time you use one—and the quicker you catch them and stamp them out, the easier it will be. They have the same potential for positive effects as any other twirk, and their use can serve to reassure people that you are part of their group. But it's so easy to get them embedded in your linguistic habits that I don't think they are often worth the risk. I suggest that you avoid them.

## Academic Regalian

On the way to getting advanced degrees, students find themselves required to master a sort of language that is used nowhere but in the academic world. It is an excellent example of what is called a *register*, meaning a form of speech that is associated with a particular role or function in life. All of us know several registers and switch among them with relative ease. The child who says "Bye, Mom" to a parent, "Gotta split, man," to a friend, and "Good-bye, Mr. Rand" to a teacher is exhibiting control of three registers. I call the academic register "Academic Regalian," after the robes, stoles, mortarboards, and hoods that academics wear on ceremonial occasions; these items are referred to as one's "academic regalia." Most words and phrases from foreign languages (especially dead foreign languages) are part of Academic Regalian—for example, *inter alia, tout court*, and *Weltschmerz*. When these items work their way out of Academic Regalian into ordinary speech they lose their foreign pronunciation; thus, an academic says "geshtawlt" while a nonacademic pronounces "gestalt" as "gesstawlt." You can sometimes judge the rarification of a given academic's status by the degree to which his or her Academic Regalian retains its foreign pronunciations.

Also part of AR are words like *albeit* and the phrase "so to speak." So long as they are used in academic contexts, they are not only harmless but may be essential to an individual's scholarly career. *Outside* the academic environment they are twirks that will either make you look foolish or provoke resentment because you appear to be putting on airs. Their only really legitimate use outside Academe is in those bizarre situations when it would actually be helpful in real-world terms for you to be able to convince someone that you really and truly are a professor of something or other. If you are the young chaperone of a group of even younger students who have become a little unruly, or have forgotten to bring some necessary paper or fill out some necessary form, a few "so to speaks" and "inter alias" flung about the linguistic environment may serve to reassure officials and the population at large that someone responsible is in control of the situation.

## Jargon

The term *jargon* refers to sets of words used only by a specialized group of individuals—more specialized than the set of all college teachers, for instance. The example that comes most readily to mind is the jargon of the computer programmers, particularly those whose jargon term for themselves is *hackers*. They talk of computer parts and pieces and processes in a way that goes far beyond the average Radio Shack customer's "hardware, software, and user-friendly" vocabulary. The rule for using jargon, whether it is the lofty jargon of the judge's bench or the intimate jargon of the fly fisherman, is simple: When you are within the group to which the jargon belongs, use it; otherwise, don't. It's rude and thoughtless to speak French with your friends when someone in your group speaks only English; it's just as bad to speak Auto Mechanic in a group that contains someone who can't tell a spark plug from an exhaust pipe. If you want to function within a group, you *must* learn its jargon; only when you have become someone with significant status in the group can you afford not to use that vocabulary. And even then, you should do so carefully, since it will create a distance between you and the other members of the group. It should be done knowing full well that that is true, and for good reasons. Be certain that you *want* to be remembered as the person who insists on calling a boat's kitchen a kitchen instead of a galley.

## Miscellaneous Word-Choice Twirks

There are necessarily vocabulary items that won't fit in the five categories above but that aren't numerous enough to make up an entire new category with a label of its own. In a miscellaneous set, nothing is going to be a *typical* example; that is why it is miscellaneous. A few examples from my personal list of things that distract me from what a speaker is saying are:

> "Listen here . . ."
> "Who says?"
> "Oh, *nev*er mind . . ."

And phrases that are taken from popular commercials, television shows, and the like quickly become twirky in a very negative way. Politicians appear to be especially insensitive to the process by which today's funny line becomes tomorrow's irritating twirk, and will go on saying "Where's the beef?" long after every five-year-old American child could tell you that *no*body says that anymore. The sensible thing to do, as a way of checking these out, is to find a five-year-old child and *ask*.

## Twirks in Syntax and Semantics

Syntax is what is usually meant by "grammar"—roughly speaking, how to put words together into sentences. Semantics is usually referred to as the study of meaning. Once it seemed possible to consider syntax separately from semantics, and linguistics departments still teach separate courses in the two subjects. However, this is yet one more of those artificial divisions that are made for the sake of convenience but cannot be maintained in the real world. We will therefore threat syntax and semantics twirks as a single category in this section.

Many of these twirks are expanded versions of the "grammar and usage" category. For example, there is the matter of "double negatives." They will have one of two effects: either "He's one of us" or "He must have grown up in a barn." For example:

> "I don't get no answer when I call Mary."
> "If you can't do no better than that, just stop."
> "I don't like eggplant nor spinach, neither!"

Use of these sentences, or sentences like them, will really set people off. (Unless you are a country singer, in which case they are obligatory; they are part of the country music register, just as "so to speak" is part of the academic one.) Traditionally teachers tell students that they're wrong because "two negatives cancel each other out"; that is manifestly false. If it were true, people would have difficulty understanding sentences like the examples—but they don't. The cancellation claim is true only in mathematics, not in language.

Furthermore, all of the following sentences are just as doubly negative as the ones above, but they cause no problems. (Each negative element is underlined for clarity.)

> "I'm <u>not</u> <u>un</u>happy or <u>un</u>comfortable."
> "They did<u>n't</u> <u>refuse</u> to leave."
> "It's <u>im</u>possible <u>not</u> to be <u>un</u>easy in this fog."

Clearly, we are once again looking at a phenomenon that is based arbitrarily on linguistic fashion. But it is anything but trivial; there is extensive research showing that people react more strongly (and appropriately enough, more negatively) to the use of double negatives than to almost any other grammatical sacred cow in English. It is therefore crucial for you to have their use under conscious control. The following rule will take care of most of the problem:

> Never use an auxiliary verb plus *not* with a following *no, not, nothing, nobody, nowhere, never, neither* in the same clause.

It's the violation of that rule that accounts for such grammatical twirks as "He isn't no doctor," "She can't get no answer," "We shouldn't send her letters neither," and "They can't do nothing right."

Another example of a syntax-semantic twirk is the pattern called a "Hedge," which has had much attention from linguists. It is a good deal like the "boundary words" in that it becomes a twirk only if you use it frequently; I'm sure that everyone uses a Hedge at least occasionally. Here are a few examples:

> "I don't want to tell you what to do, but you shouldn't eat that."
> "I know this is a silly thing to say, but I'm afraid of plums."
> "You'll probably tell me I shouldn't have told you this, but your wife just bought a sports car."

The primary function of the Hedge is to steal the listener's response by predicting it and announcing the prediction. When you begin a sentence with "I know this is a silly thing to say . . ." you are predicting that the person you are speaking to will hear your sentence, will think "That's a silly thing to say," and may very well be rude enough to say that aloud. By Hedging, you beat your listener to it; then if you do get "That's a silly thing to say" as a response, you are able to come right back with "I know! I already *said* that!" If you use Hedges in Placater Mode, they are also an attempt to get your listener to respond with "Oh, of *course* that's not a silly thing to say!" and similar words of reassurance. (Whereupon the Placater can say, "But it is—I *know* it is!" and try for another round of stroking.)

When a teacher or lecturer hears "I know this is a stupid question, but . . . ," the temptation—unworthy, perhaps, but almost overwhelming—is to ignore the question itself and just respond with "It certainly *is* a stupid question." Or "If you know it's a stupid question, don't ask it." The reaction of almost anyone to "I know I shouldn't say this, but . . ." is a crisp "Then don't say it." The Hedge is one of the most explicit of all "I'm a verbal victim; please abuse me" patterns; be aware of that, and don't issue invitations.

When a Hedge is used by someone who holds the *dominant* rank in an interaction, it creates even more resentment, because the subordinate partner doesn't feel free to respond openly. The doctor who says to a patient, "I know you're not going to understand any of this, but . . . ," or the domineering husband who says to a subordinated wife, "I know you're not going to like this, but . . . ," can count on a sullen and unhappy patient or spouse.

The only positive use for the Hedge is in a situation where, for one of a number of possible reasons, it is to your advantage to appear to be less confident and skilled than you really are. It can then serve to diminish your personal image slightly, and there are times when that is an excellent strategy.

The only way to break someone of a Hedge habit is to use an Anti-Hedge, like these:

"I know this is a brilliant question, but . . ."
"I hope you'll be angry, but . . ."

And so on.

The shock of having to process a few of these Anti-Hedges should make the habitual Hedger sufficiently self-conscious about the habit to give it up, at least in language interactions where you are present.

Finally, any of the verbal attack patterns discussed in chapter 4, or any of the Satir Modes, if used constantly and to the exclusion of other kinds of language, will constitute twirks. The incessant use of Blamer Mode for every purpose, for example, will cause people to be so aware of the Blaming that the substance of your speech will never reach them. The incessant use of Leveler Mode, especially when there is never any concession made to the feelings of others, can be so conspicuous a twirk that people will cross streets and duck into doorways to avoid talking to you, no matter *what* your subject of conversation might be. There is a science fiction cliché plot in which individuals who are telepathic find it impossible to survive because knowing exactly what others are thinking is intolerable; the undeviating Leveler who never makes an exception is the closest thing our current society has to offer along that line.

## Twirks in Discourse

The traditional way of dividing "grammar" up in linguistics and related studies is a three-way split into phonology (the sound system), syntax (roughly, the formation of sentences), and semantics (meaning). We have seen that this division is artificial, but that it is convenient for organizing a discussion. It's also convenient to put them all back together again and look at *discourse*, which is larger units of language. (In written language, for example, the paragraph is a typical "unit of discourse.")

Twirks in discourse are easy to identify but hard to describe, because they involve all elements of language simultaneously. If we want to consider the question within syntonic theory, however, we can use the unifying concept of the *action chain* to help us proceed systematically.

In Edward T. Hall's *Beyond Culture* (page 141), he defines the action chain as follows:

> An action chain is a set sequence of events in which usually two or more individuals participate. . . . If any of the basic acts are left out or are too greatly distorted, the action must be started all over again.

Hall's example is the handshake, a sequence of body language. It takes two people to carry out a handshake, and if it is interrupted there is really no way to do it without beginning again. It's both distracting and frustrating to interrupt the handshake action chain; most people, even if they don't particularly want to shake hands, will respond if someone begins the chain and will go through the motions necessary to finish it. As is usual with action chains, it's easy to make changes and variations at the level of small parts of the handshake. You can vary the amount of pressure used to grip another's hand, or the degree of tilt you give your hand at the wrist. At the level of larger units, however, making changes is difficult or impossible. You can't decide that first you'll shake someone's hand and then you'll hold out your own hand.

Action chains in discourse are not as rigid as the handshake except within rituals and formal ceremonies, but they can be clearly recognized. For example:

> A:  "Hello, how are you?"
> B:  "Fine, thanks. And you?"
> A:  "Oh, I'm fine!"

Much variation is possible in this chain at the level of word choice; the first line could be "Good morning! How are you?" or "Hi there, how are you this morning?" or any one of many other similar utterances. But the higher level is rigid in the same way the handshake is. The first speaker must offer a greeting and a query about the state of the second speaker; the second speaker must respond positively, following that with a query about the state of the first speaker; then the first speaker completes the chain with a positive response. You can't shake someone's hand without first reaching for it; similarly, you can't respond to a question and then expect it to be asked. To respond to "Hello, how are you?" with "Two and two are four" is a serious violation of the rules of language interaction.

This action chain is so rigid (perhaps especially with women) that it is a source of confusion in health care. The doctor who drops in to see the hospitalized patient on morning rounds and says, "Hello, Mrs. Smith! How are you this morning?" has initiated this chain. If the patient isn't in acute distress, the tendency to respond with "Fine, thanks" and a query about the doctor is extremely strong. The doctor who then says, "Fine, fine!" and disappears has not obtained any information about the way the patient feels. Health care personnel should avoid initiating this action chain unless they genuinely don't want to hear how the patient feels and don't mind leaving him or her feeling frustrated. All this requires is that they reword the first line of the utterance like this:

"Good morning, Mrs. Smith! Please tell me how you're feeling today."

The patient will then feel free to provide accurate information. The basic rule for action chains in discourse is very simple:

NEVER INTERRUPT AN ACTION CHAIN UNLESS YOU HAVE AN EXCEL-LENT REASON TO DO SO.

This means, of course, that it's unwise to *start* any action chain that you'd prefer not to have to finish. It *doesn't* mean that you have to go along mindlessly with any old discourse chain that someone else begins; it *does* mean that you must be aware that the chains exist and be prepared for the consequences of interrupting them. Not knowing that you are involved in an action chain, or not knowing what the steps in the chain are, can get you into serious difficulty; this is one of the most common problems in cross-cultural communication.

I remember with much distaste an emergency program for teaching English to refugees in the United States—people who had arrived here knowing almost no English at all, sometimes none at all, and who had only a few weeks to acquire a smattering of the language before they moved into the community. One of the first utterances chosen to teach to these people was the sentence "What is the matter with you?" This was convenient in the camp and in crises, when the answers included such items as "I am lost," "I can't find my visa," "I can't find my family," "I am sick," and the like. In the community, however, it put the innocent refugee (who had only a very limited set of sentences to choose from and tended to use this one as a greeting) right smack in the middle of the following action chain:

A: "What is the matter with you?"
B: "Not a damn thing! What's the matter with *you?*"

This did nothing to lessen the inevitable awkwardness between the refugees and the community.

At a different level—an interaction between subcultures within a single culture—this is what happened to Geraldine Ferraro when she answered that blueberry muffin question. She was in the middle of an action chain and didn't realize it. With unsavory results.

The deliberate interruption of discourse action chains is a twirk of monumental proportions; as with all twirks, whether it provokes positive or negative reactions will depend upon the context and the audience. (I have served on committees so helplessly entangled in one action chain after another that they could get nothing at all done; they were extremely grateful to have someone present who was willing to interrupt the chains and disentangle them.) But it will *always* attract attention that may outweigh the content of what you are saying. It may be the ideal thing to do—but it should not be done at random.

Sometimes people have this twirk without being aware of it, and that is not at all funny. It may be the source of your problem if any of the following apply to you:

a.   You feel that people involved in language interactions with you are always uneasy, or always behave oddly.
b.   You don't ever quite know what to say.
c.   People always look a little puzzled before answering you, or pause a little longer than is usual before answering you.
d.   People always seems slightly bewildered by your responses to what *they* say.
e.   It seems to you that nobody ever wants to talk to you.

Deliberate action chain disruption can be a good thing; in classical psychoanalysis, it is a primary tool of the specialist. But if it's accidental, and particularly if it is accidental and habitual, it can make your life a linguistic mess.

To get a personal look at the power of the action chain, try the following experiment. Next time you have a captive audience, tell them to listen to you very carefully; then hum the tune to "Mary Had a Little Lamb," all the way through, firmly and clearly—except for the very last note. Just stop; don't hum that last note. Every time I have done this experiment, the listeners have responded by humming the missing note in unison—they cannot stand to leave that incomplete last line just hanging there in the air. The drive to complete patterns is crucial to human survival, and is very powerful indeed; interruption of discourse action chains frustrates this drive and creates disharmony in language interactions.

It is true that when you use the suggested responses to verbal attack patterns presented in chapter 4 you are breaking an action chain. The attacker has become accustomed to the response in which you take the bait offered in the attack and then participate in a linguistic row. But you are doing that deliberately, for a carefully thought out reason, and in a systematic way; your response does not just *break* the chain but attempts to lead the attacker into a completely different one that will *not* inevitably lead to confrontation. Consider the interaction in which one member of a couple demands to know why the other never does anything to make him or her happy, and the potential victim breaks the action chain by making an offer such as "Why don't we go to New Jersey for the weekend?" That is answering a question with a question, which violates the rules of discourse; furthermore, it is failing to respond with the expected "Whadda you *mean*, I never do anything to make you happy? Why, only last week . . . ," etc. And that disrupts a chain that the attacker has come to expect and to enjoy. At the same time, it has begun a *new* action chain, because it is customary to respond to an offer with either an acceptance or a refusal, and now the attacker—who is caught off guard—will probably make the switch. This is a *good* use of the technique, done with full awareness, using the strength of the action chain in the same way that someone skilled in karate would use the strength of an opponent's lunge.

## The Permanent Twirk

So far we have discussed only twirks that can be eliminated, with varying degrees of effort and varying amounts of time, from an individual's language behavior. (Or that can be added to language behavior, if that is desired.) Not all twirks are like that. Some are to all intents and purposes a permanent feature of the speaker's life.

Sometimes these twirks sound like a problem the average person would be delighted to have—for example, it *sounds* as though nobody could object to being magnificently beautiful or handsome, to having a spectacularly perfect body, to being endowed with stunning dark violet eyes, etc. If you have one of these characteristics, however, it constitutes a permanent twirk. You will find people so distracted by your extraordinary appearance that they don't really hear what you are saying. Worse yet, your ability to use this twirk to get whatever you want may cause you to go through life without ever learning any communications skills at all. Then, when old age begins to destroy your physical appeal to others—and this is inevitable, although it comes to men much later in life than it does to women—you will suddenly be linguistically helpless.

I don't want to seem unsympathetic to the problem I've just described; it can be serious and disruptive and have tragic consequences. But my primary concern here is with the opposite side of this coin: the person whose permanent twirk is not an excess of attractiveness, but a physical characteristic that frequently provokes negative reactions. The most common twirks of this kind are physical handicaps and speech disorders.

The only effective way to handle this problem is to go right into Leveler Mode and acknowledge your problem. Like this:

> "I have cerebral palsy (or I am a stutterer, or I don't hear well) and this may interfere with our communication. Please feel free to ask me to repeat or explain whenever necessary; I won't be offended. I appreciate your patience."

And then go right on with the language interaction. And use every one of the syntonics techniques introduced in this book as mechanisms to compensate for the communication disadvantage that you must deal with. The reason that people react so drastically to your situation is because the degree of mismatch is so great; the more you can reduce that, the more effective your communication will be. And as people continue to talk with you they will become less aware of the difficulty, particularly if you have done your best to set them at ease at the very beginning, as in the example. They won't have to spend time wondering if they dare ask you to say something twice because they can't be sure whether that will cause you distress or anger; and that will make it possible for them to listen to you without being distracted by potential social catastrophes.

I have not devoted a section to body language twirks in this chapter, for the very simple reason that it isn't necessary to do so. Remember that *everything* associated with an utterance except its words—the way you dress, the way you do your hair or use cosmetics, the way you sit and stand and move, your voice quality, the location you choose for the interaction, *everything you do during the interaction*—becomes part of your language behavior and contributes to the message you communicate. If you read books on effective communication today, you will find that they devote entire chapters to such matters as how you should choose your clothing and how you should arrange the furniture in your office.

The place to go for information about these matters is to the shelves bulging with books on good manners, on proper clothing and grooming, on interior decoration, on developing your "image," and the like. There is no shortage of such materials. Review chapter 7, which has choices in nonverbal communication as its subject.

As a very general principle, the more an element of your body language is unlike that same element in the body language of your listeners, the more likely it is to constitute a twirk in that situation. Twirks call attention to themselves, which draws attention away from what you are saying—for good or for bad, depending on your communication goals at the time and in that context. Your goal is to have conscious *control* of your twirks, and to use them or avoid them systematically and for your own excellent reasons. This is as true in body language as in any other part of your communication behavior.

## Notes

1.  This is an obsolete word from English, once used to refer to twitches and twirls.
2.  There are, of course, also twirks in written language, but they won't be discussed in this chapter.

# 9

# *Syntonics and Rhetoric: Written Language and Public Speaking*

The first eight chapters of this book have focused on language used in oral interactions—in conversations, interviews, business meetings, professional appointments, sales transactions, and so on. In this chapter we will shift our attention to two other areas of the language environment: written language and what is called "public" speaking. The term *written language* as it is used here refers not to professional writing (fiction, articles, etc.) but to the written tasks of ordinary life, such as brief written descriptions, personal and business letters, memoranda, club newsletters, and similar "amateur" writing.

Certainly writing and public speaking are different, but they have a number of characteristics in common that make it appropriate to consider them in a single chapter under the heading of *rhetoric*. Let's begin with a list of some of the features that they share.

1. Both are usually more *planned* than oral language interactions are. In the case of writing, there's time for revising and polishing not available for oral language. When a speech is written before it is given, or is based on a

carefully prepared written outline, the same thing is true of public speaking.

2. Both *frighten* people! You would never know, from the way many of us react to the prospect of writing a few pages or giving a short talk, that these tasks are only variations on the ordinary language activities of our daily lives.

3. Both are highly valued in our society in a way that ordinary oral language usually is not valued. If you can write well, or do effective public speaking, you will be rewarded for those abilities; people will give up both time and money to read or hear your words.[1]

4. Both can be constructed using a single set of rhetorical principles; we'll be discussing some of these principles in this chapter.

Suppose we extend Miller's Law to writing and public speaking. We will find that its application in those situations is not very different from its application to ordinary language. In fact, because we have more time to choose our words and arrange them, it's often easier to apply the rule and to do so more successfully.

Miller's Law instructs us to share realities; in writing and in public speaking we have the leisure to do that really well, if we choose to. In conversation we have to react instantly to the language behavior of others, with very little time to think or prepare; we may provoke a sort of "Hey, get out of my reality before you wreck it!" attitude. Unless conversation is confined entirely to trivialities, it's hard to avoid that. And perhaps it doesn't matter much in conversation, because your listeners aren't exposed to the damage you might do for very long.

But when people read your written words, or listen to your public words, the situation changes drastically. Now you have a much greater opportunity to do both good and harm. Now you have a much greater opportunity to cause in your audience a phenomenon called *cognitive dissonance*, which is definitely *not* syntonic.

*Cognitive dissonance* is the name Leon Festinger gave to that disharmony created in an individual's personal reality when information is perceived that does not *fit* that reality, the way a wrong note does not fit in a chord. Every single one of us has a set of statements that make up our personal description of reality.[2] Any information a person perceives that clashes with the personal reality creates disharmony, tension, and discomfort; the person reacts to this by making adjustments to restore the state of fit. Something has to give; the new information must be changed, or the personal reality must be changed, or both. Or the new information must be rejected and denied. If you want your words (whether written *or* spoken) to be effective, you must find a way to avoid causing cognitive dissonance, because cognitive dissonance means *automatic* resistance. All the techniques presented in this chapter are designed to help you do this.

We are taught that written language and public speaking have multiple purposes. A common list includes "to inform, to entertain, to instruct, or to persuade." But we need to remember that in the final analysis *all* such language has persuasion as its purpose, even when the goal is simply to persuade the audience to read or to listen. People cannot be persuaded by words unless they either believe that they understand them or (as may be true with rituals) are convinced that it doesn't matter whether they understand them or not. They may be wrong. They may not understand at all; or they may understand something other than what was intended; or there may be almost nothing *to* understand, as in many political speeches. Nevertheless, it must be their conviction that they understand as much as they need to understand, or they will not be persuaded.

Miller's Law says: "In order to understand what somebody says, you must assume that it's true and try to imagine what it could be true of." And I have proposed a corollary to the law—an extra piece—that goes like this: "In order for people to understand what you say, you must make it possible for them to apply Miller's Law to your words." (Which includes doing your best to make your body language something that it is possible for others to synchronize *with*.) Among other things, this means that in both written language and public speaking your goal should be to avoid cognitive dissonance altogether or to minimize it when it cannot be avoided. If what you have to say is likely to create cognitive dissonance, you need to find a way to say it, or write it, so that its effects will not trigger immediate resistance. There are two primary principles to accomplishing this:

1. ALWAYS INTRODUCE THE NEW BY FITTING IT TO THE OLD.
2. ALWAYS INTRODUCE DISRUPTIVE INFORMATION SLOWLY AND GENTLY.

When you are involved in an oral interaction with someone whose speech you know will be unpleasant, you can decrease that unpleasantness by helping the other person change his or her language behavior. First you match your partner's body language; then, after the two of you are in synchrony, gradually, a little at a time, you change your *own* body language. Your goal is for the person to change his or her language behavior along with you, without ever feeling pressured to do so, a goal that you can't achieve by just telling that person to speak more slowly and more softly and without so much whining. You use exactly the same strategy when you use more formal language to persuade: First, match realities; then, when you and your audience can be assumed to be working from a base of shared perceptions, introduce a little change, slowly. If you do this well, the chances are excellent that the audience will follow.

For an excellent example of cognitive dissonance in America, consider the history of methods for dealing with physical pain. According to the reality consensus (the set of reality statements shared by almost everyone in the culture), the only reliable way to control pain was to use chemicals—painkilling drugs. Then the evidence that hypnosis and acupuncture could control pain as reliably as morphine began to be unavoidable. This created a situation of intense disharmony for the culture. For some time it was dealt with by denying it; but with the electronic media spreading information so fast and so far nowadays, it soon became impossible to ignore these alternative methods of pain control. Faced with intolerable strain, American researchers set to work and discovered the *endorphins*, which are chemicals the human body manufactures to control pain. Now, acupuncture and hypnosis for pain control were no longer problems. Once it could be said that they cause the body to manufacture its own painkilling drugs, they fit right into the reality consensus. And if evidence should begin to accumulate tomorrow that you could control pain by turning around three times and flinging salt over your shoulder, that could be fit right in as well. We would just say that the turning and the flinging stimulate the production of endorphins.

There are three conditions under which a communication breakdown due to cognitive dissonance is likely:

**1.** There is a perception for which no mechanism of communication exists, or for which the only available mechanisms are so inefficient and inadequate that they're almost useless. The most extreme case is that in which the people involved do not have a language in common and must try to manage by pantomine alone. Another example is the problem of communicating the experiences of religious mysticism; typically mystics say there is no way they can possibly describe what they have perceived.

**2.** There is a perception (expressed or unexpressed) that is not included in the set of reality statements for the culture in which the communication must take place—for example, a perception that all disease is caused by witchcraft; or a perception that every death is followed within thirty days by reincarnation. Neither of these is included in the set of statements that make up the mainstream American reality consensus.

**3.** There is a perception that is not *absent* from the reality consensus, but differs in some significant way from the consensus statement. For example, a perception that infectious disease *is* caused by bacteria, but that the bacteria are behaving with deliberate malice.

You need techniques that will let you avoid all three of these situations while using the two principles stated on page 208. Fortunately, we have some. We will begin with techniques for written language.

# Using Written Language Syntonically

First, use the techniques that you have already learned for ordinary language interactions. The Satir Modes and the Sensory Modes are just as important in written language as they are in oral language; use what you know. Write in either Computer Mode or Leveler Mode; Placating, Blaming, and Distracting are even worse when written down. If you know your audience well enough to match Sensory Modes, do so; if not, either use neutral language that does not come from any Sensory Mode or use language that includes all three major ones. Avoid using any of the verbal attack patterns, just as you would if you were talking rather than writing. And don't use the *words* of the attack patterns even if you are not using them as attacks; they may be read as attacks because the written language has no satisfactory way to indicate stresses.

Remember that in writing you don't have any body language to help you make your meaning clear. You have the English punctuation system as a very poor substitute for voice quality and intonation. You have titles and subtitles and the arrangement of sentences in paragraphs as a poor substitute for the traffic mechanisms of speech. For all the rest of body language, you have nothing but graphic format and whatever resources the medium you are using provides. That is, you have such things as the color of the paper, the amount of empty space on a page, the typeface or handwriting style, the presence or absence of illustrations, etc. And you have the inclusion of your written language in a letter, newspaper, brochure, or some other medium. Much of the time you will have little control over either of these. Unless you are a best-selling author (in which case this chapter is superfluous for you), other people will decide how your work is to look and whether there will be illustrations and even what the title will be. It is therefore crucial for you to use every bit of the control that you *do* have, and to use it as well as you possibly can.

If you take a writing class, you will learn many useful things. But you probably will not learn why the mechanics of writing—punctuation, the arrangement of text on a page, the typeface or handwriting style, the preparation of diagrams, and the like—are so important. And that's unfortunate. If people understood that mechanics in written language must do all the work done by nonverbal communication when they talk, they would feel differently about having to learn such things.

The information is not new, and it is of course taught to students. But it's scattered all around, with a little piece of it in the advertising course, a little piece of it in the technical writing course, a little piece of it in the composition course . . . Meanwhile, the principle that ties all the pieces together is never mentioned, and whatever piece happens to turn up in the class *you* take looks like arbitrary trivia that you're being asked to learn just because of your instructor's personal foibles.

Youngsters are given a list of thirty "Rules for the Use of the Comma" to memorize, without ever being told that the comma is a picture of a brief, nonfinal pause. Graduate students in seminars who *do* learn that commas represent nonfinal pauses are given one set of rules for comma use by one professor and a different set by the thesis committee, and are obliged to use still another set when submitting papers for publication. And nobody tells them that comma-rule sets reflect differences in spoken dialects. Nobody tells them that seemingly irrational rule differences correspond to differences of language *function*.

Let me give you an example or two to make this more clear.

In Standard Spoken English (to the extent that such a thing can be said to exist), there is an emphatic sentence pattern that looks like this:

"It's terrible, Frank's having to work three jobs!"

In Ozark English the equivalent sentence pattern—that is, the utterance to be used in the same context—looks like this:

"It's terrible Frank's having to work three jobs!"

The comma is not absent from the Ozark English sentence because of a "different comma usage rule" but because the pause

after "terrible" in the Standard English sentence doesn't occur in the Ozark sentence.

Now look at these two examples.

"In Paris we ate snails."
"In Paris, we ate snails."

Whether you put a comma after "In Paris" should not be determined by anyone's "style sheet."[3] When the comma is present, the sentence is part of a narrative—the writer is telling a
story. When it's not present, the sentence is a statement of fact
and not part of a narrative sequence. The presence or absence
of the comma has a purpose, like the presence or absence of
"once upon a time," in many dialects of English. You may have
no luck convincing your editor or employer or teacher of that;
you may find yourself required to follow someone else's rule;
but you should at least know the facts of the matter so that
when you *do* have a choice you know why you are making it.
Furthermore, if you understand the situation and are not allowed to make your own choices you may be able to revise
what you've written to compensate for the rule. None of this
is possible if your approach to commas, and to other punctuation, is that their primary function is to give teachers an excuse to penalize you.

The best way to find out whether your written language
sounds the way you want it to sound is also the most obvious
way: READ IT OUT LOUD AND LISTEN TO IT. Don't just read the
words; read the punctuation marks as well. If you find yourself
pausing where you have no punctuation marks, or not pausing
where you do have one; if you find your voice rising where you
have a period written; if you find that the way you've written
the words down results in oral language that is choppy, monotonous, breathless, or unpleasant in its rhythm—trust your
ear. *Fix the language!* I read aloud every word I write; if I'm
still not sure how I feel about it, I read it into a tape recorder
and listen to the recording. If my sentences don't *sound* right,
I fix them so that they will not offend the ear. A sentence that
is hard to read aloud will be hard to read silently, no matter

how flawless its logic, no matter how scrupulous its adherence to the lists of rules.

You may have been given the impression that only the professional writer, the language expert, and the occasional "born genius" are capable of judging the quality of written language. I assure you that as a native speaker of the language you are entirely competent to do that yourself. I agree that it may take years of experience to learn to judge written language when you have to read it silently and can hear it only in your mind's ear; that skill also depends on how strongly you prefer the auditory (ear) Sensory Mode. But if you are able to read it aloud and listen to what you are reading, you are a competent judge—badly written prose will betray itself aloud almost at once. The fact that something has been written by a recognized authority should not intimidate you; many of our most brilliant scholars write abominably, and the publication of their work is justified not by their writing skills but by the valuable nature of its informational content. There is no more reason to expect a great physicist to be a superb writer than there is to expect a superb writer to be a great physicist.

You may now have the uneasy feeling that you're about to repeat an experience you've had many times before, in which someone who already knows "how to write" tells you nothing useful at considerable length. Being told to trust your ear may remind you unpleasantly of those occasions when you heard that "there's no way to explain it, you just have to be able to *hear* that it sounds right," or "you just have to have an *ear* (or eye) for good writing." Followed by abandonment.

That isn't going to happen this time. I am concerned that you should have a sturdy respect for your own language skills, and be aware that you *are* an expert in such matters. And because this is not a writing textbook, I won't pretend that I'll be able to do anything drastic to change your writing. But I do have some genuinely useful things to tell you, things that have broad application to every single thing you write.

You know that your goals include the use in written language of the techniques you've already learned for oral language. Some of these—for example, the elimination of Blamer

Mode and the avoidance of the twelve verbal attack patterns—should give you no difficulty. They only require that you be careful with the words you use and with their arrangement, and that you recognize and remove the undesirable items. The same twirks that can trigger negative perceptions in response to your speech—obscenities, ethnic slurs, "ain't got none," and so on—can be watched for and replaced with some more neutral wording. When you read aloud what you've written, you will hear those items and can repair the damage. These are all matters of recognizing what must be left out (or taken out) of what you've written.

But what about the opposite side of writing? What about the choice of things to put in, rather than things to take out? I want to discuss a few techniques that you can use to make such choices—because while it's true that if you can't spell you can usually find someone to do it for you, only the very rich can afford to have someone else do the entire writing task for them from scratch. You need to be able to do it for yourself.

## Using a Written Model

The first technique I am going to suggest is one with an ancient history. I am old enough to remember when it was part of everyone's education in elementary and secondary school; but for many of you, it may be not only new but also shocking. I know that people are often shocked when I mention it in workshops and seminars.

A number of times in this book I have described techniques in which you acted by doing something *simultaneously* with language you had chosen as a model, letting your mind use the model to detect mismatches and make adjustments to eliminate them. I've emphasized the value of this procedure, as opposed to the traditional "Repeat after me" techniques, when you work with the tape recorder and the television set. When we come to the written word, however, we run into the same problems that force us to divide language into verbal and nonverbal components even when we know that division to be an illusion: Simultaneous presentation of information is largely excluded from written language by its form. This means that once again there must be a compromise.

When using a written model, the closest thing to working simultaneously with the model is the very old-fashioned process of copying out someone's written words in your own hand. In *longhand*, not on the typewriter or the computer. I do not have to be told that this is hard work; I am well aware of that. However, it requires almost no tools, it costs almost nothing, you can do it at your own speed and in complete privacy, and it *works*. I strongly recommend it.

When you copy a well-constructed piece of prose in longhand, you are involving many of your senses in the process. Your eyes are looking at the words and at their arrangement; your ears are hearing those words internally as you perceive them; and your sense of touch is flooded with information by the movements of your fingers and your hand. Your entire "bodymind" is involved in the process, in a way that is impossible when you use a typewriter, and you are providing yourself with the best available conditions for learning what the writer knows.

It's important that you copy *all* of whatever you choose as model. Only by copying the whole thing do you get a chance to participate in the building of the text—you learn how to begin, how to keep things going, how to get from one part to another, and how to bring it to an end. Copying parts of it won't give you this sense of structure.

Since this is true, and only you can know your tolerance for the task of longhand copying, choose as your model a piece that is the right size for you personally. If that means that you begin by copying well-made paragraphs that are self-contained, that's fine; from doing that you will learn how to put together sentences and paragraphs. You can move on from that to larger items.[4]

I have one caution for you about this technique. Many people have found great pleasure in listening to the speech of Jimmy Stewart, Jack Benny, Katharine Hepburn, and Ethel Merman, but these people are celebrities, for whom a distinctive style of speech is a sort of trademark. To model your speech on theirs produces a style that is not appropriate for daily life. The same thing is true when you choose a model for your written language. The flashy and exotic style that may be the one you most admire is exactly the one that will make your own writing appear to be an imitation of that style; set it aside, and choose someone equally competent but less unusual.

As a young woman I used to earn part of my living as a folksinger and guitarist. The queen of folk music in those days was Joan Baez, beyond all question. And the surest way to find yourself without work was to *sound* like Joan Baez. People who wanted to hear her wanted to hear the real thing. I knew fine singers and excellent guitarists who could not find jobs anywhere because their auditions always ended with someone saying, "You sound just like Joan Baez—sorry."

If your writing immediately makes the reader think, "Oh, you write just like So-and-So," even if So-and-So is your company's top executive, that constitutes a written twirk. The reader's attention will not be on what you are writing, but on how much your writing is like the overly recognizable model you've selected. If you write sales reports, business letters, brief product descriptions, or personal letters, the last thing you want to hear is "I always enjoy getting a letter from you, because you write just like Tom Wolfe!" Your goal is not to sound like Tom Wolfe but like yourself; this is what people mean when they talk of writers needing to find their "voice."

As is true with spoken language, don't carry the process to extremes. When you feel that your own writing is becoming more solid and satisfactory, you have done enough copying. Copying in longhand is such hard work that you are unlikely to overdo it, but the consequences would be identical to those resulting from practicing with a tape until you had achieved a flawless imitation.

## Using the Powerful Number Three

Next, I want to suggest two applications of the number three to your written language. Three is an important number in our culture; how many times have you been told that what you write must have "a beginning, a middle, and an end"? How many stories have you read that involved three wishes, or three brothers, or doing something three times? We say, "Third time's a charm!" People are comfortable with things that come in threes. Since you are working toward harmony, even when you are obliged to introduce information that you know may not be welcome, take advantage of this fact and use it to make your words less disruptive for your readers.

Suppose that you've been given the unpleasant task of informing a group that its already stressful parking problem is going to get worse because one hundred of the three hundred spaces available are going to be closed. Suppose you have to tell them that the only way they can deal with this is to start car-pooling, so that the number of cars to be parked will be reduced as well. Suppose that you must write this information for a memorandum to be posted on company bulletin boards and included in your firm's newsletter.

Use the power of threes to help you. Begin by stating your proposal; that's Part One. Continue by explaining it or arguing for it; that's Part Two. Add a concluding statement as Part Three. And Part Two should include three arguments or three explanations. Here is the skeleton of your announcement, using this pattern:

1. Starting one week from today, you will have to begin sharing rides to work.
2. Because:

    a. we are closing one hundred of the three hundred parking spaces in the lot, and
    b. there is no other space available in this area for parking, and
    c. no public transportation exists to get you here.

3. We regret that this has to be done, but are confident that car-pooling will keep it from being a serious problem for you.

Once you have that structure before you as a guide, you can begin considering the exact words that you will use—and for that task you can refer to the sections on word choice in this book. The three-part structure, and the use of three arguments in Part Two, won't make your group members any happier about the inconvenience of car-pooling, but people will tend to set up less automatic resistance, because the format is familiar and reassuring even when its content is not. As far back as rhetoric can be traced, you will find a strong recommendation for a structure that begins with an introductory statement of the situation, continues with three supporting items, and concludes with a summary or closing statement. Whatever you need to say, set up an outline for yourself like the one below, and fill in all its parts before you start trying to choose your words.

### Rule of Three Outline

1. Introductory Statement
2. Explanation or Argument

    a.
    b.
    c.

3. Concluding Statement

I warn you that this structure is not trendy; I have been criticized for teaching it from time to time. But trendiness is not your goal. What you are trying to do does not require flash and zip. People do not find flash and zip reassuring, and they tend to see the special effects and be distracted from the content; unless that is your intention, this model is reliable and effective. It's always possible to set your arguments out in at least three statements; if you have *many* arguments, it's always possible to present them as *sets* of three, so that your structure is something like this one:

1. Introductory Statement
2. Explanations or Arguments

    a. About Money
       i., ii., iii.
    b. About Safety
       i., ii., iii.

  c. About Convenience
   i., ii., iii.

 3. Concluding Statement

There is a military version of this pattern that goes, "Tell them what you're going to tell them, then tell them, then tell them what you've told them." In civilian life this is carrying things too far, and it should be avoided.

Now, within the three-part structure of what you're writing, continue to use threes generously. Not in every sentence, because if it becomes too obvious it will be either funny or irritating, but often enough to provide strength. Suppose that you are among the group told to start car-pooling, and you've been chosen to write a letter to management protesting the decision to close those parking spaces. Look at the following sentence:

> "We see your point of view; we hear and understand the arguments you have presented; and we can certainly grasp the seriousness of the problem. However . . ."

That sentence uses the power of threes to reinforce its structure; furthermore, it is carefully worded to speak to each of the three major Sensory Modes. You set up your pattern skeleton like this:

1. We need more, not fewer, parking spaces.
2. Because:

  a. we live too far apart to car-pool, and
  b. our schedules are so varied that car-pooling is impossible, and
  c. car-pooling would lead to friction and bad feeling in our group.

3. Therefore, we ask that the plan to close one hundred parking spaces be reconsidered.

And somewhere in Part One, you use the example sentence on page 31. It says, "We are looking, we are listening, we are feeling."; it says, "We share your perceptions; we are together in understanding what you have told us." Only then, after establishing synchrony, does it move on to state the *dis*agreement. This process will now be familiar to you. First, you try to match the other person or persons by tuning *to them;* then, when there is synchrony, you introduce change. The goal is to lead the others to change *with* you, slowly and gently and with minimal disruption.

As you construct your sentences, make use of all the techniques you have learned. Suppose you want to say that the problem is serious, that the solution will be hard to find, and that both sides will have to cooperate. You might do that by setting up three nominalizations, so that their existence is presupposed, like this:

> "The seriousness of the problem, the difficulty of its solution, and the necessity for cooperation have convinced us that a meeting should be held immediately."

Again, don't do this in every sentence. But do it as often as is appropriate. And examine every sentence to be sure you're not including presuppositions you don't intend, and that you *are* using all the verbal devices available to you.

There is one important exception to what I've just said about not overdoing things. Assume that you are obliged to argue for something that you disapprove of; let's say that the parking lot is a company lot, and your boss has given you a nonnegotiable order to prepare that announcement about closing the one hundred parking spaces. Assume that you've done your best to present a case against the announcement, but it has done no good and you've been left with no choice. You are required to urge people to do something that you don't feel they should be asked to do.

Now, you could just write a very bad announcement. But it's far more skillful to write one that is too *good*. It's hard for your boss to criticize you for doing the task too well. In that situation, overdo the techniques described, to the point where they will become obvious and weaken your surface message. This is something like being a Distracter on purpose; it is a strategy you can use when you intend for your communication to fail. Perhaps your boss will choose someone less skilled to be the messenger of bad tidings next time.

You can use this same technique of elaborate excess with metaphors. A metaphor draws a comparison between two things by saying "*x* is a *y*," as in "Life is just a bowl of cherries." Americans frequently use sports metaphors and associated language because they feel comfortable with that framework. We are told that "this is a whole new ball game" but that "our team has some of the finest players" there are; if things aren't going well, we are told that "the game isn't over till the referee blows the whistle." Done in moderation, this is extremely useful; done to excess, it becomes silly. If you must argue for something you can't support wholeheartedly, put a chunk of a sports metaphor in every single sentence. To make it worse, *mix* your metaphors. Put football in one sentence and tennis in the next; go back to football in the third; wind it up with a specular list of three taken from three different sports. It is astonishing, frankly, how far you have to push this sort of thing to make it fail. As an experiment, I suggest that you write something in which you overdo every technique you've learned; then give it to people to read. You may be surprised at the reaction. It will, in any case, give you a sense of how much is *too* much in such situations.

When the writing is coming *at* you, be aware of the possibility that the writer is also using these techniques, or similar ones. Look at the text carefully. Is it a three-part structure? Are there many sentences that have sets of three items—perhaps sets of three nominalizations? Is the content carefully fitted into a reassuring metaphor, as a way of tying the new information to familiar information?

And does it seem to have been overdone? If so, you should be wary. It may only be that the writer has bad taste; but it may also be a metamessage that says, "I'm only saying this because I'm required to say it—I don't mean it."

## Avoiding the Cumbersome Number Nine

Among the publications for which George Miller (of Miller's Law) is known is an article discussing what he called "the magical number seven, plus or minus two."[5] In it he establishes the fact that your short-term memory can handle only so much at a time, and that there is a systematic way to say *how* much at a time.

The part of memory that makes it possible for you to remember a phone number long enough to dial it after you look it up is called either "short-term memory" or "working memory." (I prefer the label "short-term memory," because it seems to me to make a more lucid comment about what goes on in our heads.) It's not an accident that telephone numbers are only seven digits long, or that they are divided into a group of three numbers followed by a group of four numbers. It's not an accident that when you must also remember an area code it is a group of three numbers set off by parentheses. Unless you are very unusual, you don't remember the phone number and area code as a ten-number sequence. You think of the area code as one thing to remember, three digits long, and then you think of the seven-digit phone number as a second thing to remember.

George Miller's research established that the upper limit of the short-term memory is the number seven, plus or minus two—that is, from five to nine items, with seven being about average. And his research has turned out to be so useful that it's hard to find any area of information dissemination where it is ignored.

Fortunately, this seven-item capacity can be made more efficient by a process called "chunking." Think of your short-term memory as having seven hooks that you constantly use to catch information—the more you can catch on each hook, the greater your total catch. The short-term memory is indifferent to whether the seven items are seven letters or seven words, for example; if that weren't so, reading would be physiologically impossible. Still, chunking can be carried only so far before the contents of the short-term memory start getting lost unless they are transferred to long-term memory and stored for retrieval, with indexes attached. Nobody has found a way to keep seven sentences of average length in short-term memory; our concern at this point is with the word-size chunk or very brief phrase.

Think back to the last time you had to write under the supervision of someone who was allowed to "correct" your writing. What do you remember? Most of us remember a lot of red ink and mysterious scribbles all over our work; and there are few of us who don't remember a scribble that read "AWKWARD!" The problem with "AWKWARD," which tends to speckle writing under examination like a graphic case of measles, is that no one ever explains what it means. Thanks to George Miller, it is now possible to change that in a large proportion of cases, and to change it in a way that is not dependent upon personal taste.

We can now define "AWKWARD" as follows: A chunk of language that interferes with the functioning of short-term memory is awkward. And we can set up a list of language situations in which this is likely to happen.

As you listen to a sentence, or read one, one of the things you have to do is remember the subject until you find the predicate, or vice versa. To understand the sentence, you have to go through all the following steps:

1. Locate the predicate.
2. Locate each noun phrase that is associated with the predicate.
3. Figure out, for each noun phrase, what its *role* is in relation to the predicate.

(Please be warned that the order I've listed these steps in is completely arbitrary. There's no strong evidence that they are carried out in this order, and it may be that they all go on simultaneously. It just isn't possible to *list* them without choosing an order.)

If you are dealing with a sentence that has other sentences embedded in it, each of those sentences will have a predicate of its own, for which you have to go through the steps listed above in order to understand the *whole* sentence. Consider the following example:

"John knew that Mary had forgotten that the bus didn't run on Tuesday."

Here we have the sentence "the bus didn't run on Tuesday" embedded in the sentence "Mary had forgotten that the bus didn't run on Tuesday," and this is in turn embedded in the largest sentence, "John knew that Mary had forgotten that the bus didn't run on Tuesday." Three sentences, packaged as one sentence, each with its own predicate and its own set of noun phrases.

Your mind is entirely capable of handling sentences that are more than nine words long, because it chunks pieces of the sentences together as single items. But if any of those pieces is too big, so that it's hard for the short-term memory to re-member it until it can *be* combined with other pieces, it is AWKWARD. Compare the two sentences below:

"That John refused to stop smoking his cigarette even when the air conditioning had broken down and everyone was coughing made Mary furious."
"It made Mary furious that John refused to stop smoking his cigarette even when the air conditioning had broken down and everyone was coughing."

The first sentence is AWKWARD. Its predicate is "made Mary furious." Its subject, "That John refused .. (etc.)," is way be-yond the upper limits of the short-term memory—twenty words long! It's very hard for you to keep that huge subject in short-term memory until you get to the predicate it goes with. The second example has the same chunk in it, but it now *fol-lows* "made Mary furious"; in that position, it no longer puts an excessive strain on the short-term memory. It may not be a superb sentence, but it has ceased to be AWKWARD.

The subject in the first sentence is called a "sentential sub-ject," because it contains another sentence (in this case, an-other *three* sentences!). But sentential subjects are not *in themselves* awkward. "That John smokes makes Mary fu-rious" is not awkward. It is the number of pieces contained in the sentential subject that matters.

And this is an excellent place to ask you to look once more at my definition of "AWKWARD." It was:

> A chunk of language that interferes with the functioning of short-term memory is awkward.

You will now be aware that the definition, as worded, is awkward. It has a cumbersome subject that is thirteen words long and must be kept in mind until the predicate—"is awkward"—is reached. It would be much better if it were done like this:

> The term *awkward* refers to a chunk of language that interferes with the functioning of short-term memory.

If you are a highly skilled writer, you can find ways to use long and intricate sentential subjects without causing problems for the reader; but if you are a highly skilled writer you don't need to be reading this section. The less skilled writer should behave as if there were no exceptions to the following rule:

NEVER USE A SENTENTIAL SUBJECT THAT IS MORE THAN NINE WORDS LONG—AND KEEP IT TO SEVEN WORDS OR LESS IF YOU POSSIBLY CAN.

After you are more at ease with written language you will have plenty of time to begin working out exceptions.

Here are eight more linguistic environments that tend to get cluttered up with AWKWARD chunks. I have given them their technical names for convenience, and have underlined them for clarity. You may know them by some other name; so long as you recognize the item, it's not necessary that we agree on its label.

**1. Restrictive Relative Clauses:**
"The stranger that John saw leaving a sack of old empty soft drink cans in the yard behind the house yesterday was arrested for littering."

**2. Nonrestrictive Relative Clauses:**
"Jim Smith, who works in the university lab on the experi-

ments with white mice that don't respond to normal auditory stimuli, is a new graduate student."

**3. Passives:**

"That the missing book had been dropped behind the bookshelf on the side of the room nearest the window accidentally was not discovered until after Jennifer had left."

**4. Passives PLUS Relative Clauses:**

The pizza that was served early yesterday afternoon in the faculty lounge by the Anthropology students made the visitors sick.

**5. Subjects of Cleft Sentences:**

"What John told Mary he had seen in the alley behind the restaurant last night after he left for work amazed her."

**6. Parentheticals:**

"Most eminent scientists (the term is used loosely here in view of the numerous competing and sometimes contradictory definitions) have Ph.D.s."

**7. Any Series:**

"They told us to bring scissors, pliers, bread, matches, umbrellas, needles and thread, paste, small trowels, blank notebooks, and a sack lunch to the meeting."

**8. Multiple Combinations of the Above:**

"That Norm was alarmed by the racket at the gas station (which everyone knew was under repair and which the man who had claimed to be its new owner had warned us would be left vacant for some time) was not surprising."

You may feel that this is all too complicated to bother with, but that is only a reflex that comes from the many years you have spent learning things by memorizing them instead of by finding general principles that make them easy to remember. The general principle behind those horrendous examples is this: Any *constituent* of a sentence that contains more than nine items is likely to interfere with the short-term memory. And a constituent of a sentence is just any piece of that sentence that could be the answer to a question all by itself, as "in the yard" could be the answer to the question "Where was the dog?" from the sentence "The dog was in the yard." You know that the sequence "dog was in the" can't be a constituent of that sentence, because it can't be the answer to any question about the sentence. If you remember the principle, you won't need to concern yourself with memorizing the list of examples.

You will realize that sentences like those in the examples above cause even more trouble when they are spoken than when they are written. What if I asked you the following question, aloud?

"Has anyone found out whether the fact that none of the students who were smoking in the cafeteria had been here more than a few days is an important clue?"

You'd have trouble answering me even if you knew the answer—it's just too hard to keep track of a mess like that going by only one time at normal speed. (This is often what's wrong when a speaker "gets into a sentence and can't get back out" or "loses the train of thought.") If the sentence is written down, the reader can go back and read it over as many times as necessary, until the meaning finally becomes clear. And the more times this has to be done, the more AWKWARD the language is; it is rarely necessary to use such sentences. In written language you can set the upper limit for the number of words per chunk higher than in spoken language. But the more you make your reader struggle to understand your meaning, the more you decrease your chances for successful communication.

It's possible to go too far in the opposite direction as well. No one—and that includes small children learning to read—wants to read pages of three- or four-word sentences. Keep Miller's useful numbers firmly in mind, and aim toward seven-word constituents, whether they are whole sentences or only parts of larger sentences.

I want to be very careful here not to appear to be advocating what is called the "dumbing down" of written materials. It's not the number of words in a sentence that is crucial; it's the number in a given chunk that must be held in short-term memory. If you compare the two sentences on page 188 again, you'll see that the one that is less awkward is actually longer, but moving the cumbersome chunk out of the subject position has reduced the burden on the short-term memory. Furthermore, to the short-term memory a word is a word is a word, so long as it's a word you know. The short-term memory doesn't find *locomotive* any more troublesome to deal with than *train*; each is a single chunk to be remembered.

## Public Speaking

I can begin by telling you that most of what I have said about written language holds true for public speaking. Certainly you will use everything that you have learned about ordinary speech when the speaking you do is "public"; in addition, you should use the techniques discussed above for written language.

Recently much attention has been given to a national survey (published in *Current Opinion*) showing that people rank the task of giving a speech as one of their greatest fears in life, ahead of illness, poverty, and even death. It's a dramatic comment on our national rhetorical skills, but I think there is a slight skew in the data. I am quite sure that what most people really are afraid of is not giving a speech, but giving a speech they aren't properly *prepared* to give. They are afraid of giving a speech that fails. And much of this is due to the popular myth that says the truly good public speaker is the one who can speak *without* preparation—the "extemporaneous" speaker. People tend to feel that they should be able to do that, too.

It is reasonably safe to say that in the mainstream of American culture today there are no great extemporaneous speakers, and very few good ones. It is not an oral culture. Our educational system trains us in taking notes, and looking things up, and relying on the printed word and the computer and the TelePrompTer. When you hear a good speech that is said to be "extemporaneous," you are usually hearing one of the following:

1. A speech on a subject that the speaker has talked on so often that he could do it in his sleep.
2. A speech composed entirely of ritualized elements reinforced by skillful body language.

3.  A speech that has in fact been carefully prepared, but that the speaker is able to give an "extemporaneous" delivery.

An example of the first type is the talk by a man who has spent twenty years as a stockbroker and is called on to provide a fifteen-minute explanation of money market funds. An example of the second kind is the talk by the experienced politician who can, at the drop of even half a hat, do fifteen minutes on Mom, the flag, and apple pie, with an intonation and a set of gestures that make everyone who is listening feel comfortable. Neither of these represents the gift of extemporaneous oratory. The third kind is more interesting; the distinguishing skills here are the method of preparation and the style of delivery.

The amount of time you give to writing a speech is determined by the importance of the occasion, how much warning you are given, and the interest that you have in the subject. If you have six months to get ready for a talk on a subject that matters to you, proceed just as you would if you were going to write a brief article on the topic for publication. Use all the writing techniques introduced in this chapter; read the speech aloud and listen to it carefully, recording it and listening to the recording if that seems indicated; make as many revisions as you need to make; repeat until you get it right.

It's easier to use rhetorical devices in a speech than in writing, because you can make much freer use of them and much freer use of repetition. What would seem excessive in writing becomes valuable in public speaking, because it actually helps listeners to understand and remember what is being said.

Folksingers always have in their repertoires a few "zipper songs," like this one:

> Goin' down the road feelin' bad,
> goin' down the road feelin' bad,
> goin' down the road feelin' bad, Lord, Lord,
> and I ain't gonna be treated thisaway!

Once the singer has sung this one verse and established the pattern, the song can go on until everyone present is tired of it, with the audience contributing as many new verses to be "zipped" into the pattern as they like. Any line that will fit the melody, sung three times and followed by "lord, lord, and I ain't gonna be treated thisaway!", will do. It doesn't even require rhyme.

Public speakers in the mainstream American culture don't go quite this far, because they aren't inviting active audience participation. But they do try to present patterned speech in a way that will make *passive* audience participation easy. They set their talk into a metaphor that is familiar to those listening—The Football Game, The Old West, The Proud Ship Sailing—so that when they mention any one part of the metaphor people will be prepared to hear the other parts mentioned. When a speaker says, "The first strike against us was . . . ," the audience knows that two more strikes are coming up. When the speaker says, "As we go into the first quarter, we know . . .," the audience is prepared to hear about three more quarters, complete with fumbles and touchdowns. If a speaker uses twice a pattern like "I do not speak of *x*; I speak of *y*" or "Say to *x*, we will do *y*", the audience—by the pervasive rule of three—anticipates at least one more repetition.

The more structural information of this kind an audience has, the less difficulty it will have understanding the speech. There's no time for listeners to go back over your words as they could go back over your written language, and the burden on the short-term memory and the language-processing mechanisms of the brain is heavy; any information that reduces the workload and helps in the process of anticipating what will come along next improves understanding. (It's unfortunate that more teachers who rely on lectures in their classes don't take advantage of these basic facts.)

When you have only hours, or perhaps only minutes, to get ready for a talk, fall back on the reliable Rule of Three Outline shown on page 182; grab a scrap of paper and make an outline to provide structure for your "extemporaneous" efforts. Write down your main point, plus three items to support it, and a conclusion. Like this:

1.  I am genuinely happy to be here tonight.
2.  Because:

    a.   this is my hometown, and

    b.   you are all my dear friends, and

    c.   I have been away far too long.

3.   Thank you for asking me to join you.

1.   I regret to tell you that we must raise our annual dues.

2.   Because:

    a.   inflation is now at 8 percent, and

    b.   our membership is now so large that we have to rent a larger building, and

    c.   all the members have voted to change our newsletter from a quarterly to a monthly.

3.   I'm sure we will all feel that we're getting our money's worth.

1.   It is with great pleasure that I introduce Tracy Smith,

2.   Because:

    a.   Tracy is responsible for our new convention center, and

    b.   Tracy grew up in this state and understands its needs, and

    c.   Tracy has never been associated with an unsuccessful business project.

3.   I'm sure we will all enjoy hearing the speech that Tracy is now going to make.

If you feel that such speeches are not memorable, you are right. What's more important, however, is that they are *not unbearable*. The obligation of the casual public speaker is like the obligation of the physician: First, do no harm. Cause no pain! You have no right to make people suffer just because you are trying to be memorable. People will forgive you for making speeches like those outlined above—they will even ask you to make more of them. They will *not* forgive you for tormenting them with disorganized ramblings that go on and on and on, no matter how brilliant each sentence might be in isolation; *nor should they.* Few communicative acts cause greater hostility toward the speaker than the boring public talk, and there is absolutely no reason why you should be on the receiving end of that emotion.

I am always astonished, and shall no doubt go to my grave astonished, at the obligation people feel to speak at LENGTH, even when they don't want to give the talk in the first place. It must be a horrible experience to look out at the audience and see them trying desperately not to yawn, and to know that when you finally do get to the end of your speech they are going to lean toward one another and moan that they thought you would *never* stop. Here is a rule for you: NOTHING THAT YOU HAVE TO SAY CANNOT BE SAID IN FIFTEEN MINUTES. Anything that you say in fifteen minutes will be understood and remembered far better than if you had used the same material and talked twice as long. To ensure that you don't talk longer than fifteen minutes, *time* your speech when you practice it aloud, so that you know exactly how long it takes. As a rule of thumb, assume that you will need three minutes to deliver each double-spaced page properly—that means that no fifteen-minute speech should ever be more than five typed pages long.

The one-hour scholarly "keynote address" that you occasionally see advertised is not intended primarily to be heard, although it will be listened to with respectful attention; it is intended to be read. It will be read aloud at the formal occasion for which it was prepared, and then it will be published, to be gone over at leisure. Any other sort of talk that lasts more than twenty minutes is rude; one that lasts more than half an hour is unforgivable.

In order to get a feeling for the way good speeches are put together, write out a few of the great ones in longhand. Your public library will have copies of the speeches of Franklin D. Roosevelt, of John F. Kennedy, of Martin Luther King, Jr.; write some of them down, so that you can involve all your senses in the process.

To get a feeling for how good speeches are delivered, *say* a few of the great ones, preferably along with their original speakers. Most libraries will have recordings that you can use for this purpose. Write out a fine speech in longhand, and then read it aloud along with the recording. You are not trying to learn to talk like Roosevelt or Kennedy or King, and you don't want to do this over and over in the way suggested for improving voice quality and eliminating pronunciation twirks. Your goal is simply to get a sense of *phrasing*: where speakers speed up or slow down; where they pause; when and where they take a breath. You can't learn those things just from reading the speeches, because—as usual—the writing system is not adequate. But now that most good speeches are recorded, it's possible to obtain as much of that information as you need and want.

Obviously, if you can also work with a videotape or film of such a speech, you will be able to learn a substantial amount about the body language that goes along with it. If you want to try this as a project, and have the necessary equipment to do so, proceed as follows.

1. Copy out the speech in longhand.
2. Play the film, but don't watch it this time; just listen, and read the text aloud with the speaker.
3. Play the film again, but this time don't play the sound— just watch the body language.
4. Now play the film one more time; this time you will both watch and listen.

To be able to say the speech along with the speaker while you watch the film would require you to memorize the speech. That's not necessary, because you aren't trying to learn to "perform" that particular piece of language. The point of the project is to let you experience, as far as possible, what it feels like to give a successful speech and give it well. You are trying to share that experience so that when you are the one speaking you will know what it is supposed to be like.

You want your audience to be syntonic with you. You want them breathing with you, moving in synchrony with you, aware of little but the sound of your voice and the body language that accompanies it, feeling a strong rapport with you. You don't want them to be wondering whether their parking meters have run out, or how much longer you're going to talk, or why the air conditioner is so loud in the room. You want them to be so completely attuned to you that for the moment you have their *total* attention. You want them to feel that the talk is an experience that they share with you, not something that you do *to* them while they pray for it to end.

Another reason for fear of public speaking is the "question and answer session" that often follows the talk itself. You won't have to face that if your own talk is intended to introduce the main speaker or something of that kind, but if you are the featured attraction it is a very real possibility. To refuse to participate in such a session makes you look as though you were afraid you couldn't answer the questions. Never refuse unless you are willing to state your refusal like this and stick to it: "I'm sorry. I never do question and answer sessions." Better to appear eccentric than to appear a coward. And best of all is to agree to do the session and to appear delighted at the opportunity.

You prepare for the question and answer session by sitting down in advance of the talk and writing down all the questions that you can reasonably expect to hear asked, together with their answers. If you're likely to need a particular date or statistic or reference, write it down—don't leave it in your briefcase, where you'll have to fumble for it while people wait. If you find yourself staring at a question you can't answer, you have time to *get* the answer; make some calls, go to the library, or consult an expert. With the list of questions and answers in hand, you're ready, and you face only two more problems, one trivial and the other a bit more serious.

The trivial problem is the matter of what you do about questions that you didn't expect and aren't prepared for. If you're prepared for most of them, this truly doesn't matter. Just say that you don't know, and you're sorry about that, and take the next question. *Never* try to fake it.

The more serious problem is what you do about the person who stands up allegedly to ask you a question and proceeds to talk and talk and talk, from the floor. These people are of two kinds: those who really do want an answer but aren't able to get their question formulated properly or bring their question to an end; and those who don't want an answer at all—they want to give their *own* talk. What do you do about these ice-bergs suddenly looming up on your oratorical bow?

Proceed as follows.

1. If possible, make eye contact with the individual and maintain it—do not look away.
2. Whether you have eye contact or not, begin nodding, matching your nods to the individual's rhythm so that the two of you are synchronized.
3. If you do have eye contact with the individual, start nodding more slowly—or, if the questioner is dragging along, more rapidly; your goal is to lead the individual to match *your* body language.
4. Now begin talking *along with* the individual, synchronizing the rate of your speech to his, saying, "It would be very RUDE for me to answer your question while *you* are TALKing!"
5. Keep this up, with variations if necessary, until the floor hog fades away. The longer it takes you to accomplish this, the more foolish said floor hog will appear; don't be concerned if it takes you a few minutes to get his or her attention. If you haven't been able to make eye contact, you may have to speak rather loudly to get *ear* contact; that is also all right.

If you view this as being rude to the floor hog, you have it backwards. Your responsibility is not to that individual, but to your audience, which is being cheated of what it has come to hear, and which has a right to expect that you will be able to maintain control of the floor.

Action chains do occur in public speaking. If you are giving a standard talk, even if it is to be followed by questions and answers, you needn't worry—it is the audience that is involved in an action chain. Your listeners are supposed to sit quietly until you are through talking, no matter how bored they are, no matter how much they disagree with what you are saying. They break that chain at their own risk. It is often a considerable shock to the American mainstream speaker to give a talk to a cultural group for whom the rule "Only one person talks at a time" does not apply—it is a powerful rule for the Anglo speaker. If you would find it intolerable to give a talk during which people in the audience spoke freely to one another, wandered in and out, and so on, do not accept invitations to speak cross-culturally without checking for this rule difference first.

There is a special kind of public speaking, usually called either a "workshop" or a "seminar," in which a high degree of audience participation *is* expected. If you head one of these, and if the material you are presenting falls into an area that the audience members consider part of *their* turf, you will run into a problem of a different kind. This is especially true when they are present not because they want to hear what you have to say or take part in the workshop activities but because someone (usually their employer) has ordered them to be there.

I have done many language or linguistics workshops at which the audience was made up of teachers with a great deal of classroom experience. And I learned very early to refuse to do work of that kind unless I was given twice as much time as I would actually need for my own presentation. For a half-day workshop, I would schedule the entire day, and for just one purpose: so that my audience could have the other half-day in which to completely get rid of their "What I do in MY class is . . ." compulsions. It was absurd for me to start talking before they had done this, because they were not going to listen to me—their entire attention was focused, often *grimly* focused, on their own experiences and their own methods for dealing with them. I could of course have forced them to listen to me despite their internal turmoil, and after a while I might well have managed to make them *forget* about it. But that would have required valuable time and energy that I preferred to spend in providing them with useful information that they were ready to hear.

Always, if you have any control over the situation, allow your listeners to exhaust their objections before you present your alternative. This is as true of an audience composed of one administrator as it is of fifty workshop participants. Wait patiently and courteously until all the stored-up "This is how *I* do it" and "This is what I *know* should be done" has been dumped, giving each individual your full attention. Listen *syntonically*, so that the speaker will not feel that you are just tolerating what is being said. When the dumping is over, some space will exist for what *you* are going to say. Interfere with this drive and you will accomplish very little.

This is extremely hard to do in our mainstream culture; it's hard even to get permission to try it. If you've been brought up to believe that most of life must revolve around a fixed schedule, you may find the process frustrating (and some of your audience may help you out by expressing that frustration and motivating the others present to hurry up). In such a situation, think of the cultures in this world in which, for any meeting that concerns the entire group, the rule is that everybody who wants to speak must be allowed to speak, until everybody has said everything that they want to say, and until the entire group has reached an agreement. Not a majority vote, mind you, but an agreement. A consensus! Remind yourself, with the seconds ticking away in your brain, that you don't have that to deal with; it should restore your perspective on the matter.

It is worth mentioning that doctors will never really know what is wrong with their patients until they learn to allow this sort of dumping; in America, this means that most doctors simply never will know. It wouldn't take *that* long—this is an irrational fear that physicians have been taught by the medical curriculum and by their accountants. Doctors today are perceived as rude, callous, uncaring, and money-mad because they spend most of their time with their patients breaking into, cutting off, and otherwise interfering with action chains. That is perhaps why doctors in our culture are said to "see" patients; certainly, they do not listen to them.

## Uphill All the Way—Persuasion in Adverse Circumstances

Through this chapter I have written from the best-case viewpoint. That is, I have written as though you would never have to face obstinate and obstreperous resistance to your written language and your public speaking. I want to close by discussing briefly how to proceed when you have the *worst* case to deal with: when you know in advance that the people you are speaking or writing to are going to react negatively, and that they have their minds absolutely made up to reject what you propose.

Sometimes this happens because of nothing more than a strong dislike for you personally, but this is very rare; most of the time what is perceived by you as a rejection for personal reasons is in reality caused by something else. In most cases, the something else will be one of these two factors: (a) what you are proposing or presenting would create severe cognitive dissonance; or (b) there are negative real-world consequences for your listeners-readers if they allow themselves to be persuaded by your language. Worst of all, of course, is the situation in which both of these factors are involved. If you go into a language interaction like that unprepared, you are going to fail in your communication goals; in addition, you may be in for a very unpleasant experience. More than run-of-the-mill rhetorical skills are needed.

The major problem in this situation is that people are not ordinarily consciously aware of the reasons for their determination not to be persuaded by you. They may in fact *believe* that a personal dislike for you is their only reason. But they cannot present their objections to you either as "because I say so, and that's the only reason I've got" or as "because I don't like you." Not without sounding childish or irrational or worse. Therefore, the chances that the reasons you hear for their objections will be the *real* reasons are very slim, and this means that for you to try to deal with them would be a great waste of time and energy. If you deftly dispose of the phony reasons, you will only have provided yourself with a group of people who now have their backs to the wall and are risking substantial loss of face. Let's consider a hypothetical example of a situation of this kind.

In the United States today, it is claimed that there is a "literacy crisis." Ignore for now the question of whether that crisis really exists. If people believe that it exists, and behave as if it exists, there will be serious real-world consequences of that belief.

Assume that you have discovered or devised a foolproof method for solving the alleged literacy crisis. Let's go all the way with this—let's assume that you have devised a system that will allow someone with reading and writing skills at third-grade level or below to improve those skills to the level of the high school graduate, in about three weeks' time, without the assistance of a teacher.

You would no doubt be very proud of your work, and you would perhaps take it for granted that when you presented your solution to those struggling with the crisis they would receive you with the sort of respect, admiration, and gratitude—perhaps even financial reward—that people receive who discover cures for diseases.

You would be wrong. All over this country there are platoons of people deeply involved in the literacy-crisis problem. Most of them are educators or administrators, and most of them have spent many years achieving their *own* level of literacy. One of the statements that is part of their personal reality, and that is so widely shared as to be part of the reality consensus of our culture, is this one:

> It takes a *long time* and a lot of *hard work* to become truly literate.

If you come along with a three-week low-effort road to literacy, you are going to represent a direct and violent challenge to that reality statement. You are going to represent cognitive dissonance of the very worst kind. That's your first problem.

Your next problem is that these people are part of a vast industrial complex in America. The remedial-education industry and the testing industry involve many many thousands of people. There are Study Skills Departments, Basic Learning Labs, literacy volunteers, private coaches and consultants; there are institutes and centers and businesses and publishers and literally packs of experts. ALL OF THEM OWE THEIR LIVELIHOOD TO TWO PROPOSITIONS:

1. The literacy crisis *does* exist, and is extremely serious.
2. It takes a long time and a lot of hard work to become literate.

You cannot expect them to greet you and your solution with the joy they would feel toward a 37¢ cancer vaccine that needed no refrigeration! On the contrary. You, with your quick fix for a problem to which they are devoting their lives, are going to meet the kind of resistance you'd meet if you walked into the executive offices of a major oil company with a safe and nonpolluting automobile fuel that could be manufactured for a penny a gallon.

Your opponents in this context will work much harder to prepare arguments against either you or your proposal, or both, and to support those arguments, than they would if they could just admit the truth. And they will make a far greater effort to resist *your* arguments. Suppose that you, in Blamer Mode and full attack stance, ask them, "Don't you even CARE if hundreds of thousands of Americans are going to be kept in ignorance just to protect your jobs and your personal fortunes?" If you do that, your literacy cure will never reach the people it could help; and you will find yourself ridiculed, suppressed, unemployable, disgraced, and systematically rejected by one and all. The brief moment of satisfaction you gained from attacking the ethics of the literacy industry would not be worth those consequences. Don't you even CARE if people go on being illiterate when they don't have to be, just because you can't keep your big mouth shut?

I have chosen an extreme example because it makes the point quickly and clearly. But it is just as accurate when what you propose is no more earthshaking than a longer coffee break at your workplace or a different brand of sandwich bread at your home as when it threatens to destroy an industry. The scale is different, but the principle is the same:

IF YOUR PROPOSED CHANGE WOULD HAVE SERIOUS NEGATIVE CONSEQUENCES FOR THOSE IN POWER IN THE SITUATION, IT MAKES NO DIFFERENCE HOW GOOD IT IS—IT WILL NOT BE ALLOWED TO HAPPEN.

Not to anticipate this, and not to be prepared for it, is the most foolish kind of naïve behavior, and the least syntonic. Before proposing *any* change, you must give serious thought to what the consequences of the change would be for *everyone* concerned.[6]

One of the reasons why the changes proposed by Ronald Reagan have met with so little mainstream resistance is that they were all carefully packaged as changes back to the familiar. Back to the Good Old Days. Reagan's space program is Norman Rockwell in Space or, at the very worst, The Old West in Space. Remember that the first automobiles were called horseless carriages and were built with sockets for buggy whips!

So there you are. You have the cure for the literacy crisis, cheap and fast and effective. Or you have the solution to racism, or sexism, or ageism. You have found a way to dispense with the water-squandering flush toilet without the psychologically off-putting side effects of the composting toilet. You know how to put an end forever to the excessive expenditures of your Kiwanis Club. You know how to make it possible for your spouse to quit smoking. You have in your possession, in short, Something Good that everyone concerned will hate. Now what?

In the *Co-Evolution Quarterly* for Summer 1976, there is a fine description of the manner in which NASA's Jesco Von Puttkamer tackled just this kind of a situation.[7] Moving humankind out into space—in some manner, at some speed, for some purpose—is clearly the eventual goal of NASA. But real-world considerations make it impossible to sit down and plan for that in a straightforward fashion. Still, while the wrangling over how and when and at what cost is going on, NASA is required to be *doing* something. Obviously, it would be best if it did something that could be useful in achieving the eventual goal. "So what Jesco did," Stewart Brand tells us, "was put down a list of all the interesting distant visions and then see what intermediate steps they all have in common." This is a variation on a technique called "normative planning," in which you plan by working *backward* from your goal to the present instead of trying to go in the other direction.

If you have a change in mind, and it is so disruptive a change that it hasn't a prayer of getting past those with the power to make or break it, your proper strategy is to sit down and work backward, making a list of all the intermediate steps that would have to be made on the way to that change. They will have to be done anyway—doing them is not a waste of time or resources. If these steps still constitute disruptive change (which is likely if the problem is a large one), break them down again, into *their* intermediate steps. The graphic form you'll have when you finish this will look like a Christmas tree, with the ultimate goal at the very top like a finial, and the subgoals below, and each subgoal divided into *its* subgoals, and so on down to the base of the tree, where the earliest steps toward change would have to be taken.

When you find a substep toward the goal, or toward one of the subgoals, that is small enough and nonthreatening enough, something that will not send everyone screaming into their cubicles shrieking "The sky is falling!", propose *that* substep. Using all the techniques for persuasion in written language and public speaking that have been described in this chapter, as well as all the techniques for one-on-one interactions that were presented earlier in the book. Once the substep has been accomplished, go back to your planning tree and find another one like it to move on to.

This is exactly like the technique you use for encouraging another person toward a change in language behavior. You will get nowhere if you say, "Hey! The way you talk is all wrong! Stop it right now, and talk the way I tell you to talk, and everything will go much better!" That threatens the other person with loss of face; it is rude, abusive, and crude; and you have no right whatsoever to proceed in so bizarre a manner with another human being. But you know that all the parts of the human language system work together, in an orderly fashion, and that change in one will always result in change in others. You begin by trying to get the other person to change some very small thing—perhaps the rate of breathing. The resistance to that is slight enough so that it's usually possible for you to get someone to do that just by setting an example, without any overt move toward persuasion. When you have larger changes in mind, you do exactly the same thing.

You can ordinarily count on others not to realize that small changes have any significant potential consequences. Unless you have absolute power to enforce the decisions you make, introduce all threatening change in very small and gentle steps. Be absolutely certain that they are substeps necessary to the accomplishment of the ultimate large change, so that they aren't wasted steps. One small step at a time, adjusting as you go to reduce dissonance and disharmony—syntonically.

# Notes

1. The experts who serve as communicators in hostage negotiations, law enforcement crises, labor struggles, etc., are doing a specialized kind of public speaking that uses a dialogue format. Their language behavior in these roles is also highly valued.

2. When enough of those statements are shared by a group, you have the reality consensus that holds a culture together.

3. This characteristic, for some dialects of American English, was first discussed by Gary Underwood.

4. If you want to write fiction, that is what you should copy; you'll learn more about how a novel is made by copying a good one from beginning to end than you will ever learn in a class. But the writing of fiction is beyond the scope of this book.

5. George Miller, "The Magical Number Seven, plus or minus Two: Some Limits on Our Capacity for Processing Information," *Psychology Review* 63 (1956): 81–97.

6. I strongly recommend in this connection a Prentice-Hall book called *The Change-Resisters*, by J. Dan Rothwell.

7. Stewart Brand, "Apocalypse Juggernaut, Hello," *Co-Evolution Quarterly*, Summer 1976, p. 4.

# 10
# Communication Plans and Goals

In 1960, George Miller, Eugene Galanter, and Karl Pribram published a book titled *Plans and the Structure of Behavior* New York: (Henry Holt, 1960). They proposed that all organisms respond to recognition of a mismatch between the state they are experiencing and the state that is their goal by carrying out an action which they keep repeating until the mismatch is eliminated. They called this feedback loop a TOTE. The organism Tests for mismatch, Operates in an attempt to get rid of it, Tests again, and repeats those steps until—on perceiving that no more mismatch exists—it Exits from the loop. TEST; OPERATE; TEST; EXIT—the TOTE.

These authors offered the example of hammering a nail into a board. You TEST (by judging the distance between the head of the nail and the surface that you want it to be exactly flush with); then you OPERATE (by striking the head of the nail with the hammer); then you TEST again, judging the distance once more. When the result of your TEST is that there is no difference between the height of the nailhead and the surface of the board, you EXIT (by ceasing to strike the nail with the hammer). The process of tuning a guitar string is a TOTE of the very same kind.

Communicating with other people is also a TOTE, one in which we all participate, constantly striving to achieve our goals. And here we reach a crucial point: We have *no choice* about participating in this process, unless we are willing to live in complete isolation from other human beings. We all must do this particular TOTEing, whether we like it or not. But we *do* have a choice about the way that we define our terms.

Whether there is or isn't a distance between the height of a nail and the surface of a board, or between the pitch of a guitar string and the concert tone it's tuned to, is not a matter for argument. In both instances we have clear and scientifically verifiable evidence that defines the terms for us. But communication is different. Every one of us will define mismatch in the same way—as deviation from our communication goal; but the goal itself may be defined in a multitude of ways.

One person's communication goal may simply be "to be heard and understood," in the most elementary sense of those terms. The parent whose idea of conversation with a child is to say, "Hey—go make your bed!" may consider the goal achieved and all mismatch eliminated when the bed has been made. Such persons will perceive mismatch only when those they speak to appear unable or unwilling to hear what is said, and they will feel free to EXIT just as soon as their TEST indicates the most minimal sort of communication.

Others may feel that the goal has been reached only if the listener responds with a particular utterance or body language unit. "Yes, ma'am," or "I love you," or "I'm sorry," or "You're absolutely right," or "The square root of sixteen is four," or "I'll lend you the money." A kiss may be their goal, perhaps; or a handshake. When the goal is defined like this, speakers won't feel free to EXIT until the specific response or a close approximation of it has been obtained—which can lead to interminable wrangles. Or, alternatively, to a situation of almost noncommunication, because others would rather provide the desired response and end the interaction than go on talking.

Very domineering people may define the goal in communication as getting what they want, regardless of the manner in which that takes place, and will see a mismatch until *that* goal has been achieved. There is a difference between the parent who says "Go make the bed" and is satisfied with "Yes, Mother," even if nothing happens to the bed, and the one who doesn't care whether anything at all is said so long as the bed gets made.

Very antisocial persons may feel free to EXIT from the language TOTE when they have succeeded in making the people they are interacting with withdraw and leave them alone.

I would be pleased, of course, if you defined syntonicity—the state of being syntonic with the listener or reader—as your communication goal. I would prefer for you to find your mismatch not in an unmade bed or a withheld apology but in a perception that you and the person you are communicating with are not in tune with each other. However, that is your choice; I can only do my best to convince you that getting syntonic is well worth the effort, and explain to you how that goal can be achieved if it *is* your choice.

If you do define your goal as syntonicity, you may tend to think that it should be reserved only for important occasions—that it's too much trouble to bother with in casual interactions. I would suggest to you that this is a poor strategy, because the skills you need must be automatic. You would be wise to take advantage of the opportunity to practice them in the thousands of situations where the outcome is trivial and failure won't affect you seriously. The well-honed expert skill that you need to have ready when it really matters will come from that risk-free practice. If you were learning one of the classic martial arts, you would not feel that practice was unnecessary so long as you "remembered how" to carry out the moves in a crisis; syntonics is no less a skill to be taken seriously. However, practice in the physical martial arts requires trained partners, and they may be in scarce supply; for syntonics, every language interaction is a potential practice session. With no special equipment required, and no fee.

What if you want to define your goal as the ability, in communication, to please everybody? Could you do that? Is it even a sensible target in abstract terms?

Probably not. For most of us, most of the time, it won't be possible to please everybody. Not in the real world. However, syntonics offers you the alternative goal of not *dis*pleasing—

*except when that is your own deliberate choice.* For most of us, most of the time, this goal is within our grasp if we choose to work toward it.

There is always a way to say whatever you want and need to say, without sacrificing your own values and principles, and without destroying the syntonic relationship between yourself and your listener or reader. Always. This book has been devoted to providing you with the information necessary for that purpose. Getting syntonic is a tuning operation; it is a matter of speakers tuning to the signal provided by their listeners' reactions. When your communication is syntonic—even if its content is not welcome—people are not likely to feel displeasure. They are therefore not likely to set up a resistance to your message that is based not on its content but on a negative reaction to *you as communicator.* This is a goal that you can achieve.

I've never done a talk or a workshop where I made this claim without having to respond to at least one person who was convinced that even if we *can* do this, we *shouldn't* do it. I do not argue with these persons. If your personal position is that when people react negatively to your language behavior, you don't care, or "that's their problem," you are entitled to feel that way. If you are convinced that making adjustments in your language on the basis of others' reactions is a weak and wimpy way to behave, you have every right to that opinion. (I have applied Miller's Law to the statements made to me by people who feel this way, and I have carefully considered what they could be true of. I do not like the reality in which those statements are true; but nothing obliges me to live in it.) My suggestion, if *you* feel this way, is that you do an honest experiment based entirely on your own self-interest; never mind what it might mean to others. *Try* the syntonics techniques for a month or two and see if you don't find the results surprisingly to your taste. Find out whether things will go better for *you* if you use syntonics. You can always go back to your previous language behavior if you don't like what happens. Do not forget, as you carry out your experiment, that the purpose of syntonics is to achieve effective, efficient, and satisfying communication *without dishonor.*

# The Phony Leveler

There is one group of speakers who come far closer to having the ability to please everybody than others do. I have warned you against these individuals before in this book, and now we are going to take a closer look at them. They are the Phony Levelers—whose primary communication goal is to deceive.

Phony Levelers are people who can use the techniques in this book superbly, along with many other specialized techniques that have not been mentioned. In addition—and most importantly—they are both willing and able to *lie*. They are able to give a false impression of a completely syntonic *internal* state (often called *congruence*), as if there were no mismatch whatsoever between their feelings and their expression of those feelings in words and in body language.[1] Not only are they able to make their body language match what their voices say, they can do that when the inner channel—their feeling about what is being said—is in conflict with both external ones. They are constantly testing, adjusting, retesting, readjusting, based on the feedback they get from their listeners. Always TOTEing, those Phony Levelers! And the more ignorant you are about them, the more successful they are. You need information that will help you spot Phony Levelers and protect yourself against them. Since their communication is based on deception, the place to begin is with some hard facts about *lying*.

Most of what people "know" about lying is folklore. We don't keep up with scientific research literature on the subject; we rely on "gut feelings" and the occasional scrap of news that catches our eye or ear. Furthermore, where lying is concerned it hasn't been all that easy to *do* scientific research. You can set up experiments in which one set of people is instructed to lie to another set, and then you can observe the results, but it's a slippery procedure. Consider the obvious fact that a lie told because you are instructed to lie as part of a scientific experiment about lying is not at all the same thing as a lie told for ordinary reasons. And tricking people into spontaneous lying, even if experiments could be devised to do so, presents many ethical problems. Only recently have we begun to accumulate reliable information about what really happens when people lie and to organize it in such a way that it's possible to make practical use of it. And many breakthroughs in this research have resulted not from deliberate efforts to study lying but from more general studies of such things as facial expression and tone of voice.

My way of writing about lying may be less elegant than that preferred by most authors. They write of "fibbing" and "hedging" and "exaggerating"; they make a careful distinction between the deliberate lie and the deliberate failure to tell the truth that involves no *active* lie. They devote considerable space to the delicate question of what is and what is not a lie, based upon the reason the speaker has for not speaking the truth. They do not use the ugly word *lie* to refer to the custom of telling children there is a Santa Claus.

Within syntonics, we can approach this subject more directly. We are not concerned at this point with whether a lie is told out of kindness—as when a doctor tells a dying patient that there is still hope when in fact there is none—or is told for the wickedest of reasons. We can fall back on this unambiguous statement: IF IT'S NOT TRUE, AND IT'S NOT JUST A MISTAKE, IT IS A LIE. We need to be able to tell when we are being lied to; discovering *why* we are being lied to, and deciding whether the lie is justified, is a separate skill.

We can rely on two primary principles in learning to spot lies. The first is nothing new—it is the old reliable rule: WATCH FOR MISMATCH. But there is such a lot to watch! To use the first principle effectively, you need the second, which is:

THE MORE EASILY ANY PART OF LANGUAGE BEHAVIOR CAN BE VOLUNTARILY CONTROLLED, THE MORE EASILY IT CAN BE USED TO LIE; PAY ATTENTION, THEREFORE, TO THOSE PARTS OF LANGUAGE BEHAVIOR THAT ARE <u>HARD</u> TO CONTROL.

It's because of this second principle that words alone are such unreliable clues to lying. The words of a lie can be worked out by the speaker in advance and rehearsed over and over again until they are its most flawless possible expression.

By comparison with the rest of the body, the face is also easy to control voluntarily. People can assume almost any facial expression they choose, and can do so quickly and easily; the face is flexible and responsive. It is also an obvious target of attention, and it's reasonable to expect that your facial expression *will* be noticed by others.

The rest of the body is harder to bring under voluntary control in communication; and the voice is the hardest of all. As a general rule, then, for the detection of lies you should pay the greatest attention to the speaker's voice, then to the speaker's body, then to the face, and least of all to the words.

The best-known expert on human facial expression today is Paul Ekman, a University of California psychologist whose research has made possible the exact specification, muscle by muscle, of more than seven thousand different facial expressions. From Ekman we have learned that *certain parts* of the face are extremely difficult to control voluntarily and are therefore worth watching. For example, most people cannot control the muscles that raise their inner eyebrows. This means that the facial expression characteristic of distress, in which the eyebrows slant like an inverted V—higher over the nose than over the cheeks—is usually genuine. And its absence, when a person is claiming distress, is a clue to be wary; it is just as hard to suppress this expression deliberately as it is to fake it. Similarly, most people are not able voluntarily to control the dilating of their pupils; when they are interested in something, the pupils will dilate; when they are not interested, dilation will not take place. Although dilated pupils can be misleading—since they indicate emotional arousal, but do not tell you whether the interest is in what you are saying or in something else—their absence is a reliable clue. The person who says to you, "Oh, how fascinating!", but whose pupils remain undilated, is probably not being truthful.

Ekman has recently confirmed one piece of folklore, by the way. Your mother probably told you, when you were a child, that if you'd just keep smiling you would actually feel happier; for most people this is true. In his books on telephone communication, Gary S. Goodman reports that many telephone companies provide their operators with mirrors at the workplace, so that they are better able to keep on their faces the smiling expression that is expected of them and that is reflected in their voices as well as in the mirrors. Clearly, one of the characteristics of the Phony Leveler is the ability to maintain an inner feeling that is *not* in tune with his or her facial expression.

Probably the most useful information Ekman has for us is something that he learned almost accidentally, from a combination of already established neurological facts and an ingenious experiment done with photographs.[2] Neurologists are aware that the brain has one pathway to the facial muscles for unplanned spontaneous expressions and another pathway for deliberate ones. There are neurological disorders that clearly demonstrate this. In one, a patient who will smile if you tell him a joke is unable to smile if you just *ask* him to; in the other, a patient who can smile if asked to do so will not respond with a smile to jokes. Ekman discovered a specific and directly observable difference between spontaneous facial expressions and deliberate ones, related to this difference in the brain. Spontaneous expressions, he found, are much more *symmetrical* than deliberately planned ones. The deliberate ones show a mismatch between the left and right sides of the face that reflects the mismatch between the true feelings and the way that they are presented in body language. Thus, the important thing about smiling and lying is not the old cliché about people who smile all the time being untrustworthy. The important thing is that when a smile is not symmetrical—when the left and right sides of the smiling face do not match—it is a clue to deception.

Be careful, however. As always, it is deviation from the norm that is deserving of attention. You will remember from the discussion of tone of voice as a clue to lying that if the person you are talking to *always* speaks in a high-pitched voice, the pitch doesn't tell you anything—it is only a *change* from the typical pitch to a higher one that should make you suspicious. In the same way, if a person's smile is always asymmetrical, perhaps because of the shape of the mouth itself or some other facial characteristic, lack of symmetry is not reliable as a clue to lying. But when you see both kinds of smiles on someone's face (or both a symmetrical and an asymmetrical version of any other expression), it is the asymmetrical ones that are most likely to be false.

Another mismatch indicator reported by Ekman is eyebrow movements that are not synchronized with the loudness of the voice, or that are not synchronized with the emotional attitudes being expressed by the voice. Ordinarily there will be a very brief upward movement of the eyebrows as the voice gets louder, and a corresponding downward movement as it gets softer; the eyebrows and the volume of the voice should rise and fall together. The eyebrows also tend to move upward briefly when the content of the words is positive, but downward with the expression of negative content. The deliberate faking of this rapid synchronization of movement is difficult to manage.

When you are dealing with the average person, attention to this kind of nitpicking detail is probably not necessary. The average person will provide you with much more obvious signs of mismatch. You'll be able to observe that although the words used are pleasant, the fists are clenched and the body is tense, or vice versa. You will see easily detectable conflicts between the words spoken and the body language used with them. But Phony Levelers are not average people, and they will not make obvious mistakes. In dealing with *them*, Ekman's minute details may be exactly what you need.

All of the research on lying agrees on one thing: The ear is better at hearing lies than the eye is at seeing them. This is why I advised you, if you are not sure whether you will be facing a Phony Leveler or not, to talk to the person on the telephone before you have a meeting in person. Remember that when there is an intention to deceive, the pitch of the voice tends to rise above the baseline pitch already established in the person's speech. And the intonation will often give away the best-rehearsed falsehood, if you know what to pay attention to. No amount of "sweet talk" will cover up the abnormal heavy stresses on words and parts of words in the verbal attack patterns. We can hear a sneer, smirk, a snarl, *in the voice itself*, that appears nowhere in the words used and may not be apparent in the facial expression or other body language of the Phony Leveler.

Suppose that as you are talking with someone you suddenly notice a visual clue to deception, perhaps an obviously asymmetrical smile. Switch your attention at once to the *sound* of the speech if you can. Stop watching, and concentrate on listening. If the situation is one where you can get away with closing your eyes as you listen, by all means do that. Perhaps you can say, "I think I could understand what you're saying better if I closed my eyes while you talk—I can concentrate better that way." Chances are, the Phony Leveler will immediately know that you're doing that because you are suspicious. That may be a good thing—you may want to serve notice that you don't trust this person and that you are on the alert. But it should be a choice *you* make, not just one more advantage for the skillful liar.

This is tricky. Of course it's tricky. Unless you are yourself a Phony Leveler—in which case what's happening is a kind of contest between experts—anything you do to reduce your visual attention and increase your focus on information for the ear is going to be obvious to your opponent. It will show on your face, and in your eyes. Unless you can plausibly turn your back, or move to a dimly lighted area, or put on dark glasses, it may not be possible for you to keep the Phony Leveler from knowing right away that you are deliberately *not watching*. If that's the situation, and there's no possibility of shifting the conversation from the in-person context to a telephone context, your best strategy is to be completely up front about it. You can't hide what you're doing from the Phony Leveler anyway; don't burden yourself with the distraction of trying to maintain a doomed pretense. That just makes extra work for you at a time when you need all your energy and attention for other purposes.

You may not be able to determine precisely what the Phony Leveler's lies *are*; that will depend on your skills and the opponent's skills, as well as on the amount of real-world knowledge each of you brings to the situation. But with a little practice you should be able to increase your skill at knowing that you are *facing* a Phony Leveler (or any other variety of liar), and this in itself is a major improvement. Lying to someone who suspects nothing is not at all the same thing as lying to someone who is aware and alert.

# When the Communication Goal Is Power over Others

In the formal sense, as I have pointed out before, there is no such thing as neutral communication. When you attempt to get someone to listen to what you are saying, that is verbal manipulation—it is the use of language as a mechanism to control another person's behavior. If you are not going to try to at least influence people to listen to what you say, there is little reason to talk or write at all. Not one of us is innocent of verbal manipulation in this formal sense of the term.

However, like any other sort of power, verbal manipulation can be used for good or for bad. The parent who uses language to convince a child not to run into the street where she might be struck by a car is using language as a mechanism for control, and is doing so for the best of reasons. The trial lawyer who uses language as a mechanism to break down the testimony of an uncooperative witness and bring a criminal to justice is using verbal manipulation for a good cause. But the very same parent, the very same lawyer, can use verbal manipulation to terrify and abuse and do harm.

There are a number of situations in our culture in which verbal manipulation is used systematically and routinely, and in which it is an accepted part of the situation. The psychotherapist uses language to force patients to look closely at things in their lives they do not want to look at and that may cause them much pain. The physician uses verbal manipulation with patients who are reluctant to undergo medical procedures or comply with medical instructions, to impress them with the seriousness of their condition and the hazards of not following orders. Hypnotists use the most powerful techniques of verbal manipulation for a number of purposes—to keep the client from feeling pain, to modify undesirable behavior such as excessive eating, to get access to information that has been suppressed and is badly needed by law enforcement, etc. Lawyers use verbal manipulation to convince juries and judges of the guilt or innocence of their clients. Teachers use it to convince students that what they are hearing is important and should be remembered, so that examinations will be passed and degrees granted. Preachers use it to help their congregations build a solid foundation of moral and ethical principles, and to convince their listeners that they are preaching the truth. Salespeople use verbal manipulation to convince customers to buy the products they are selling; they could not keep their jobs if they refused to do so. Politicians, unless they are willing to resort to bribery and mob violence, have nothing but verbal manipulation as a tool for both getting an office and keeping it. Practitioners of systems such as Neuro-Linguistic Programming use verbal manipulation as a way to enable others to bring about changes in their lives.

In all such situations, verbal manipulation is the accepted mode of behavior for the dominant person in the interaction. When we enter into one of these, we not only expect to encounter verbal manipulation, we are willing to pay the manipulators for what they do.

As a culture, we have set up measures to safeguard us from many types of *incompetent* verbal manipulation. That is what bar exams, medical boards, and state licensing boards are for. That is why we have laws requiring voluntary consent to these sorts of manipulation before they can be used; that is why we require adult guardians to give or deny such consent when children are involved; that is why we have courts to see to it that those guardians do not abuse their privileges. And that is why it is made difficult to declare an adult person incompetent to refuse such manipulation. That is why our politicians are for the most part elected rather than appointed. Our safeguarding systems do not always work, by any means, but they are in place, and we do our best to make good use of them.

However, incompetence is not the only hazard. There are times when the dominant person in one of these systems of verbal manipulation is a fully qualified—even magnificently qualified—Phony Leveler. When that happens, the safeguards are not enough. The superb psychotherapist, teacher, politician, or other "licensed" verbal manipulator, who has passed every one of the tests required by law and by custom *and who is a Phony Leveler,* is dangerous.

Against these people, your only ready defense is knowledge. You need to be aware that they exist, aware of the techniques that they are likely to use against you, and aware of the methods available to you for countering those techniques. The more you know, the less likely they are to be able to make you their victim. And the less likely you are to *appeal* to them as a victim. They are so sensitive to signals from others that they will know you are on to them; unless they are people who approach verbal manipulation as they would a sport, always looking for a greater challenge, they will prefer not to bother with you. They'll look for easier prey.

When you are facing someone whose clear communication goal is to deceive you, especially if that someone in any significant way "outranks" you, you are under attack. This is the time when you will be deeply grateful that you've done a lot of practicing in safe situations. You will need every bit of skill that you can muster.

It often happens that I am asked this question: "Doesn't your system of verbal self-defense techniques teach people how to *be* Phony Levelers? Aren't you teaching people how to use verbal manipulation for abuse, and to do it so well that they can't be detected?" I understand the question, and I agree that syntonics is like any other martial art—it has a potential for abuse. But if it is your nature to be a Phony Leveler, you will find a way to do that whether you read this book or not. The truly dangerous Phony Levelers have one characteristic that cannot be learned from a book: They are without a conscience. They can lie flawlessly because they really do not feel *any* kind of unease when they deceive others; they are entirely lacking in empathy. They are sociopaths. You are very unlikely to be without a conscience, or to be a potential sociopath, and syntonics techniques and information will not change that.

The more you know about the use of language to defend yourself, the less need you will feel to use it for aggression. People who are secure in their knowledge of their own competence feel no obligation to prove that competence by showing off, and will be reluctant to abuse their skills; they will not stoop to verbal bullying. But neither will they be easy victims for those who *do* misuse language.

# Notes

1.  Because there is more than one kind of syntonic state in communication, I also use the term *metasyntonics*. There is the *internal* syntonic state, in which all channels of communication in a single individual are perfectly in tune with one another. There is the *external* syntonic state, in which two or more human beings are as perfectly in tune with each other for purposes of transmitting information as possible. In order to talk about both systems of syntonics, we need the prefix *meta-*, which allows us to include both in a single larger system.

2.  Daniel Goleman, "The 7,000 Faces of Dr. Ekman," *Psychology Today*, February 1981, pp. 43–49.

# 11
# Conclusion

Throughout this book, I have been talking about syntonics in general terms. I am going to be somewhat more specific in this concluding section, beginning with a list of the eleven statements that make up the theoretical foundation for syntonics. The point of a set of statements of this kind, whether they come from aerobics or from physics or from any of the "ologies," is that they make it possible to test the claims of the system. Experiments can be devised to check them for accuracy, and that is crucial. You will not find this set obscure or excessively technical—the statements have not been written in Academic Regalian. Here they are.

### The Theoretical Propositions of Syntonics

1. DISHARMONY in the linguistic environment is *harmful* to the human being physically, mentally, and emotionally.
2. HARMONY in the linguistic environment is *beneficial* to the human being physically, mentally, and emotionally.
3. It is possible to distinguish systematic patterns of language behavior that encourage or increase DISHARMONY in the linguistic environment; it is also possible to dis-

tinguish systematic patterns of language response to such behavior that will eliminate it or increase it.

4. It is possible to distinguish systematic patterns of language behavior which encourage or increase HARMONY in the linguistic environment; it is also possible to distinguish systematic patterns of language response to such behavior that will facilitate or increase it.

5. The use of patterns of language behavior that lead to DISHARMONY constitutes verbal abuse of human beings and pollution of the linguistic environment.

6. The use of patterns of language behavior that lead to HARMONY constitutes verbal self-defense and a nurturing of the linguistic environment.

7. The single principle upon which all the patterns mentioned above are based is the principle of SYNTONICITY.

8. A shared syntonic state is necessary to the establishment of linguistic HARMONY and to a sound ecology of the linguistic environment.

9. The only reliable method for achievement of a shared syntonic state between human beings in any language interaction is the use of a system of feedback.

10. In the ideal communication situation all persons involved would be perfectly syntonic with respect to one another. It is probable that no such ideal situation can exist in the real world except as a theoretical formulation of a target goal for use in a feedback system.

11. By the principle of resonance, the more the language behavior of one person in a language interaction tends toward syntonicity, the more that of other persons involved will do so, even if they are unaware of the phenomenon.

For any set of theoretical propositions of this sort, it's customary to provide definitions of the terms used—and those definitions can be excruciatingly detailed and technical. In this case, however, no terms have been introduced that are not already well-defined in common use; and none have been used in a way that makes further definition necessary. The only term about which there might be confusion is *resonance*; it should clarify that term if I mention that resonance is what causes a piece of crystal glassware to give off a musical tone when precisely the *right* tone is sung nearby, without any need to touch the glassware in any way. Resonance alone will cause the glass to sound a tone in harmony with the singer's note.

Testing the statements above would require controlled scientific experiments. Many experiments have been suggested in this book, but they have always been what are called "uncontrolled" experiments. When you respond to a person who is using the visual Sensory Mode by using that mode yourself, you are testing Proposition 4. A speaker who uses a consistent Sensory Mode provides information about his or her view of reality that is helpful in communication; for you to respond by matching that Sensory Mode uses the information provided to increase harmony in the linguistic environment. If you do this and it works, your experiment has been successful; if you do it and the only result is friction and misunderstanding, your experiment has failed.

What makes your experiment "informal" is the fact that it is full of *uncontrolled variables.* You have not proved that what led to the good results was your Sensory Mode matching; theoretically, it could have been the color of your shirt, or the fact that you and your partner in the interaction were at the beach at the time. It could have been because you are so charismatic that it makes no difference what you say—the results will always be good. In a formal and controlled experiment all these factors would be provided for, so that they could not contaminate the experiment.

For example, if it were suspected that using Sensory Mode matching at the beach worked only because of the physical location, the experiment would be repeated in other settings; a classroom, a hospital lobby, a bus station, a dentist's office. Everything else, such as the color of the experimenter's shirt, would be kept exactly the same as in the experiment at the beach, insofar as that was possible. Each and every possible factor (including your personal charisma!) that could be causing the good results would be tested for in that way, until it could be said—without any doubt—whether or not the factor responsible for the results was the technique of matching Sensory Modes.

You will see that this could take a long time, a lot of work, and a large sum of money. This is why it takes so long to get federal approval of a new drug. It's not enough to give the drug and report that it made the patients feel better; you must prove that it was only the drug that led to the improvement, and not any of the dozens of other things that might have been involved. And you must also prove that the drug had no harmful results that outweighed the good ones.

You don't have to wait for federal approval of the techniques presented in this book; unlike drugs, they are readily available for use in your own life. If you use them consistently, in a variety of situations and with many different people, and they work for you, the lack of scientific proof does not make them any less useful to you. By the same token, if one of the techniques seems to work badly for you, you are not in the situation of a patient taking a drug with unpleasant side effects, who is advised that it *must* be taken nevertheless. If it doesn't work, and you've given it a fair trial and are satisfied that it's not useful for you, you need only drop it from your linguistic behavior.

The important thing is not the perfection of your experiments or their results; the important thing is that you understand that there are things that you can try, to improve your own linguistic environment and that of others around you, and that you do try them.

I wish you the very best of luck, and would always be interested to hear about your experiences with getting—and being—syntonic.

# References and
# Bibliography

## Articles

Abramowitz, S. F., et al. "The Politics of Clinical Judgment: What Nonliberal Examiners Infer about Women Who Do Not Stifle Themselves." *Journal of Consulting & Clinical Psychology* 41 (1973): 385–91.

Addington, D. W. "The Relationship of Selected Vocal Characteristics to Personality Perception." *Speech Monographs* 35 (1968): 492–503.

Anderson, S. "How to Get *Even*." *Language* 48 (1972): 893–906.

Andrews, L. B. "Mind Control in the Courtroom." *Psychology Today*, March 1982, pp. 66–73.

Argyle, M. "Non-Verbal Communication and Mental Disorder." *Psychological Medicine* 23 (1978): 551–54.

Aronovitch, C. D. "The Voice of Personality: Stereotyped Judgments of Their Relation to Voice Quality and Sex of Speaker." *Journal of Social Psychology* 99 (1976): 207–20.

Atkinson, R., and R. Schiffrin. "The Control of Short-term Memory." *Scientific American* 225 (1971): 82–90.

Austin, W. M. "Some Social Aspects of Paralanguage." *Canadian Journal of Linguistics* 11 (1965): 31–39.

Barroshuk, L. "Separate Worlds of Taste." *Psychology Today*, September 1980, pp. 48–63.

Bateson, G., D. D. Jackson, J. Haley, and J. H. Weakland. "Toward a Theory of Schizophrenia." *Behavioral Science* 1 (1956): 251–64.

Beattie, G. W. "Planning Units in Spontaneous Speech: Some Evidence from Hesitation in Speech and Speaker Gaze Direction in Conversation." *Linguistics* 17 (1979): 61–78.

———. "The Regulation of Speaker-Turns in Face-to-Face Conversation: Some Implications for Conversation in Sound-Only Communication Channels." *Semiotica* 34 (1981): 55–70.

———, et al. "Why Is Mrs. Thatcher Interrupted So Often?" *Nature* 300 (1982): 744–47.

Bedell, G. "The Arguments about Deep Structure." *Language* 50 (1974): 423–45.

Bellugi, U. "Learning the Language." *Psychology Today*, December 1970, pp. 32–55, 66.

———, and E. S. Klima. "The Roots of Language in the Sign Language of the Deaf." *Psychology Today*, June 1972, pp. 60–64, 76.

Benderly, B. L. "Dancing Without Music." *Science '80*, December 1980, pp. 54–59.

Bohannon, L. "Shakespeare in the Bush." *Natural History*, August–September 1966, pp. 28–33.

Bolinger, D. "Accent Is Predictable (If You're A Mind-Reader)." *Language* 48 (1972): 633–44.

———. "Accents That Determine Stress." In M. R. Key, ed., *The Relationship of Verbal and Nonverbal Communication* (The Hague: Mouton, 1980), pp. 37–47.

———. "Contrastive Accent and Contrastive Stress." *Language* 37 (1961): 83–96.

Brand, S. "Apocalypse Juggernaut, Hello!" *Co-Evolution Quarterly*, Summer 1976, pp. 4–6.

Broverman, I., et al. "Sex-Role Stereotypes and Clinical Judgments of Mental Health." *Journal of Consulting and Clinical Psychology* 34 (1970): 1–7.

Brown, P., and S. Levinson. "Universals in Language Usage:

Politeness Phenomena." In E. Goody, ed., *Questions and Politeness: Strategies in Social Interaction* (Cambridge: Cambridge University Press, 1978), pp. 56–289.

Burns, T. "Nonverbal Communication." *Discovery*, October 1964. pp. 31–35.

Cain, W. S. "Educating Your Nose." *Psychology Today*, July 1981, pp. 48–56.

Charrow, V. R. "Linguistic Theory and the Study of Legal and Bureaucratic Language." In L. K. Obler and L. Nenn, *Exceptional Language and Linguistics* (New York: Academic Press, 1982), pp. 81–101.

Clynes, M., and N. Nettheim. "The Living Quality of Music: Neurobiological Patterns of Communicating Feeling." In M. Clynes, ed., *Music, Mind, and Brain: The Neurophysiology of Music* (New York: Plenum Press, 1982), pp. 47–82.

Cole, R. A. "Navigating the Slippery Stream of Speech." *Psychology Today*, April 1979, pp. 77–87.

Condon, W. S. and L. W. Sander. "Neonate Movement Is Synchronized with Adult Speech: Interactional Participation and Language Acquisition." *Science* 183 (1974): 99–101.

———, "The Relation of Interactional Synchrony to Cognitive and Emotional Processes." In M. R. Key, ed., *The Relationship of Verbal and Nonverbal Communication* (The Hague: Mouton, 1980), pp. 49–65.

Conley, J. M., W. M. O'Barr, and A. E. Lind. "The Power of Language: Presentation Style in the Courtroom." *Duke University Law Journal* 6 (1978): 1375–99.

Conway, F., and J. Siegelman. "The Awesome Power of the Mind-Probers." *Science Digest*, September 1983, pp. 72–75, 91.

Craik, F. I. M., and R. S. Lockhart. "Levels of Processing: A Framework for Memory Research." *Journal of Verbal Learning and Verbal Behavior* 11 (1972): 671–84.

Crosby, F., and L. Nyquist. "The Female Register: An Empirical Study of Lakoff's Hypotheses." *Language in Society* 6 (1977): 313–22.

Donovan, H. "The Enigmatic President." *Time*, May 6, 1985, pp. 24–33.

Dubois, B. L., and I. Crouch. "The Question of Tag Questions in Women's Speech: They Don't Really Use More of Them, Do They?" *Language in Society* 4 (1975): 289–94.

Duncan, S. "Toward a Grammar for Dyadic Conversation." *Semiotica* 9 (1973): 29–47.

Dykema, K. "Where Our Grammar Came From." *College English* 22 (1961): 455–65.

Edelman, M. "Language, Myths and Rhetoric." *Society*, July–August 1976, pp. 14–21.

Edelsky, C. "Who's Got the Floor?" *Language in Society* 10 (1981): 383–421.

Ekman, P., and W. V. Friesen. "Nonverbal Leakage and Clues to Deception." *Psychiatry* 32 (1969): 88–106.

_____. "The Repertoire of Nonverbal Behavior: Categories, Origins, Usage, and Coding." *Semiotica* 1 (1969): 49–68.

Elgin, S. "Why *Newsweek* Can't Tell You Why Johnny Can't Write." *English Journal* 65 (1977): 29–35.

Ervin-Tripp, S., M. C. O'Connor, and J. Rosenberg. "Language and Power in the Family." In C. Kramarae et al., eds., *Language and Power* (Beverly Hills: Sage Publications, 1984), pp. 116–35.

Fisher, S. "Experiencing Your Body: You Are What You Feel." *Saturday Review of Science*, July 8, 1972, pp. 27–32.

Fishman, J. A. "A Systematization of the Whorf Hypothesis." *Behavioral Science* 5 (1960): 323–39.

Frankel, R. M. "The Laying On of Hands: Aspects of the Organization of Gaze, Touch and Talk in a Medical Encounter." In S. Fisher and A. D. Todd, *The Social Organization of Doctor-Patient Communication* (Washington, D.C.: Center for Applied Linguistics, 1983), pp. 19–54.

Fromkin, V. "Slips of the Tongue." *Scientific American* 229 (1973): 110–17.

Gantt, W. H., et al. "Effect of Person." *Conditional Reflex* 1 (1966): 18–35.

Gardner, H. "Gifted Worldmakers." *Psychology Today*, September 1980, pp. 92–96.

_____. "Strange Loops of the Mind." *Psychology Today*, March 1980, pp. 72–85.

Geldard, F. A. "Body English." *Psychology Today*, December 1968, pp. 43–47.

Gibbs, J. R. "Defensive Communication." *Journal of Communication* 11 (1961): 141–48.

Giles, H. "Evaluative Reactions to Accents." *Educational Review* 22 (1970): 211–27.

Goleman, D. "Can You Tell When Someone Is Lying to You?" *Psychology Today*, August 1982, pp. 14–23.

———. "People Who Read People." *Psychology Today*, July 1979, pp. 66–78.

———. "The 7,000 Faces of Dr. Ekman." *Psychology Today*, February 1981, pp. 43–49.

———. "Who's Mentally Ill?" *Psychology Today*, January 1978, pp. 34–41.

Grice, H. P. "Logic and Conversation." In P. Cole and J. L. Morgan, eds., *Syntax and Semantics*, vol. 3: *Speech Acts* (New York: Academic Press, 1975), pp. 41–58.

Grotstein, J. S. "The Higher Implications of Langs' Contributions." In J. Raney, ed., *Listening and Interpreting: The Challenge of the Work of Robert Langs* (New York: Jason Aronson, 1984), pp. 3–20.

Hall, E. "Giving Away Psychology in the 80's: George Miller Interviewed by Elizabeth Hall." *Psychology Today*, January 1980, pp. 38–50, 97–98.

Hall, E. T. "Proxemics." *Current Anthropology*, 9 (1968): 83–104.

Hall, J. A. "Gender Effects in Decoding Nonverbal Cues." *Psychological Bulletin* 85 (1978): 845–57.

Halle, M. "Stress Rules in English: A New Version." *Linguistic Inquiry* 4 (1973): 451–64.

Hennesee, J. "Some News Is Good News." *Ms.*, July 1974, pp. 25–29.

Hess, E. "The Role of Pupil Size in Communication." *Scientific American* 233 (1975): 110–19.

Jonas, G. "Manfred Clynes and the Science of Sentics." *Saturday Review*, May 13, 1972, pp. 42–51.

Kagan, J. "Do Infants Think?" *Scientific American* 226 (1972): 74–82.

Kartunnen, L. "Implicative Verbs." *Language* 47 (1971): 350–58.

———. "Presupposition and Linguistic Context." *Theoretical Linguistics* 1 (1974): 181–94.

Katz, J. J., and D. T. Langendoen. "Pragmatics and Presupposition." *Language* 52 (1976): 1–17.

Kempton, W. "The Rhythmic Basis of Interactional Micro-Synchrony." In M. R. Key, ed., *The Relationship of Verbal and Nonverbal Communication: Student Edition* (The Hague: Mouton, 1980), pp. 65–75.

Kendon, A. "Gesticulation and Speech: Two Aspects of the Process of Utterance." In M. R. Key, ed., *The Relationship of Verbal and Nonverbal Communication: Student Edition* (The Hague: Mouton, 1980), pp. 207–27.

Kinzel, A. "Body-Buffer Zone in Violent Prisoners." *American Journal of Psychiatry* 127 (1970): 59–64.

Kiparsky, C., and P. Kiparsky. "Fact." In M. Bierwisch and K. E. Heidolph, eds., *Progress in Linguistics* (The Hague: Mouton, 1970), pp. 143–73.

Klima, E. A., and U. Bellugi. "Poetry without Sound." *Human Nature*, October 1973, pp. 74–83.

Korsch, B. M., and V. F. Negrete. "Doctor-Patient Communication." *Scientific American* 227 (1972): 66–73.

Kotker, Z. "The 'Feminine' Behavior of Powerless People." *Savvy*, March 1980, pp. 36–42.

Kramer, C. "Folk Linguistics: Wishy-Washy Mommy Talk." *Psychology Today*, June 1974, pp. 82–85.

———, et al. "Perspectives on Language and Communication." *Signs* 3 (1978): 638–51.

Ladd, D. R. "Stylized Intonation." *Language* 54 (1978): 517–40.

Laib, N. K. "Territoriality in Rhetoric." *College English* 47 (1985): 579–93.

Lakoff, G. "Hedges: A Study in Meaning Criteria and the Logic of Fuzzy Concepts." In P. Peranteau et al., eds., *Papers from the 8th Regional Meeting of the Chicago Linguistic Society*, 1972, pp. 183–228.

Langer, E. J., and R. A. Abelson. "A Patient by Any Other Name: Clinician Group Differences in Labeling Bias."

*Journal of Consulting and Clinical Psychology* 42 (1974): 4–9.

Lennenberg, E. H. "On Explaining Language." *Science* 164 (1969): 635–43.

Leonard, G. B. "Language and Reality." *Harper's*, November 1974, pp. 46–52.

Loftus, E. "Words That Could Save Your Life." *Psychology Today*, November 1979, pp. 100–137.

Longfellow, L. "Body Talk: The Game of Feeling and Expression." *Psychology Today*, October 1970, pp. 45–55.

Lynch, J. J. "Interpersonal Aspects of Blood Pressure Control." *Journal of Nervous and Mental Diseases* 170 (1982): 143–53.

————. "Listen and Live." *American Health*, April 1985, pp. 39–44.

McCawley, J. D. "Conversational Implicature and the Lexicon." In M. Shibatani, ed., *Syntax and Semantics*, vol. 9 (New York: Academic Press, 1978), pp. 245–259.

McConnell-Ginet, S. "Intonation in a Man's World." In B. Thorne et al., eds., *Languge, Gender and Society* (Rowley, Mass.: Newburg House, 1983), pp. 69–88.

McDowell, J. J. "Interactional Synchrony: A Reappraisal." *Journal of Personality and Social Psychology* 36 (1978): 963–75.

Mamis, R. A. "Name-Calling." *INC.*, July 1984, pp. 67–74.

Marcus, M. G. "The Power of a Name." *Psychology Today*, October 1976, pp. 75–78.

Mehrabian, A. "Nonverbal Betrayal of Feeling." *Journal of Experimental Research in Personality* 5 (1971): 64–73.

Miller, G. A. "The Magical Number Seven, plus or minus Two: Some Limits on Our Capacity for Processing Information." *Psychology Review* 63 (1956): 81–97.

Milstead, J. "Verbal Battering." *BBW*, August 1985, pp. 34–35, 61, 68.

Miron, M. S., and T. A. Pasquale. "Psycholinguistic Analyses of Coercive Communications." *Journal of Psycholinguistic Research* 7 (1978): 95–120.

Moore, M. S. "Some Myths about 'Mental Illness'." *Archives of General Psychiatry* 32 (1975): 1483–97.

Morgan, J. L. "Conversational Postulates Revisited." *Language* 53 (1977): 277–84.

Newcome, T. "An Approach to the Study of Communicative Acts." *Psychological Review* 60 (1953): 393–404.

O'Barr, W. M. "Speech Styles in the Courtroom." In W. M. O'Barr, *Linguistic Evidence: Language, Power, and Strategy in the Courtroom* (New York: Academic Press, 1982), pp. 61–91.

Osgood, C. E., and P. Tannenbaum. "The Principle of Congruity in the Prediction of Attitude Change." *Psychological Review* 62 (1955): 42–55.

Pearce, W. B., and F. Conklin. "Nonverbal Vocalic Communication and Perceptions of a Speaker." *Speech Monographs* 38 (1971): 235–41.

Philips, S. U. "Sex Differences and Language." *Annual Review of Anthropology* 9 (1980): 523–44.

Preston, I. "Inconsistency: A Persuasive Device." In J. H. Campbell and H. W. Hepler, eds., *Dimensions in Communication: Readings* (Belmont, Calif.: Wadsworth Publishing Company, 1965), pp. 95–102.

Rice, B. "Between the Lines of Threatening Messages." *Psychology Today*, September 1981, pp. 52–64.

Richardson, J. I. "The Manipulative Patient Spells Trouble." *Nursing '81*, January 1981, pp. 48–53.

Rosenhan, D. L. "On Being Sane in Insane Places." *Science* 179 (1973): 250–58.

Rosenthal, R., and L. Jacobson. "Teacher Expectations and the Disadvantaged." *Scientific American* 218 (1968): 19–23.

Rossman, P. L. "Organic Diseases Simulating Functional Disorders." *General Practitioner*, August 1963, pp. 78–83.

Ruesch, J. "Communications and Human Relations: An Interdisciplinary Approach." In K. Giffin and B. R. Patton, eds., *Basic Readings in Interdisciplinary Communication* (New York: Harper and Row, 1971), pp. 3–20.

Sacks, H., et al. "A Simplest Systematics for the Organization of Turn-Taking for Conversation." *Language* 50 (1974): 696–735.

Schane, S. A. "The Rhythmic Nature of English Word Accentuation." *Language* 55 (1979): 559–602.

Scheflen, A. E. "The Significance of Posture in Communication Systems." *Psychiatry* 27 (1964): 316–31.

Schegloff, E. A., G. Jefferson, and H. Sacks. "The Preference for Self-Correction in the Organization of Repair in Conversation." *Language* 53 (1977): 361–82.

Schegloff, E. A., and H. Sacks. "Opening Up Closings." *Semiotica* 8 (1973): 289–327.

Shuy, R. W. "The Medical Interview: Problems in Communication." *Primary Care* 3 (1976): 365–86.

Siple, P. "Signed Language and Linguistic Theory." In L. K. Obler and L. Menn, *Exceptional Language and Linguistics* (New York: Academic Press, 1982), pp. 313–38.

Snyder, M. "The Many Me's of the Self-Monitor." *Psychology Today*, March 1980, pp. 33–40, 92.

Thorndike, R. L.. "Review of Rosenthal, R., and Jacobsen, L., *Pygmalion in the Classroom.*" *American Educational Research Journal* 5 (1968): 708–11.

Trillin, A. S. "Of Dragons and Garden Peas: A Cancer Patient Talks to Doctors." *New England Journal of Medicine*, March 19, 1981, pp. 699–701.

Underwood, G. "How *You* Sound to an Arkansawyer." *American Speech* 48 (1976): 208–15.

Word, C. O., M. P. Zanna, and J. Cooper. "The Nonverbal Mediation of Self-Fulfilling Prophecies in Interracial Interactions." *Journal of Experimental Social Psychology* 10 (1974): 109–20.

Ziegler, H. P. "The Sensual Feel of Food." *Psychology Today*, August 1975, pp. 62–66.

## Books

Argyle, M. *Bodily Communication.* London: Methuen, 1975.

────── . *Social Interaction.* London: Methuen, 1974.

Atwater, E. *"I Hear You": Listening Skills to Make You a Better Manager.* Englewood Cliffs, N.J.: Prentice-Hall, 1981.

Austin, J. L. *How to Do Things with Words.* London: Oxford University Press, 1962.

Beattie, G. *Talk: An Analysis of Speech and Non-Verbal Behav-*

*iour in Conversation.* Milton Keynes, England: Open University Press, 1983.

Bierwisch, M., and K. E. Heidolph, eds. *Progress in Linguistics.* The Hague: Mouton, 1970.

Birdwhistell, R. L. *Kinesics and Context: Essays on Body Motion Communication.* Philadelphia: University of Pennsylvania Press, 1970.

Bolinger, D., ed. *Intonation.* Harmondsworth, Middlesex, England: Penguin Books, 1972.

Bolton, R. *People Skills: How to Assert Yourself, Listen to Others and Resolve Conflicts.* Englewood Cliffs, N.J.: Prentice-Hall, 1979.

Boulding, K. *The Image.* Ann Arbor: University of Michigan Press, 1956.

Carnegie, D. *How to Win Friends and Influence People.* New York: Pocket Books, 1972.

Clynes, M. *Sentics: The Touch of Emotions.* New York: Doubleday, 1977.

———, ed. *Music, Mind, and Brain: The Neurophysiology of Music.* New York: Plenum Press, 1982.

Cole, P., and J. L. Morgan, eds. *Syntax and Semantics,* vol. 3: *Speech Acts.* New York: Academic Press, 1975.

Critchley, M. *Silent Language.* London: Butterworths, 1975.

Crystal, D. *The English Tone of Voice.* Bristol: Edward Arnold, 1975.

Dale, P. *Language Development, Structure and Function.* 2nd edition. New York: Holt, Rinehart and Winston, 1976.

Daniels, H. *Famous Last Words: The American Language Crisis Reconsidered.* Carbondale, Ill.: Southern Illinois University Press, 1983.

Denes, P., and E. Pinson. *The Speech Chain.* New York: Anchor Books, 1973.

Edwards, B. *Drawing on the Right Side of the Brain.* Los Angeles: J. P. Tarcher, 1979.

Ekman, P. *Telling Lies.* New York: W. W. Norton, 1985.

———, and W. V. Friesen. *Unmasking the Face.* Englewood Cliffs, N.J.: Prentice-Hall, 1975.

Ekman, P., et al. *Emotion in the Human Face.* New York: Pergamon Press, 1972.

Elgin, S. H. *The Gentle Art of Verbal Self-Defense.* Englewood Cliffs, N.J.: Prentice-Hall, 1980.

———. *The Gentle Art of Verbal Self-Defense Workbook.* New York: Marboro Books, 1986.

———. *Manual for Syntonics Trainers: Level One.* Huntsville, Arkansas: Ozark Center for Language Studies, 1986.

———. *More on the Gentle Art of Verbal Self-Defense.* Englewood Cliffs, N.J.: Prentice-Hall, 1983.

———. *What Is Linguistics?* 2nd edition. Englewood Cliffs, N.J.: Prentice-Hall, 1979.

Everstine, D. S., and L. Everstine. *People in Crisis: Strategic Therapeutic Interventions.* New York: Brunner/Magel, 1983.

Festinger, L. *A Theory of Cognitive Dissonance.* Evanston, Ill.: Row, Peterson & Company, 1957.

Fisher, S., and A. D. Todd. *The Social Organization of Doctor-Patient Communication.* Washington, D.C.: Center for Applied Linguistics, 1983.

Fodor, J. A., T. G. Bever, and M. F. Garrett. *The Psychology of Language.* New York: McGraw-Hill, 1974.

Friedman, M., and R. Rosenman. *Type A Behavior and Your Heart.* New York: Alfred A. Knopf, 1974.

Giles, H., and P. F. Powesland. *Speech Style and Social Evaluation.* New York: Academic Press, 1975.

Goodman, G. S. *Reach Out and Sell Someone.* Englewood Cliffs, N.J.: Prentice-Hall, 1983.

———. *Winning by Telephone: Telephone Effectiveness for Business Professionals and Customers.* Englewood Cliffs, N.J.: Prentice-Hall, 1982.

Gordon, T. *Parent Effectiveness Training.* New York: Peter H. Wyden, 1970.

Grinder, J., and R. Bandler. *The Structure of Magic: I.* Palo Alto: Science and Behavior Books, 1975.

———. *The Structure of Magic: II.* Palo Alto: Science and Behavior Books, 1976.

———. *Trance-Formations: Neuro-linguistic Programming and the Structure of Hypnosis.* Moab, Utah: Real People Press, 1981.

Gumperz, J. *Discourse Strategies*. London: Cambridge University Press, 1982.

Haley, J. *Uncommon Therapy: The Psychiatric Techniques of Milton H. Erickson, M.D.* New York: W. W. Norton, 1973.

Hall, E. T. *Beyond Culture*. New York: Anchor Books, 1977.

Halle, M., and S. J. Keyser. *English Stress: Its Form, Its Growth and Its Role in Verse*. New York: Harper and Row, 1971.

Heider, F. *The Psychology of Interpersonal Relations*. New York: John Wiley and Sons, 1958.

Henley, N. *Body Politics: Power, Sex, and Nonverbal Communication*. Englewood Cliffs, N.J.: Prentice-Hall, 1977.

Herndon, J. *A Survey of Modern Grammars*. 2nd edition. New York: Holt, Rinehart and Winston, 1976.

Hofstadter, D. *Gödel, Escher, Bach: An Eternal Golden Braid*. New York: Random House, 1980.

Holt, J. *How Children Fail*. New York: Pitman Publishing, 1974.

_____. *How Children Learn*. New York: Pitman Publishing, 1967.

Hunt, M. *The Universe Within: A New Science Explores the Human Mind*. New York: Simon and Schuster, 1982.

Key, M. R., ed. *The Relationship of Verbal and Nonverbal Communication*. The Hague: Mouton, 1980.

Kernberg, O. F. *Internal World and External Reality: Object Relations Theory Applied*. New York: Jason Aronson, 1980.

Kleinke, C. L. *First Impressions: The Psychology of Encountering Others*. Englewood Cliffs: Prentice-Hall, 1975.

Kramarae, C. *Women and Men Speaking*. Rowley, Mass.: Newbury House, 1981.

_____, et al., eds. *Language and Power*. Beverly Hills: Sage Publications, 1984.

Kuhn, T. S. *Structure of Scientific Revolutions*. Chicago: University of Chicago Press, 1970.

Labov, W., and D. Fanshel. *Therapeutic Discourse: Psychotherapy as Conversation*. New York: Academic Press, 1977.

Ladefoged, P. *Elements of Acoustic Phonetics*. Chicago: University of Chicago Press, 1962.

Lakoff, R. *Language and Woman's Place*. New York: Harper and Row, 1975.

Lang, R. *The Bipersonal Field.* New York: Jason Aronson, 1984.

————. *The Listening Process.* New York: Jason Aronson, 1978.

Lynch, J. J. *The Broken Heart: The Medical Consequences of Loneliness.* New York: Basic Books, 1977.

————. *The Language of the Heart: The Body's Response to Human Dialogue.* New York: Basic Books, 1985.

Macneilage, L. A., and K. A. Adams. *Assertiveness at Work: How to Increase Your Personal Power on the Job.* Englewood Cliffs, N.J.: Prentice-Hall, 1982.

Mehrabian, A. *Nonverbal Communication.* Chicago: Aldine, 1972.

Miller, G. A. *The Psychology of Communication.* New York: Basic Books, 1975.

————, et al. *Plans and the Structure of Behavior.* New York: Henry Holt, 1960.

Montagu, M. F. A. *Touching: The Human Significance of the Skin.* New York: Harper and Row, 1971.

Myers, W. E. *Aliens and Linguists.* Athens, Ga.: University of Georgia Press, 1980.

Nairn, A. *The Reign: The Corporation That Makes Up Minds.* Washington: Center for the Study of Responsible Law, 1980.

Nierenberg, G. I., and H. H. Calero. *How to Read a Person Like a Book.* New York: Pocket Books, 1971.

Norman, D. *Memory and Attention: An Introduction to Human Information Processing.* New York: John Wiley and Sons, 1969.

O'Barr, W. M. *Linguistic Evidence: Language, Power, and Strategy in the Courtroom.* New York: Academic Press, 1982.

————, and J. F. O'Barr, eds. *Language and Politics.* The Hague: Mouton, 1976.

Obler, L. K., and L. Menn. *Exceptional Language and Linguistics.* New York: Academic Press, 1982.

Odiorne, G. S. *The Change Resisters: How They Prevent Progress and What Managers Can Do About Them.* Englewood Cliffs, N.J.: Prentice-Hall, 1981.

O'Rourke, T. J. *A Basic Course in Manual Communication.* Silver Spring, Md.: National Association for the Deaf, 1973.

Pratt, M. L. *Toward A Speech Act Theory of Literary Discourse.* Bloomington: Indiana University Press, 1977.

Qubein, N. R. *Communicate Like a Pro.* Englewood Cliffs, N.J.: Prentice-Hall, 1983.

Riekehof, L. *Talk to the Deaf.* Springfield, Mo.: Gospel Publishing House, 1981.

Rivlin, R., and K. Gravelle. *Deciphering the Senses: The Expanding World of Human Perception.* New York: Simon and Schuster, 1984.

Rogers, C. R. *On Becoming a Person.* Boston: Houghton Mifflin, 1961.

Rosenthal, R., and L. Jacobsen. *Pygmalion in the Classroom: Teacher Expectations and Pupils' Intellectual Development.* New York: Holt, Rinehart and Winston, 1968.

Rothwell, J. D. *Telling It Like It Isn't.* Englewood Cliffs, N.J.: Prentice-Hall, 1982.

Samovar, L. A., and R. E. Porter. *Intercultural Communication: A Reader.* 4th edition. Belmont, Calif.: Wadsworth Publishing, 1985.

Satir, V. *Conjoint Family Therapy.* Palo Alto: Science and Behavior Books, 1964.

_____. *Peoplemaking.* Palo Alto: Science and Behavior Books, 1972.

Schrank, J. *Deception Detection.* Boston: Beacon Press, 1975.

Searle, J. *Speech Acts.* Cambridge: Cambridge University Press, 1969.

Siegman, A., and B. Pope, eds. *Studies in Dyadic Communication.* New York: Pergamon Press, 1972.

Smith, F. *Psycholinguistics and Reading.* New York: Holt, Rinehart and Winston, 1973.

_____. *Understanding Reading.* New York: Holt, Rinehart and Winston, 1971.

Spender, D. *Man Made Language.* London: Routledge and Kegan Paul, 1980.

Sperber, P. *Fail-Safe Business Negotiating: Strategies and Tactics for Success.* Englewood Cliffs, N.J.: Prentice-Hall, 1983.

Thompson, W. N. *Quantitative Research in Public Address and Communication.* New York: Random House, 1967.

Thorne, B., C. Kramarae, and N. Henley., eds. *Language, Gender and Society.* Rowley, Mass.: Newbury House, 1983.

Thorne, B., and N. Henley, eds. *Language and Sex, Difference and Dominance.* Rowley, M.A.: Newbury House, 1975.

Trent, J. D., J. S. Trent, and D. J. O'Neill, eds. *Concepts in Communication.* Boston: Allyn and Bacon, 1973.

Uris, D. *A Woman's Voice.* New York: Barnes and Noble Books, 1978.

Watzlawick, P. *The Language of Change.* New York: Basic Books, 1978.

Whorf, B. L. *Language, Thought, and Reality,* ed., J. B. Carroll. Cambridge, Mass.: MIT Press, 1956.

Wiener, R. *The Human Use of Human Beings: Cybernetics and Society.* New York: Avon Books, 1971.

# Index

# *About the Author*

Suzette Haden Elgin, best-selling author of *The Gentle Art of Verbal Self-Defense* and *More on the Gentle Art of Verbal Self-Defense,* is a retired professor of applied psycholinguistics who lives in Huntsville, Arkansas. She is the founder of the Ozark Center for Language Studies and gives lectures and seminars on verbal self-defense across the country. Elgin has also published several popular science fiction novels.